Economics Gone ASTRAY

Economics
Gone
ASTRAY

Bluford H Putnam
Erik Norland
K T Arasu

CME Group, USA

WS Professional

NEW JERSEY · LONDON · SINGAPORE · BEIJING · SHANGHAI · HONG KONG · TAIPEI · CHENNAI · TOKYO

Published by

WS Professional, an imprint of
World Scientific Publishing Co. Pte. Ltd.
5 Toh Tuck Link, Singapore 596224
USA office: 27 Warren Street, Suite 401-402, Hackensack, NJ 07601
UK office: 57 Shelton Street, Covent Garden, London WC2H 9HE

Library of Congress Cataloging-in-Publication Data
Names: Putnam, Bluford H., author. | Norland, Erik, author. | Arasu, K. T., 1954–   editor.
Title: Economics gone astray / Blu Putnam and Erik Norland ; edited by KT Arasu.
Description: New Jersey : World Scientific, 2018. | Includes bibliographical references and index.
Identifiers: LCCN 2018046977 | ISBN 9781944659585 (hardcover : alk. paper) |
    ISBN: 9781944659615 (pbk : alk. paper)
Subjects: LCSH: Economics. | Economic policy. | Monetary policy. | Fiscal policy.
Classification: LCC HB171 .P88 2018 | DDC 330--dc23
LC record available at https://lccn.loc.gov/2018046977

British Library Cataloguing-in-Publication Data
A catalogue record for this book is available from the British Library.

For any available supplementary material, please visit
https://www.worldscientific.com/worldscibooks/10.1142/Y0019#t=suppl

Desk Editor: Sylvia Koh

Printed in Singapore

Dedication

We dedicate this book to our loving families.

Acknowledgements

We want to thank Terry Duffy, the chairman and chief executive officer of CME Group, for the supportive culture he has helped foster and for giving us the opportunity to practice our skills and share our insights with the company's clients.

We would like to acknowledge the mentorship and guidance we have received over the years and at various points in our careers from D. Sykes Wilford and Jose M. (Pepe) Quintana. Sykes is an amazingly talented economist and has been a valued friend and colleague, always willing to read our research and offer insightful comments and suggestions. Pepe introduced us to Bayesian inference analysis, and while we served as colleagues, Pepe was always our statistics teacher. We owe him a great debt.

Praise for *Economics Gone Astray*

Economics Gone Astray is a major contribution for economic forecasters and researchers in helping them recognize and measure the costs of simplifying assumptions, models or global contexts. The stakes of ignoring these costs and their effects have grown exponentially in recent years with globalization, increased trade, risk management techniques and instruments, improved communications, technology and new payment systems.

— **Susan M. Phillips**, Former Governor of Federal Reserve Board, Former Chair of the Commodity Futures Trading Commission, and Retired as Dean and Professor of Finance Emeritus of the School of Business, George Washington University

---

This book is worth reading — whether you're a sophisticated advocate of certain economic theories or a consumer or businessperson trying to make plans around what might happen next in the economy and the markets. Whether the discussion revolves around the efficacy of tax cuts, the impact of interest rates, the significance of regulation or simply the vagaries of human nature, you'll get the arguments on both sides of the coin. And at the end, even if you don't agree with all the authors' conclusions, you'll have a much better perspective on the dangers and opportunities ahead."

— **Terry Savage,** Author of *The Savage Truth on Money* and nationally syndicated Tribune financial columnist

---

Just brilliant! Finally, a fun read that describes the financial world we live in with clear coherent thought and wonderfully crafted charts rather than linear equations based on unrealistic assumptions. This book should be required reading for any economics or finance major.

— **Clemens Kownatzki**, PhD, MBA, Academic Director MS Applied Finance, Practitioner Faculty of Finance, Pepperdine University

---

Those of us who are reductionists appreciate the relative simplicity mathematics can bring to increasingly complex situations. Those of us who are human appreciate that the complexities of the systems that are inherently part of life and living cannot be reduced simply to a series of mathematical equations. Putnam and Norland's take on economics is thought-provoking, sometimes irreverent, and written in good old English. Well done!

— **Tuajuanda C. Jordan**, PhD, President, St. Mary's College of Maryland

---

This insightful volume provides readers with a thorough, systemic explanation of modern macroeconomic policies responding to recent social and economic trends. It is required reading supplementing standard college-level macroeconomics textbooks as well as an essential resource in courses examining current issues in economics and finance. This thought-provoking book helps college instructors educate well-informed engaged citizens.

— **Lucjan T. Orlowski**, Ph.D., Professor of Economics and Finance, DBA in Finance Program Director, Department of Economics and Finance, Jack Welch College of Business, Sacred Heart University

---

How do economic policies, financial market vacillations, new technologies and disruption affect our prosperity and our future? Two great economists, Blu Putnam and Erik Norland, help us by bringing unprecedented clarity to our complex, fast changing world. With their analyses and insights in *Economics Gone Astray*, we can plan, adjust and get better outcomes in our business and personal lives.

— **The Honorable Mary K. Bush**, President of Bush International, LLC, member, board of directors of Mariott International, Discover Financial Services, ManTech International Corporation, and T. Rowe Price Group, Inc., and formerly the US representative on the IMF Board.

Grounded in research and stripped of the traditional jargon, *Economics Gone Astray* is a unique perspective on the economic patterns of the past, present, and future. From interest rates to Bitcoin, *Economics Gone Astray* boldly challenges why traditional economics misses the mark in an ever-evolving landscape. The book challenges us to consider — if the economic landscape is constantly evolving — why have we not adapted our traditional assumptions and interpretations? Before you invest in the next sexy trend, read *Economics Gone Astray*.

— **Karen Natkin**, Founder and President, Moonstone Asset Management

---

This collection of essays on some of the most pressing topics of our time brings to light the shortcomings of blindly applying empirical models. In a straightforward and entertaining way, the authors lay out the questions that need to be addressed in comprehensive ways without assuming away the inconvenient bits. Of course, no coverage of economics and markets today would be complete without the obligatory chapter on Bitcoin and here too, the authors have taken a market-based approach to analyzing the topic. Definitely worth reading.

— **Matthew McMaster**, Director, The Rock Creek Group

Do economists lead us down a hazy financial path because their 'assumptions' mean we make decisions based on unrealistic concepts? With a mixture of history, pragmatic prose and pertinent examples, Blu Putnam and Erik Norland answer the above with fascinating how's, why's and a few really's in this easy-to-read *Economics Gone Astray*. With key macroeconomic essays, they re-write a variety of economic wrongs with relevant material ranging from Yield Curve Recessions to Death by Simulation. There is potential here to encourage a range of financially-inclined average Joes and Joannes like myself, (with maybe a president or central bank or two) to reassess generally accepted economic sound bites.

— **Peta Adams,** Managing Director, Liquiditv Limited

Bravo! Tight logic, deep expertise and original thinking make this the new economics' book every marketer must read. Enlightening content/thought starters for my class lectures and business practice.

– **Judy Galloway**, Managing Partner, G-group Marketing & Adjunct at New York University

---

A unique and smart way to look at things, deconstruct and decipher them and challenge our current thinking. A must-read!

– **Zoé Charny**, Executive Director and Head of Marketing, TOBAM

One of the contributions this book makes is to link essays on economic topics with essays on the types of computational and statistical methods needed to turn economic theories into practical prediction models. The chapters on machine learning, portfolio optimization, quantitative simulations, and implied volatility are a most welcome addition and will be extremely helpful to those wanting to make the transition from theory to practice.

– **Professor Simon Scheidegger**, Department of Finance, HEC, University of Lausanne

---

Investment professionals are diving into new quantitative tools, from machine learning to artificial intelligence. *Economics Gone Astray* provides some great insights into how to use these new tools, while staying firmly grounded in solid economic analysis. This book will be a great read for the hedge fund community.

– **Molly Hall,** Founding Partner, Miramar Alternatives LLC

Disclaimer

Foreword

Macroeconomic trends have a significant impact that reaches from Wall Street to Main Street, yet they are often misinterpreted not just by novices but by experts as well. In their new book, *Economics Gone Astray*, Blu Putnam and Erik Norland look beyond traditional assumptions and mathematical models. With great insight, they analyze the behavioral dynamics that often provide a better explanation of our ever-changing economic environment. Clearly written in a highly engaging style, the book upends and expands our thinking about economics in an intriguing and entertaining way.

Terry Duffy, Chairman and Chief Executive Officer, CME Group

Introduction

Blu Putnam & Erik Norland[1]

Economics Gone Astray is aimed at providing practical explanations for some of the key macro-economic topics of the day. We cut through the assumptions that economists often employ and describe how many traditional practices often lead them woefully astray. Our topics range from inflation, taxes, and debt, to demographics and crypto-currencies. Our objective is to provide thoughtful and clear explanations of complicated subjects without resorting to mathematical equations or technical jargon, often used by economists to obscure flawed arguments rather than to tighten the logic and guide the reader.

Philosophically, we believe that economics has gone astray for three key reasons which underlie the inability of economists to reach their potential in understanding economies and markets.

First, despite so many warnings to the contrary, too many economists continue to ignore or dismiss behavioral feedback effects in their models and theories. Flat-earth thinking enshrines linear models and limits feedback loops from economic agents that may have different objectives, different risk tolerances, and may not always act in the manner of the infamous "rational" man. Incorporating lessons from behavioral finance often leads one to an enhanced appreciation of the non-linear world in which we live.

Second, and closely intertwined with the first observation, is our belief that too many economists build models and theories that fail to appreciate or even totally assume away the dynamic, ever-changing, and complex nature of the institutional, political, regulatory, and

---

demographic environment. Context always matters, and failing to incorporate a dynamic view of the underlying state in which economies and markets operate can lead to very poor policy prescriptions and off-the-mark forecasts.

Finally, we argue that many economists use mathematics inappropriately and as a crutch, putting too much emphasis on simplifying assumptions and constantly forgetting just how heroic and unrealistic many of these assumptions truly are. When we read the classic economists who wrote before the extreme "mathematization" of economics after the 1950s, we are often struck by the elegance and clarity of their thinking.

In particular, we have been drawn to words of one of the great economists at the turn of 19th century, namely Professor Alfred Marshall, who also authored the best-selling economics textbook of his day. Sir Arthur Lyon Bowley, an English economist and statistician, had written to his friend, Alfred Marshall, back in the early 1920s, asking what he thought about the growing use of mathematical equations in economic writing and thinking. Marshall's response was classic and deserves highlighting today:

> "But I know I had a growing feeling in the later years of my work at the subject that a good mathematical theorem dealing with economic hypotheses was very unlikely to be good economics: and I went more and more on the rules — (1) Use mathematics as a short-hand language, rather than as an engine of inquiry. (2) Keep to them till you have done. (3) Translate into English. (4) Then illustrate by examples that are important in real life. (5) Burn the mathematics. (6) If you can't succeed in 4, burn 3. This last I did often."[2]

---

[2] A.C. Pigou. *Memorials of Alfred Marshall.* Published by MacMillan, London, 1925. In preparing this book, Professor Pigou was honoring a specific request which he explains in his introduction: "In the will of the late Alfred Marshall there is a clause in which he requests his successor in the Chair of Political Economy at Cambridge to edit, from his manuscripts, 'such material as he considers to be of value, aiming at brevity, suppressing controversial matter, and also deciding in the negative when he has any doubt at all whether any

Inappropriate use of mathematics, reliance on overly heroic assumptions, failure to appreciate behavioral dynamics and complex systems, and emphasis on linear extrapolations in a decidedly non-linear world — Economics Gone Astray!

---

matter should be published'. In the volume that follows I have endeavored to carry out the trust with which Dr Marshall honored me, and have ventured so far to depart from his directions as to include, along with selections from his writings, the memorial notices which form the first Part of this book, and a number of letters which form the third Part."

Contents

Dedication   v

Acknowledgements   vii

Praise for Economics Gone Astray   ix

Disclaimer   xiii

Foreword by Terry Duffy, Chairman and CEO, CME Group   xv

Introduction   xvii

1.   Inflation: Why So Low for So Long   1

2.   Debt: Dangers of Excess   13

3.   Taxes and Growth: Why Tax Cuts do not Necessarily Stimulate Economic Growth   33

4.   Yield Curve: Predicting Recessions   45

5.   Demographics: Appreciating Economic Growth Potential   59

6.   Wages and Productivity: Structural Changes are Crucial to Understand   69

7.   Bitcoin Economics   81

8.   Market Regulation: Origins and Cultural Perspectives   95

9.   Volatility and Uncertainty   109

10.   Machine Learning: Challenges for Financial Market Predictive Analytics Suggest a Bayesian Solution   121

11.   Portfolio Optimization:
            Revolutionizing Risk Assessment Systems   131

12.   Beyond Implied Volatility: Estimating Robust
            Risk-Return Probability Distributions   149

13.   Death by Simulation   161

14.   Quantitative Easing: Evaluating QE's Impact   171

15.   Financial Crisis: Lessons from Different
            Management Approaches   197

16.   Taylor Rule: A Bayesian Interpretation of the
            Federal Reserve's Dual Mandate   219

About the Authors   243

List of Figures   245

Index   249

Chapter 1

Inflation: Why So Low For So Long

Blu Putnam & Erik Norland[1]

Editor's Note: As the economic expansion in the US after the Great Recession of 2008–2009 chugged along, as millions of new jobs were created, as the Federal Reserve embarked on massive asset purchases and held short-term rates near zero, both monetarist and labor market economists were confounded by the lack of more inflation. This essay explores the heroic assumptions in their models and tracks the changing state of the regulatory framework, not to mention how technology has altered how money changes hands, to explain the failure of many popular theories to explain or anticipate inflation patterns correctly. – KT

US inflation has been subdued for well over two decades, as in all the major, mature industrial economies. This is not a recent phenomenon, and is not due to the lagged impact of the 2008 financial panic. Indeed, whether measured by the consumer price index (CPI) or the Federal Reserve's (Fed's) favorite personal consumption price deflator (PCE), core inflation, which excludes the more volatile food and energy categories, has been stuck in a 1% to 3% range in the US since 1994 and into 2018.

---

[1] **Disclaimer**: All examples are hypothetical interpretations of situations and are used for explanation purposes only. The views expressed here reflect solely those of the authors and not necessarily those of their employer, CME Group or its affiliated institutions. The information herein should not be considered investment advice or the results of actual market experience.

Figure 1-1: US Inflation

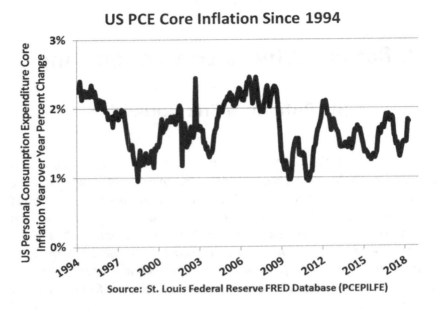

Source: St. Louis Federal Reserve FRED Database (PCEPILFE)

During this 25-year period of subdued inflation in the US, there were two big cycles in unemployment; a stock market technology rally and tech wreck; a housing boom and massive housing recession; short-term rates above 5% as well as near zero; plus, some massive Fed experiments with unconventional monetary policy (i.e., asset purchases or quantitative easing, QE). Thus, to evaluate different scenarios for inflation, analysts need to step back and examine the underlying causes of more than two decades of subdued inflation. And, in so doing, we will look at several simplified theories of inflation forecasting. By examining the often heroic (and incorrect) assumptions, we will get an improved sense of why most inflation theories totally failed to have any predictive value.

Our central thesis comes straight from basic economics: price rises (i.e., inflation) occur when spending demand exceeds the supply of goods and services. As we take a tour of various approaches to inflation forecasting, we will be highlighting the changing patterns in the demand for spending or the supply of goods and services. A common theme will be that structural changes in our information-age economy have vastly changed how spending demand is created and how goods and services are supplied. And the results of these information-age pattern shifts effectively rendered virtually all the simplified inflation forecasting approaches useless.

Monetary Policy Is Now More Limited In Its Ability to Encourage Growth

In the 1950s and 1960s, Professor Milton Friedman of the University of Chicago became famous for his research on money supply as the primary cause of inflation, even if the lags in monetary policy were long and variable. The monetarist theory of inflation fit the inflation data exceptionally well during the 1960s and 1970s, but it fell apart in the late 1980s and never regained empirical support in later decades.

What went awry with the monetarist theory? The assumed relationship between money supply and spending demand totally broke down. Back in the 1950s, if one wanted to buy goods or services, one paid with cash or with a check drawn on a basic bank account that paid no interest. There were savings accounts in the 1950s, yet they did not have check-writing privileges. Credit card use was minimal and the ability to borrow through a credit card was constrained. The ability to move funds instantly and efficiently from investment accounts to payment accounts was a dream. Neither cash management nor brokerage accounts allowed check writing. The ability to transfer money over the internet or with a smart phone was not possible. In this bygone era, the money supply was very tightly correlated to spending, and thus rapid increases in the money supply served as a good predictor of future spending and future inflation, assuming the supply of goods and services was constrained to grow at a slower rate than the money supply growth.

The 1980s and subsequent decades ushered in massive changes in the way spending demand was created and severed the link with any and all measures of the money supply. Checking accounts could pay interest. Checks could be written on brokerage accounts. Credit cards came with lines of credit to be used (up to a limit) at the discretion of the spender. These changes in how spending was facilitated alone were enough to destroy the correlation of money supply measures with inflation, and the Fed stopped setting money supply target ranges in the late 1980s. Then came the 1990s and subsequent decades. The information age brought a myriad of ways to transfer money and manage credit, with smart phones and internet.

The story does not stop here, though. Even if the measured money supply was no longer a good predictor of future inflation, one might still expect interest rate policy or quantitative easing to have an influence on future inflation. Yet, neither interest rate policy nor central bank asset purchases produced any evidence of correlation with inflation over the two and a half decades, starting in 1994.

There seems to have been two critical forces at work that contributed to the lack of influence of monetary policy over inflation and the real economy since the early 1990s. The first was increased prudential bank regulation focused on capital requirements, and the second is the rise of sophisticated interest rate risk management in the financial sector.

When banks and other lending institutions are capital constrained by prudential regulations, they are unable to expand credit, which could drive spending demand. Even if short-term interest rates are relatively low and below the prevailing inflation rate, credit growth may be constrained by capital requirements. Even if the Fed buys massive quantities of US Treasury and mortgage-backed securities, bank lending may be constrained by capital requirements. The rise of prudential regulation to safeguard the financial system, which gained substantial momentum after the collapse of savings and loan institutions in the recession of 1990–1991, had the unintended consequence of making monetary policy less effective in terms of inflation management. As the policy pendulum swung toward bank regulation and reducing systematic risk, the influence of central bank macro-economic tools waned. The embedded assumption made by most academic economists in their macro-economic models that the policy environment is stable and has no influence on the efficacy of monetary policy could not have been more wrong.

The Savings & Loan (S&L) crisis of 1990–1991 also had another impact. S&Ls were basically institutions that borrowed short-term (savings accounts) and lent longer-term (home mortgages and later high yield debt). They took on substantial interest rate risk, and many S&Ls did not hedge or otherwise manage that risk — earning the premium for taking the risk of maturity intermediation was an integral part of their business model. After the S&L crisis there were effectively no financial institutions of any importance left in the US economy that did not adopt sophisticated interest rate risk management processes.

One of the interesting consequences of improved interest rate risk management in the financial sector is that the profitability of financial institutions would be less impacted by small changes in interest rate policy. That is, small changes in Fed interest rate policy would no longer impact financial sector profitability.

With interest-rate risk being more effectively managed, the big risk left on the books of financial institutions was credit risk. That is, the risk of a recession that substantially diminishes the credit quality of bank loan portfolios. And even in the credit risk sector, financial institutions over the decades vastly improved their ability to assess and manage credit risk — not enough to handle a deep recession, such as 2008–2009, but effective credit risk management does limit the ability of the Fed to tap the brakes or hit the accelerator to influence the real economic growth.

Make no mistake, if the Fed were to raise short-term interests sharply above the prevailing rate of inflation, the Fed could, no doubt, trigger a recession, but macro-economic management and fine-tuning has become less and less possible. This latter point illustrates some of the asymmetry in Fed policy outcomes. The Fed can still cause a recession by tightening too much — often measured by the shape of the yield curve. When short-term rates are equal to long-term bond yields (flat yield curve) or when short-term rates are set above long-term bond yields (inverted yield curve), recessions often follow in one or two years. The other side does not work so well any more. Near-zero rates and asset purchases can raise equity and bond prices above what they otherwise would have been, but the impact on the real economy and inflation is virtually non-existent. Put another way, the Fed can still create asset price inflation, as it did in the 2010–2016 period of emergency low rates and QE, but the Fed has very limited ability to encourage more growth in an economy that is already creating jobs at a good pace. [See Chapter 4 for an in-depth analysis of why we believe a relatively flat or inverted yield curve remains an excellent indicator of future economic deceleration even if highly positively-sloped yield curves are no longer effective at stimulating more economic growth or inflation].

A few important caveats are in order. When an economic recession is caused by a financial market failure, such as 2008-2009, then central bank buying of assets (i.e., the Fed's approach) or provision of emergency liquidity loans (i.e., the European Central Bank's approach) can limit the damage of the recession and prevent a downward spiral into a depression. This ability to contain a recession, however, does not translate into an ability to promote additional economic growth when an economy is already growing again.

Moreover, the tendency of analysts and policy-makers to embrace linear, or as some might call it — flat-earth thinking — should be avoided. The European Central Bank (ECB) and the Bank of Japan (BoJ) experimented with negative short-term rates on the deposits of commercial banks held at these central banks. The idea was that if lowering rates from 4% to 2% could encourage inflation, and then from 2% to 0%, why not go negative? Unfortunately, economics is virtually never a linear relationship. As short-term rates approached zero and then went negative, commercial banks saw their profits squeezed, as they could not pass on the negative rates to their depositors. Lower profits hurt lending, which was exactly the opposite of what the central bank was trying to do.

If Not Monetary Policy, What About Fiscal Policy?

After monetary policy failed to produce the additional economic growth and inflation pressure desired by policy makers, the US turned to fiscal policy. With legislation passed at the end of 2017, the US embarked on a rather grand experiment to see if a large permanent corporate tax cut could encourage economic growth and possibly push inflation a little higher. The long-term outcome will be interesting to observe, and is not so clear, because the link between tax cuts and spending is quite loose. (See Chapter 3 for an in-depth analysis of tax cuts and economic growth.) Corporations may choose to buy back shares, pay larger dividends, refinance debt, or make acquisitions – all of which have excellent potential to increase shareholder value and yet may have no impact on the real economy. Only if corporations use the tax cut to pay higher wages or to invest in expansion plans in the US will the domestic real economy see higher spending. Some of this may, indeed, happen. The big question is how much and will it be enough to make a material difference in the growth of the economy. If one assumes tax cuts unambiguously increase spending on goods and services, then higher real growth and inflation pressure follow from the assumption of higher spending demand. If one assumes the permanent tax cuts to corporations and the temporary rate cuts for relatively well-off individuals will not raise spending demand by very much, then, of course, the impact on growth and inflation will also be small. [Note: Chapter 2 on "Taxes and Economic Growth" provides and in-depth analysis of these issues.]

  While not on the policy agenda in the US when the corporate tax cut was enacted, our analysis also suggests that increases in government spending is a more direct way to stimulate spending demand. After all, gross domestic product is the arithmetic sum of consumption, investment, and government expenditures, plus net exports. Raising government spending goes directly toward increasing spending demand in the domestic economy without any confusion or debate as there is with corporate tax cuts. Indeed, the restraint in the growth of US federal government spending during the 2010–2017 period – after the one-time emergency fiscal spending of 2009 — was arguably one of the reasons that economic growth was not stronger even with near-zero short-term interest rates.

Another fiscal policy issue for analysis is the rise of the national debt. At least in the short-term, both tax cuts and increased government spending would work to increase the deficit. Only if materially higher economic growth appeared down the road would tax revenues rise to partly offset the tax rate cuts or the increases in government expenditures. We carefully note, though, that rising debt loads do not signal future recessions. Over the long-term, growing economies typically take on more debt relative to GDP. As the debt to GDP ratio grows, though, the economy becomes more fragile and more interest rate sensitive. That is, higher interest rates mean higher interest expense, and so rising national debt raises the risk of a monetary policy mistake – that is, moving too fast to a flat or inverted yield curve — and causing a recession. Our conclusion is that higher debt loads may well translate over the long-term into a more cautious Fed in terms of raising short-term interest rates.

And, Why Haven't Tight Labor Markets Resulted in Rising Inflation?

Moving on to the labor market theories of inflation, the assumption labor economists, such as former Chair of the Federal Reserve Board Janet Yellen, typically make is that low unemployment rates are indicative of tight labor markets, meaning stiff competition for scarce labor and thus leading to higher hourly wages, which signals increased spending demand. There is, indeed, a loose contemporaneous correlation between wage inflation and consumer price inflation, but that relationship is not necessary causal — just an empirical association. And, as labor markets have shifted over the decades to more and more service sector jobs and less and less manufacturing jobs, the case for a causal relationship running from hourly wages to inflation was weakened if not destroyed.

To focus on spending demand, our preference is to look at the growth in total labor income. Total labor income growth is the sum of employment growth (more people working), growth in hourly hours worked (people working longer), and growth in hourly wages (people getting paid more). If you only look at any one of these items in isolation, you risk getting the wrong answer. In Janet Yellen's defense, she strongly preferred a holistic approach to labor market data — looking at every measure possible to assess in a qualitative way what was really happening.

The focus many analysts put on hourly wage growth, though, is misguided. The problem is — yes, you guessed it — in the assumptions. The link between hourly wage growth and total labor income has a lot to do with what kind of jobs of being created, and most models that economists create assume that the job distribution within the economy is stable. Nothing, of course, could be more wrong in this era of corporate disruption. The economy is creating many more low-paying service jobs and losing relatively better paid manufacturing jobs. This is a multi-decade trend, so why so many academic and policy-oriented economists do not give it more emphasis in their inflation forecasting models is a mystery to practitioner economists. The only relatively highly paid sector that saw job growth during 2010–2017 was business professionals, including those in finance, accounting, insurance, and legal professions, and this sector was too small to move the inflation needle. The basic point is that if the job mix is shifting to relatively lower paid professions, then the overall average hourly wage growth will be biased downward regardless of the path of consumer price inflation.

There is more to this story, too. Spending demand is a function of both ability and willingness to spend. The growth in total labor income measures the changes in the ability to spend, but it does not necessarily reflect the willingness to spend. Our view is that fear of losing one's job is the primary factor affecting the willingness to spend.

After the 2008–2009 Great Recession, many companies shed jobs. If you kept your job, you may have witnessed family, friends, or co-workers lose their jobs. This is the province of behavioral finance and psychology. But we would argue that the recovery from a recession involves much more than job creation — the fear that swept through the labor force from the job losses in the recession may take much longer to diminish. Hence, spending demand undershoots a linear extrapolation of total labor income growth until the job-loss fears abate. And, in this era of corporate disruptions, fears of losing one's job have not abated very quickly. For example, brick-and-mortar retailing is being disrupted, and goods delivery jobs are being created. Overall, job growth is doing fine, unless you are in one of the disrupted sectors, and then fear of job loss remains. This means that in the long-lasting yet modest economic expansion after the Great Recession of 2008–2009, spending demand was held back by the very slow recovery in confidence in maintaining one's job and income. Each year of the expansion, the fear declines, but it is a slow process in this era of disruption.

Bottom line

When analyzing inflation, assumptions about the stability of the financial regulatory environment and about innovations in the payments system can make a huge difference. Economic models of inflation that hold these factors to be constant over long periods of time should be viewed with great suspicion if not rejected outright. It may make the mathematics underlying these theories easier to manage and more adaptable to empirical analysis to assume stable and unchanging financial regulations and an absence of innovations in the payments systems, but it also makes them less relevant to the analytical challenge, prone to large forecasting errors, and may lead to poor policy choices.

We also note that the tendency of many analysts and policy-makers to assume linear relationships needs to be avoided as well. Economic systems are complex feedback loops involving behavioral interactions. This means that assumptions of linear relationships are likely to hold only for very small increments before the curvatures resulting from behavioral feedback loops and structurally embedded non-linearity's and boundary value constraints take their toll.

Chapter 2

Debt: Dangers of Excess

Erik Norland & Blu Putnam[1]

Editor's Note: It is truly amazing that so many economic models and theories of how economies work have chosen to ignore debt. This essay explores the perils of not appreciating the role of debt in the economy, for good and not so good.
— KT

Debt is among the most fundamental and least understood aspects of the macro-economy. The dominant schools of macroeconomic thought — classical, Keynesian and monetarist — pay it inadequate attention. From the perspective of these schools of thought, economies with low levels of debt operate in exactly the same fashion as those with extremely high levels of debt. From their point of view, debt ratios essentially do not matter. The problem with that is in real life, debt levels not only matter, debt burdens influence critical facets of the economy, from the pace of growth to the level of interest rates.

Only a comparatively small number of economists at the fringes of the profession, such as post-Keynesian Hyman Minsky, put the consequences of debt front and center in their understanding of how the economy works. Although economists largely overlooked Minsky's work during his lifetime (1919–1996), interest in the liability side of the economic balance sheet has grown exponentially since the 2008 financial crisis.

---

[1] **Disclaimer:** All examples are hypothetical interpretations of situations and are used for explanation purposes only. The views expressed here reflect solely those of the authors and not necessarily those of their employer, CME Group or its affiliated institutions. The information herein should not be considered investment advice or the results of actual market experience.

The basics of debt are easily and widely understood. Debt represents a claim on future cash flows. In exchange for borrowing funds today, governments, corporations and individuals promise repayment in the future with interest.

What is less well understood is how pervasive debt is, especially in the world of fiat currencies. When a government issues a currency, it creates a liability for which there is no current asset. Rather than being backed by a hard asset, like gold or silver, fiat currencies serve as a standard of deferred payment that are accepted based on the implied promise that government debts could be paid off via taxation. As such, even in the abstract, fiat money is debt backed by the faith in the creditworthiness of the issuer government's central bank. Since the central bank can create money at will to satisfy the financing of government liabilities, there is almost no risk of sovereign default unless the government in question has borrowed in a foreign (or supranational) currency that it does not control.

In a modern fiat-currency economy, only a small portion of transactions are made using actual money. Most transactions are conducted through credit. Some of the credit is extended over the very short term — the time it takes for a check or an electronic debit of a bank account to clear, typically a few days. Other transactions, such as those financed by credit cards, are revolving lines of credit than can be extended over a few months or years. The majority of debt is much longer term in nature, including auto loans, mortgage bonds and most government and corporate debt. The availability of credit makes possible all sorts of transactions that would otherwise be difficult or impossible. This provision of liquidity raises the overall standard of living, supporting both investment and aggregate demand.

Low-Debt Versus High-Debt Economies

When debt levels are low, governments, households and corporations can live beyond their means by borrowing to spend in excess of their incomes. Debt-fueled spending exceeding income tends to expand GDP as one person's or entity's expenditure is another's income. As debt levels rise, however, the nature of borrowing and its impact on spending changes. With increasing levels of debt, borrowing gradually ceases to spur new spending and investments and increasingly favors reimbursing the interest and principal payments on the existing debt. In the case of the economy, growth slows. When total debt levels become too high, lenders eventually become nervous about the credit quality of the borrowers and tend to shut off the tap, causing a loss of confidence — the so called "Minsky Moment." This threatens to send the debt-fueled expansion into a reverse spiral.

When people discuss debt-to-GDP ratios, they tend to focus almost exclusively on public debt. This is a big mistake. In most countries, public sector debt is only a small portion of overall debt (Figure 2-1). However, financial crises do occasionally result from excessive levels of public sector debt. Greece and Italy are excellent cases in point. More often, crises emerge from the private sector, as was the case in Japan in the early 1990s and in the US in 2007. Crises can even be triggered by the private sector in countries with very low

Figure 2-1: Most Debt has Been Issued by the Private Sector, not the Public Sector

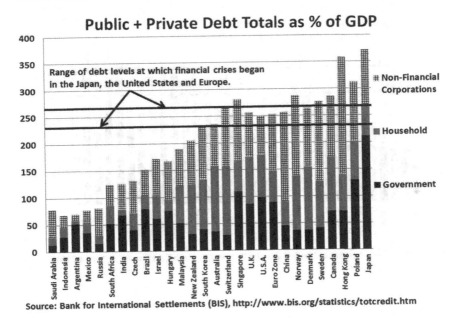

Source: Bank for International Settlements (BIS), http://www.bis.org/statistics/totcredit.htm

levels of public debt, as happened in Ireland and Spain in 2009. The crisis in both nations began when public debt was below 30% of GDP but their private sectors were highly leveraged, with debt levels exceeding 200% of GDP.

Since the early 1980s, debt-to-GDP ratios have been spiraling higher in the developed world, rising to especially stark levels between 2000 and 2017 (Figure 2-2). The rise in debt levels forced a fundamental change in the way that monetary policy works in most developed economies. So long as debt-to-GDP ratios remained relatively low (below about 230% of GDP), central banks generally kept interest rates close to the rate of nominal GDP growth. This is to say that if real growth was 3% and inflation was 2%, a central bank's policy rate was typically close to 5%.

Figure 2-2: Debt Levels have Soared in Most Nations

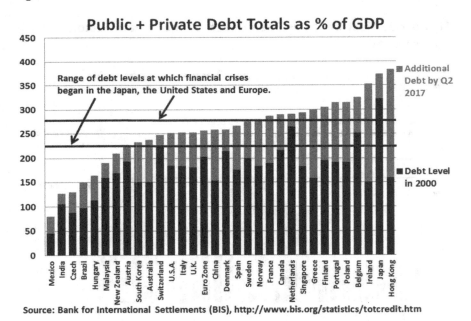

Source: Bank for International Settlements (BIS), http://www.bis.org/statistics/totcredit.htm

Since the crises in Japan in 1990 and in Europe and the United States circa 2008, central banks, by all appearances, had to keep interest rates very close to zero in order to maintain economic growth. This caused all sorts of interest rate models, including the famous "Taylor Rule," to lose their explanatory power.

A Brief History of Sovereign Debt Crises

When it comes to debt crises, Japan was the canary in the coal mine. It was the first country since the end of World War II to suffer a debt crisis in a modern, non-gold linked fiat currency of its own making. Prior to the war, debt crises were common. Under the gold standard, national central banks could not control the money supply as easily as they could later when they delinked their currencies from precious metals. The essential problem with the value of money linked to metals is that the mining supply of gold and silver grows too slowly to meet the needs of rapidly expanding modern economies. Under metallic standards, such as the gold standard, countries typically got out of debt crises by devaluing their currencies with respect to metals, as the United States did in 1933 when incoming President Franklin Roosevelt shut down the US banking system for 100 days while the government confiscated gold and devalued the US dollar by 33% with respect to the yellow metal, from US$20/ounce to US$35/ounce.

Following World War II, the US and its allies established the Bretton Woods system of fixed exchange rates which still allowed for convertibility of currencies, including the US dollar, into gold. During the 1950s and 1960s, this system laid the foundation for strong economic growth in the US, Europe and Japan as the world recovered from the war. By the late 1960s, however, the US economy began to overheat as a result of President Lyndon Johnson's Great Society program and the Vietnam War. On August 15, 1971, his successor, President Richard Nixon, delinked the US dollar from gold and ushered in the era of free-floating fiat currencies.

The first decade of this new regime was tumultuous. Commodity prices and inflation soared. By 1980, central banks had hiked interest rates to double digits to contain inflation, producing a deep economic downturn and the first set of debt crises post-Bretton Woods.

During the 1970s commodities boom many Latin American nations borrowed heavily in the belief of a prolonged period of profitable commodity exports. When commodity prices collapsed during the early 1980s, they were unable to pay their debts and many of them defaulted on their loans to Western banks. What differentiated this debt crisis from the subsequent debt crises in Japan and the United States is that the Latin American nations had borrowed in currencies over which they had no control. Most of the loans were denominated in US dollars while others were in British pounds, French francs and German deutsche marks.

Currency devaluation improved Latin American export competitiveness but did nothing to change loan values denominated in the dollar, pound, franc or Deutsche mark. Under the leadership of US Treasury Secretary Nicolas Brady, these loans were taken off the balance sheets of US banks, securitized and sold to financial markets while the Latin American countries gradually reimbursed their loans over of the course of the 1980s and 1990s. The deleveraging process was painful. In the 1980s and early 1990s, much of Latin America experienced a "lost decade" characterized by stagnant economic growth.

By contrast, Japan was an economic powerhouse during the 1980s, sporting growth rates of around 5% per annum for much of the decade, building upon the even faster pace of growth the country had experienced during the previous three decades as it recovered from World War II and transformed itself into an economic and industrial juggernaut. What changed over the course of the 1980s was that Japan, to maintain the high rates of growth to which it had become accustomed, transformed itself from a low-debt to a high-debt society. In 1980, Japan's total debt-to-GDP ratio was below 200% (still quite high by the standards of the time) but exceeded 250% by the end of the decade (Figure 2-3).

Figure 2-3: Japan had Fun Levering Up During the 1980s — Paying for it Ever Since

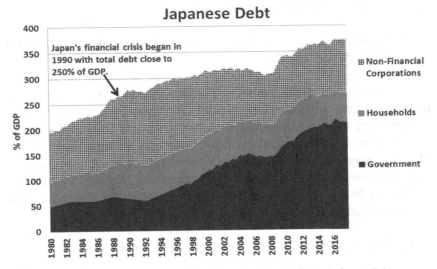

Source: Bank for International Settlements (BIS), http://www.bis.org/statistics/totcredit.htm, Trading Ecomomics for Public Debt Before Q4 1997

During this time stock and real estate prices soared. By 1989, Japan's stock market had a larger market capitalization than that of its US counterpart even though Japan's economy was only two-fifths the size of the US economy. The value of Tokyo real estate exceeded that of the entire United States. In 1989, the Bank of Japan began to tighten interest rate policy and burst the bubble. Equity prices collapsed in 1990 and real estate prices began to decline in 1991, eventually falling by more than 60%.

Following the implosion of Japan's real estate market and bursting of its equity bubble, there were three major items to note:

➤ The Bank of Japan was forced to lower interest rates to zero where they remained for over two decades, despite two failed attempts to get off the zero-interest-rate zone.

> Japan's economy barely grew in the quarter century since its debt crisis reached its "Minsky moment" and consumption and investment both remained weak.

> Japan never de-levered: in fact, its debt ratios expanded to over 370% of GDP by 2017.

During the 1990s and early 2000s, Japan was an economic curiosity. Western economists looked at Japan as an oddity. Low interest rates and massive public spending programs could not seem to boost economic growth. The country's attempts to deal with its bad debts by merging banks and keeping interest rates low were the subject of a great deal of criticism and advice. Meanwhile, Western Europe and the United States slowly transformed themselves into gigantic, but somewhat distinct versions of Japan.

The New Japans: The US and European Debt Bubbles

From 1950 through 1980, US debt ratios were essentially stable. Over the course of the three decades, the US reduced public sector leverage from nearly 100% of GDP following World War II and the Korean War to around 30% of GDP by 1980. Private sector indebtedness, however, rose from 25% of GDP following the war to just below 100% of GDP by 1980. The total debt level remained stable at around 125% of GDP during both Democratic and Republican Administrations. During this time, Depression-era banking regulations remained in force and while Americans could and did find credit, lenders generally did not extend it in an aggressive manner.

Late in the Carter Administration and early in Ronald Reagan's presidency, this began to change. During the 1970s, the US economy was beset by high inflation. International trade represented only 5% of GDP. China, India and the Soviet bloc were essentially cut off from the world economy. Labor unions retained significant strength, even in the private sector. While technology was advancing, it was doing so in a manner that posed little threat to the average worker. All of this gave labor substantial pricing power. As prices rose, workers could successfully demand higher wages. Higher wages in turn fueled more consumption. With more money chasing a relatively slowly-growing supply of goods, inflation surged.

Presidents Ford and Carter tried unsuccessfully to break this dynamic. Under the Carter Administration, public policy did, however, begin to pivot, first with the deregulation of certain sectors, including airlines. In 1979, Carter appointed Paul Volcker as head of the Federal Reserve Bank. Volker wasted no time in putting US interest rates at nearly 20%, sending the economy into a severe recession that helped to scuttle Carter's re-election.

His successor, Reagan, ran for the presidency on a platform that advocated supply-side economics.[2] This vision advocated tax cuts, especially for higher-income earners, deregulation, expansion of free trade agreements and support for management over organized labor. One of his first acts as president was to fire striking air traffic controllers, signaling a reduction in union bargaining power. In 1981, he signed the Kemp-Roth tax cut which brought tax rates for top earners down from 70% to 50% over a three-year period. During his second term, Reagan signed the 1986 Tax Reform Act that further reduced top rates from 50% to 28%. While top earners saw their taxes slashed, middle and lower-income workers got a tax increase as a result of the 1983 Social Security Reform that raised payroll taxes and caused the Social Security system to begin running large surpluses, which it lent to the rest of the government, masking the true amount of red ink from the 1981 tax cut. Meanwhile his administration began to deregulate numerous economic sectors, from banking to energy.

International trade also vastly expanded as China, India and the Soviet Union and its satellites came onto to the global markets. Particularly in the wake of the 1997–98 Asian crisis, many nations around the world built up enormous central bank reserves, which they lent to Western nations, depressing interest rates and encouraging the boom in lending. Moreover, as their labor forces connected to the global economy, it depressed wages in the developed world, contributing to the rise of inequality and producing substantial

---

[2] See Chapter 3 for an in-depth analysis of supply-side economics and the "Laffer Curve".

dislocation even as consumers benefitted enormously from a wider variety of products at a lower cost.

In some respects, supply-side economics has been a failure. Tax cuts on top earners and corporations failed to spur sufficient growth to pay for them. Budget deficits exploded. In other respects, however, supply-side economics did what its proponents hoped it would. Average annual productivity growth improved from 1.1% per annum during the 1973–1982 period to 2.3% in the decade from 1983–1992 and then to 3.0% in the subsequent 10-year period. Only in the aftermath of the 2008 crisis, as debt stopped growing and consumer demand remained soft, has productivity slowed again to pre-1981 levels (Figure 2-4). Moreover, the combination of more rapid productivity growth and stagnant inflation-adjusted wages allowed inflation rates to fall dramatically. As inflation rates fell, the Federal Reserve began to ease monetary policy and equity markets soared.

Figure 2-4: Productivity in the US

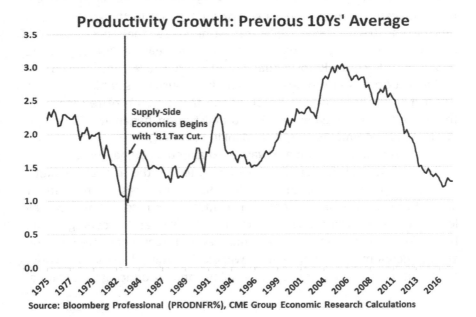

Source: Bloomberg Professional (PRODNFR%), CME Group Economic Research Calculations

Lower inflation and falling interest rates, combined with side-effects of supply-side economics and rising inequality, fueled a massive Reagan-Bush era boom in lending. Between 1981 and 1993 not only did government debt (including what the rest of the government owes to the Social Security Administration) double from 34% to 68% of GDP, but the private sector sank deeper into debt as well. Household debt rose from 48% to 61% of GDP and non-financial corporate debt edged up from 51 to 56% of GDP (Figure 2-5). From 1979 to 2007, the share of income going to the top 1% of earners rose from 9% to over 20% (Figure 2-6) as wages stagnated and productivity soared (Figure 2-7).

Figure 2-5: Supply-Side Economics Lowered Inflation, Increased Inequality and Sent Debt Soaring

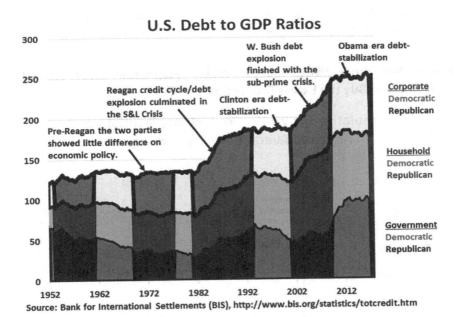

Source: Bank for International Settlements (BIS), http://www.bis.org/statistics/totcredit.htm

Figure 2-6: Tax Rates and Inequality

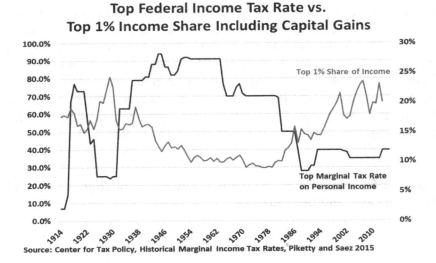

Source: Center for Tax Policy, Historical Marginal Income Tax Rates, Piketty and Saez 2015

Figure 2-7: Productivity Soared, Wages Stagnated: Debt Helped Consumers to Buy the Excess Production

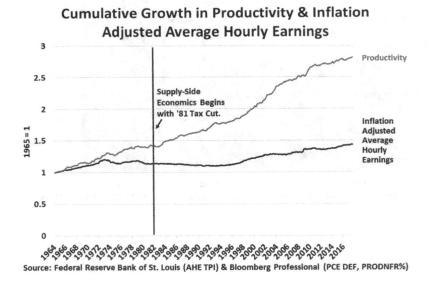

Source: Federal Reserve Bank of St. Louis (AHE TPI) & Bloomberg Professional (PCE DEF, PRODNFR%)

That debt levels increased should be of little surprise. When wages grow more slowly than productivity, three things must happen:

➢ The owners of capital (i.e. the rich) benefit disproportionately from economic growth.

➢ Inflation remains under downward pressure as the supply of goods grows while workers' ability to buy those goods does not.

➢ The only way for consumers whose incomes are stagnating to purchase that growing quantity of goods is to supplement their stagnant wages by taking on ever-increasing amounts of debt.

To offset the impact of massive government budget deficits, Congress exacted tax increases in 1990 and in 1993, bringing the marginal tax rate on top earners to 39.6%. During the 1990s, government debt levels fell from 69% to 51% of GDP. Overall debt did not decline, however, as household and corporate debt rose in a manner than offset the decline in government debt ratios.

In 2001 and again in 2003, President George W. Bush convinced Congress to cut taxes on top earners, capital gains and dividends. Once again, debt ratios exploded as real estate prices soared. In 2007, as the debt ratios crossed 230% of GDP, investors lost confidence in the ability of borrowers to service their debts, credit markets seized up and the economy entered into a deep recession that was only halted in 2009 after the Fed cut interest rates to (near) zero and began a quantitative easing program.

Europe's experience closely resembled what transpired in the United States. In 1979, Margaret Thatcher came to power in the United Kingdom and enacted policies that in many ways resembled those of Reagan. Under her government, the top marginal tax rate on top earners fell from 82% to 40%. During the 1990s, many other European countries, from France to Germany to Sweden, made analogous reductions in their top income tax rates. European nations also slashed corporate income taxes from 35% to around 20%, on average, between the mid-1980s and the early 2000s. Taxes on capital gains also fell.

In Europe too, wages stagnated, productivity growth improved and inflation rates fell, allowing interest rates to decline. This, in turn, enabled, and indeed required, a move towards higher leverage ratios. Between 2000 and 2009, the UK's total-debt-to-GDP ratio soared from 177% to 261% of GDP (Figure 2-8). Europe's debt ratios rose from 198% of GDP in 2000 to above 240% by 2008 (Figure 2-9). Just as in the US and in Japan, debt crises ensued. Both the UK and Europe have failed to de-lever after the crisis as modest reductions in private sector debt ratios were offset by even larger increases in public sector debt. Moreover, European countries also had extremely low levels of interest rates given the level of unemployment, inflation and economic growth right up through at least 2017 and slim prospects of a full normalization of monetary policy any time in the near future.

Figure 2-8: UK Debt Ratio Stabilized but Didn't Fall Much in the 10 Years After Crisis

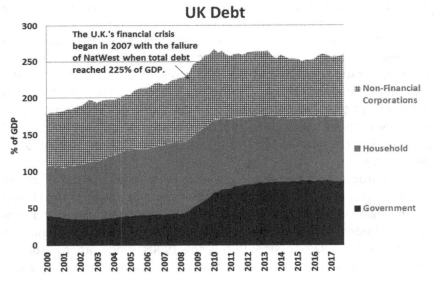

Source: Bank for International Settlements (BIS), http://www.bis.org/statistics/totcredit.htm

Figure 2-9: Eurozone Debt Ratios Remained Above Pre-Crisis Levels for at Least a Decade

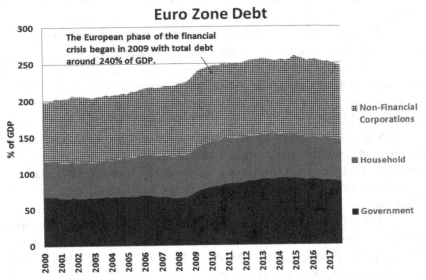

Euro Zone Debt

Source: Bank for International Settlements (BIS), http://www.bis.org/statistics/totcredit.htm

Japanese Lessons: What Europe and the US learned and didn't learn from Japan

After Japan's debt crisis began in 1990, it took the Bank of Japan eight years to get interest rates to zero. By contrast, the US Federal Reserve (Fed) and the Bank of England (BoE) had rates close to zero within 18 months of their crises beginning in 2007. Within 21 months of their crises' start, both central banks were actively engaged in quantitative easing — as they responded to the panic in September 2008 that was triggered by the forced bankruptcy of Lehman Brothers and the extraordinarily messy bailout of AIG. The massive asset purchases by the Fed and the BoE took toxic exposures off the books of banks and helped the US and UK economies to avoid falling into the deflation trap that haunted Japan's economy for decades. Both the UK and the US economies grew slowly after 2009 but by 2018 unemployment rates had fallen to exceptionally low levels by any historical standard.

A major factor that differentiated the Eurozone experience with that of the UK and the US is was the creation of the Euro. With the Euro, the nations of the Eurozone had given up sovereign control of their currencies to a supranational entity, the European Central Bank (ECB). In some respects, this made Europe's debt crisis a bit more like the Latin American debt crisis during the early 1980s and the Asian debt crisis in 1997–98. Owing money in a fiat currency over which they lacked control created a possibility of sovereign default that is generally absent in countries that control their own currencies. Greece, Portugal and Ireland received bailouts to prevent them from defaulting on their obligations.

The ECB's slow response to the crisis exacerbated Europe's situation. In contrast with the Fed and the BoE, the ECB did not take a leaf from the Japanese experience. Instead of putting interest rates close to zero like its counterparts did, it cut interest rates only to 1% in 2009 and then, fearing inflation, raised them to 1.5% during 2011. This put their economy into a double-dip recession and nearly triggered the default of Italy and Spain during the summer of 2012 (Figure 2-10). Only in late 2012 did the ECB finally begin to lower interest rates to zero and eventually embark upon a quantitative easing program. By 2013, Europe's economy hit bottom and began to grow again but its recovery was about three years behind those of the UK and the US.

Europe and the US do share one key thing in common with post-crisis Japan. Neither has achieved any de-leveraging since the crisis began. As of 2018, debt ratios remained mired at levels similar to or slightly above those that sparked the crisis in 2008. While the Fed and the BoE managed to raise rates by 2018, in both cases rates remained far below the levels that one might have expected previously given the pace of nominal GDP growth.

Figure 2-10: With Near Zero Rates and Aggressive QE, UK and US Expansions Led the Way

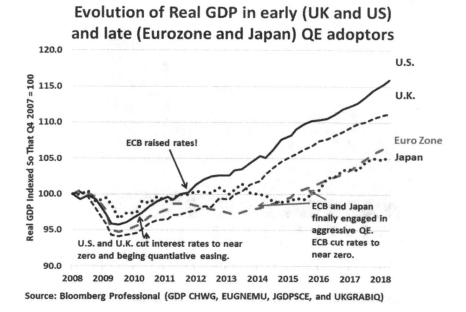

Source: Bloomberg Professional (GDP CHWG, EUGNEMU, JGDPSCE, and UKGRABIQ)

Other Nations Join the Deep-in-Debt Club

Just as the US and Europe failed to learn the dangers of high debt levels from the Japanese in the decade since the 2008 financial crisis began, other nations have also sunk deeply into debt. China, in particular, used massive leveraging to offset the slowing of its economy in 2008. It took its debt ratio from 140% of GDP in 2008 to over 250% by 2016. Initially this produced a strong wave of growth in 2010 and 2011 as China's economy rebounded quickly from the financial crisis. Since 2011, however, China's growth mostly slowed as the positive impact of higher debt ratios has been counteracted by the negative consequences of higher debt burdens.

Figure 2-11: China Joins the Club

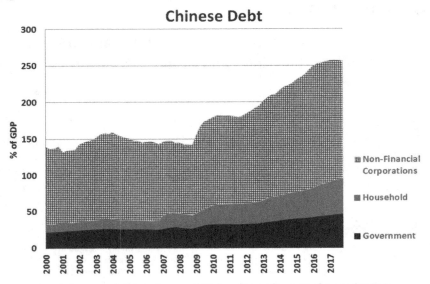

Source: Bank for International Settlements (BIS), http://www.bis.org/statistics/totcredit.htm

In addition to China, a number of other nations including Australia, Canada, Singapore and South Korea have also seen their debt levels reach US and European proportions since 2008. As of 2017, none of these nations had experienced an acute debt crisis in the manner of Europe, Japan and the US, but that could be explained by their keeping their interest rates at extremely low levels. If their central banks were to increase interest rates too much prior to a deleveraging taking place, any of these nations could experience a severe debt crisis, assuming that they also fail to reduce their leverage ratios.

Conclusion

Wage growth lagging the growth in productivity from 1980 to 2007 helped to lower inflation and enabled a more than 30-year decline in interest rates while causing several nefarious side effects. Inequality grew and debt levels soared as consumers borrowed money in order to consume the goods produced in excess of their wage growth. In 2007, confidence broke down. Lenders seized up and banks failed as real estate prices fell. Policy makers quickly lowered interest rates towards zero in order to prevent an economic collapse.

In the decade after 2007, the West lived in a new normal characterized by soft economic growth, falling unemployment, weak investment and slow productivity growth. This was accompanied by extremely low interest rates and basically no overall deleveraging. Meanwhile, China's massive borrowings supported global growth in the wake of the global financial crisis right through President Xi Jinping being installed in October 2017 for another five-year term ending in 2023. China may also one day face its own Minsky Moment and a debt crisis.

High-debt-level economies appear to operate only under conditions of very low short-term interest rates and generous central bank money supply, a temporary "new normal" that could last until a more significant deleveraging takes place in the future. Another possibility is yet another phase of levering up, perhaps the last gasp in a decades-long cycle of rising inequality and debt.

The bottom line:

➢ Macro-economic models that ignore levels of debt are seriously flawed.

➢ Focusing only on public sector debt and not the combination of public and private debt is another huge (and common) omission by economists.

➢ It matters a lot if the debt of country is largely denominated in a currency it controls through its own central bank or whether the currency is out of its control.

➢ Debt crises are common and macro-economists need to include debt loads explicitly in their theories of economic growth if they want to be relevant to the real world.

Chapter 3

Taxes and Growth:
Why Tax Cuts do not Necessarily
Stimulate Economic Growth

Blu Putnam & Erik Norland[1]

Editor's Note: The original version of this article, "Tax cuts: Fuel share prices, not necessarily a catalyst for economic growth", appeared in **The Capco Institute Journal of Financial Transformation,** *Volume 46,* **November 2017.** *This edited version focuses on why tax cuts often lead to bloated government deficits and rising national debt rather than to sustained economic growth. And, the essay makes clear the heroic assumptions some economists are willing to make to justify the political outcomes they prefer. – KT*

Tax cuts are typically politically popular. And, they are often justified by their potential to stimulate economic activity. The concept is that lower tax rates lead to higher real GDP growth, and faster GDP growth leads to higher tax revenues down the road. The link between lower tax rates and future economic growth is, however, exceedingly tenuous. The statistical evidence for tax cuts leading to higher economic growth is mixed and not very convincing. A number of the critical assumptions in the economic theory of tax cuts are often ignored. When one replaces these heroic assumptions with a more realistic view of the world, it goes

---

[1] **Disclaimer:** All examples are hypothetical interpretations of situations and are used for explanation purposes only. The views expressed here reflect solely those of the authors and not necessarily those of their employer, CME Group or its affiliated institutions. The information herein should not be considered investment advice or the results of actual market experience.

a very long way in helping to explain why tax cuts do not seem to contribute to economic growth, when the intuition is otherwise. Even so and despite the lack of impact on economic growth, tax cuts unambiguously seem to help equity markets and raise share prices.

Our research focuses, first, on the economics of tax-rate reductions. Economic theory sees lower marginal tax rates as driving more investment and economic activity; however, such an outcome depends on whether meaningful tax reform and simplification accompanies the marginal tax cuts. Unfortunately, meaningful tax simplification and reform rarely make it through the political process. So, loopholes, not tax cuts, continue to drive investment decisions, meaning that tax-rate reductions often disappoint in terms of the political promise of higher future economic growth.

Second, we take the US as a case study. The US had major marginal tax rate reductions during the presidency of Ronald Reagan in the 1980s, and there was some tax simplification as well. After the end of the 1980-1982 recession, economic growth was quite robust in the rest of the 1980s, although not quite as high as in the previous decade. The US national debt ballooned from 31% of nominal GDP in 1980 to 62% in 1992 as the tax cut experiment worked to worsen the finances of the US federal government. Adding to the evidence was the impact of the modest tax increases in the 1990s, which did not appear to meaningfully hinder economic activity, yet dramatically improved government finances. Indeed, the Clinton Administration left the country with a balanced budget, which was a milestone that may never be achieved again.

Taxation Theory and the "Laffer Curve"

The debate over the economic impact of tax cuts was energized back in the 1970s with the work of economist Arthur Laffer and became known in the political discourse of the Reagan years as supply-side economics. Laffer[2], and various co-authors, including Victor Canto, Marc Miles and

---

[2] Victor A. Canto, Douglas H. Joines, and Arthur B. Laffer, 1982, *Foundations of Supply-Side Economics: Theory and Evidence*, New York: Academic Press. Also, see an excellent summary: Laffer, Arthur B., 2004, "The Laffer Curve: Past, Present, and Future", *Heritage Foundation Backgrounder* No. 1765, pp. 1176–96.

Douglass Joines[3], produced some brilliant research. The theoretical model they developed linking tax cuts to future economic growth was both elegant and intuitive. The model also depended on some heroic simplifying assumptions; and as we can observe with hindsight, the devil was in the details of these unrealistic assumptions.

The essence of the relationship between tax rates and economic growth is intuitively visualized in the Laffer Curve. Starting from a zero top marginal tax rate, as tax rates rise, so do tax revenues as a percent of GDP — up to a point. That is, as the top marginal tax rate gets higher and higher, it ultimately serves as a disincentive for individuals and corporations, and tax revenues as a percent of GDP start to fall even as the top tax rate goes higher and higher

Figure 3-1: Laffer Curve

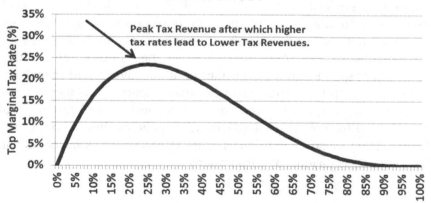

Source: Created as an Illustration by CME Group Chief Economist.

---

[3] Victor A. Canto, Marc A. Miles, 1981, "The Missing Equation: The Wedge Model Alternative", *Journal of Macroeconomics*, 3(2): 247–269. https://doi.org/10.1016/0164-0704(81)90017-3.

Please note that the Laffer Curve is a stylized representation of the theory and the actual peak point of tax revenues related to tax rates is highly controversial, not to mention the shape of the curve itself.[4]

The Achilles heel of the Laffer Curve is the heroic assumption that the top marginal tax rate drives personal spending and corporate investment decisions. Unfortunately, tax codes are exceptionally complex and full of special deductions and loopholes. As a result, the link between the top marginal tax rate and actual consumer spending and business investment is tenuous, if non-existent.

Moreover, even if corporations or individuals were to receive a large realized tax cut, there is little to guarantee that the cuts will impact the components of GDP. For example, corporations might decide to use the newfound money to buy back their stock, refinance their debt, raise dividends paid to shareholders or make a strategic acquisition. While all of these activities have the potential to increase shareholder value, they do not contribute at all to real GDP growth. Only if corporations increase domestic business investment is there likely to be any link to future GDP growth. It works the same way for individuals, especially the wealthy. High-income individuals are much more likely to save more of their tax reduction than average wage earners. So, it matters in a significant way if the tax cut is tilted toward the wealthy or not. And then there is the question of whether government spending is held constant or not. If government spending is reduced to offset the short-term negative impact on budget deficits, then the actual spending from the tax cut will almost certainly not compensate for the reduced government spending due to part of the tax cut being saved by individuals or going toward stock buybacks and higher dividend payouts by corporations.

---

[4] Legend has it that the original "Laffer Curve" was drawn on a paper napkin late at night in a bar in Washington, DC, in the mid-1970s. The version drawn here deviates from Laffer's typical symmetrical diagram and also inverts the axes, to place the tax rates on the vertical and the revenue on the horizontal.

The strongest case for tax reform promoting economic growth is when there is meaningful tax simplification. Tax simplification opens the possibility for marginal tax rates to have more influence over economic decisions, since it would eliminate loopholes. Politically, there is often a lot of rhetoric about tax rate decreases being accompanied by tax simplification, but in practice it is exceedingly rare.

The Case of the US

The US has been a very interesting laboratory for analyzing tax changes. The personal and corporate income tax rate, as well as special deductions and loopholes, have been adjusted many times over the past century. Take the top marginal tax rate on personal income as an example. The rate started out in 1913 at below 10% and applied to only the wealthiest of individuals. By the 1950s, the top rate was around 90% but still applied to relatively few.

Figure 3-2: US Top Marginal Tax Rates

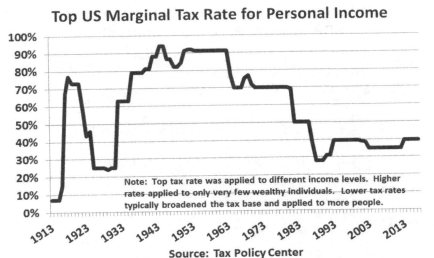

Source: Tax Policy Center
http://www.taxpolicycenter.org/statistics/historical-highest-marginal-income-tax-rates.

During the 1960s, the top tax rate was lowered to 70%, the tax base was broadened and many deductions and loopholes were included in the tax code. The 1980s under President Reagan saw large cuts in the top rate, down to 28%, and some meaningful tax simplification, and the tax base for the top rate was considerably broadened. The 1990s, under Presidents George H. W. Bush and William J. Clinton, saw some increases in the top tax rate. In short, US top tax rates have been all over the map and have applied to very different tax bases as well over time.

None of these tax rate changes had a discernible impact on the pattern of the last six decades of slowly decelerating economic growth rates. In the 1960s, the US was arguably a 5% real GDP annual growth economy. Each decade since then, however, has shown a steady deceleration down to the 2% annual growth trend seen in the 2010–2017 period in the economic expansion following the Great Recession of 2008–2009.

Figure 3-3: US Economic Expansions

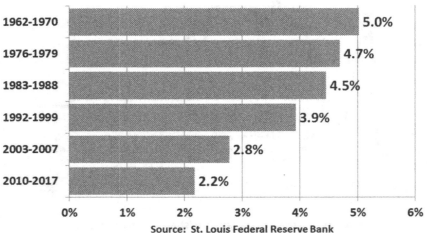

Source: St. Louis Federal Reserve Bank
FRED Database (GDPC1)

Indeed, we would argue that since 1950, the US has experienced three growth drivers. The 1950s and 1960s were about recovery from World War II, building a modern economy and improving the infrastructure, such as building the interstate highway system as well as investing in education through the GI Bill. The result was rapid growth in labor productivity and well-above average GDP growth. The 1970s and 1980s were about the arrival of the large baby boomer generation into the work force. Baby boomers, born after WWII and into the early 1960s, resulted in very rapid expansion of the labor force as they matured into their twenties in the 1970s and 1980s, keeping post-war economic growth elevated as these new workers were absorbed into the economy. From the 1990s onward, the drivers changed direction. The arithmetic is informative. Real GDP growth can be decomposed into growth in the labor force and in labor productivity.

Figure 3-4: US Government Receipts and Expenditures

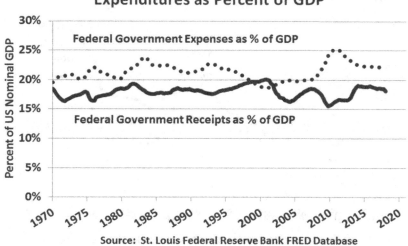

US Federal Government Receipts and Expenditures as Percent of GDP

Source: St. Louis Federal Reserve Bank FRED Database (FGEXPND, FGRECPT, GDP)

While labor productivity growth has ebbed in the 2000s, the demographic trend has been even more powerful, with aging boomers retiring and the smaller, later generations not fully replacing them, leading to very low growth rates in the labor force — below 1% in the US in the expansion period after the 2008–2009 Great Recession. Hence, it is hard to find an impact from all the different tax regimes when demographic patterns explain such a substantial part of the deceleration of potential GDP growth.

Nevertheless, one cannot study the impact of tax rate cuts on GDP growth without special attention to the 1980s. In two stages, the highest marginal tax rate went from 70% to 28%, and there was some tax simplification. Economic growth in the 1980s held up very well for demographic reasons, too, since baby boomers were in their prime working years.

Figure 3-5: US National Debt

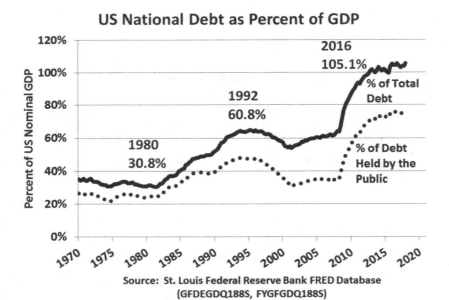

Source: St. Louis Federal Reserve Bank FRED Database
(GFDEGDQ188S, FYGFGDQ188S)

While tax revenues as a percent of GDP remained in the 17.5% to 18.6% zone during 1983–1990, budget deficits increased and the national debt soared. Indeed, the total outstanding US national debt was about 31% of GDP in 1980 and was over 53% in 1990. The idea that lower tax rates, even with some tax simplification, would close the budget deficit by spurring substantial additional GDP growth, just did not happen.

Subsequent US presidents in the 1990s, both Republican and Democrat, made the decision to close the budget gap with increases in tax rates. Federal debt fell from 64% of GDP in 1993 to 55% of GDP in 2001. This process was reversed in the 2000s, as government expenses soared in the immediate aftermath of the Great Recession. By 2013, the US national debt as a percent of GDP was 101%. From 2013 through 2016, with tight controls over government spending and modest economic growth, national debt ratios remained relatively stable at just under 105% of GDP.

Lessons for Analyzing Tax Policy Changes

The implications of tax policy changes for future economic growth typically focus on three main challenges: (1) whether lower (higher) taxes will increase (decrease) future economic growth as analyzed here, (2) the possibility of tax simplification, and (3) the implications for future budget deficits and the national debt.

The debate about tax cuts and future economic growth largely pits economists against politicians. Politicians in favor of a tax cut are going to consistently argue that higher growth will follow, allowing for lower projections of future deficits and national debt levels. Many economists, not all of course, will follow along the lines argued in this research, and will be very cautious in projecting higher economic growth in the face of severe demographic headwinds.

Our initial, or naïve, scenario typically assumes very little tax simplification because the special interest groups associated with each deduction and loophole are exceedingly strong. If one is willing to make the assumption of major tax simplification, then the case for stronger economic growth is much easier to make.

We can take US corporate taxes as an illustration to emphasize the importance of tax simplification to the economic growth story. Before we examine US corporate tax data, though, we need to note that US corporate tax data is quite tricky to interpret. Let's take the 2016–2017 tax data as an example. Corporate tax receipts received by the US federal government in the four quarters from July 2016 through June 2017 were reported as US$409 billion. This headline number, used by many to analyze the size of the potential tax cuts, includes taxes paid by the Federal Reserve Banks, and that poses a big problem for tax analysis.

Figure 3-6: US Federal Corporate Taxes and Profits

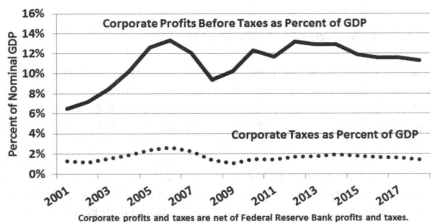

Corporate profits and taxes are net of Federal Reserve Bank profits and taxes.
Source: St. Louis Federal Reserve Bank FRED Database.
Corporate Profits = A053RC1Q027SBEA, Federal Reserve Profits = B397RC1Q027SBEA,
Federal Corporate Taxes = B075RC1Q027SBEA, F

Since the Great Recession, Federal Reserve Banks went through a period of massive asset purchases known as Quantitative Easing (QE) and earned substantial profits on their huge portfolios of US Treasury securities and mortgage-backed securities. After keeping a very small surplus to add to their paid-in capital, the Federal Reserve Banks make quite large contributions to the US Treasury. From July 2016 through June 2017, these contributions, reported as corporate taxes paid by the Fed, totaled US$86 billion, based on earnings of US$87 billion, or an effective rate of almost 99%. Clearly, the Fed is a special case and should be excluded from an analysis of US corporate taxes.

This means the Q3/2016 through Q2/2017 annual level of corporate taxation in the US, not including the Fed, was about US$323 billion, or about 1.7% of GDP. This is not that high a level of taxation for an economy approaching an annual GDP of US$20 trillion. So, on that note alone, one might want to be very cautious about expecting any tax cut to trigger a significant increase in future economic growth, just because the GDP contribution of the tax cut is not that impressive. For countries where the corporate tax burden is a much higher percentage of the economy, of course, the scope for a large tax cut impacting economic growth is proportionately larger.

Bottom Line

Our main observation with the US case study, however, is to emphasize the role of tax loopholes that are assumed not to exist in most theories of how tax cuts impact an economy. US corporate profits on a GDP basis before taxes (and not including earnings of Federal Reserve Banks) were running at 11.35% of GDP for the Q3/16 — Q2/17 period.[5] As noted earlier, corporate tax receipts, not including the Federal Reserve tax payments, ran at 1.7% of GDP over the same period. Given that the top marginal rate was 35% in the US in 2017, it is clear that corporations mostly do not pay the top rate, as that would imply corporate tax receipts of almost 4% of GDP. Indeed,

---

[5] Source: St. Louis Federal Reserve Bank FRED Database. Corporate Profits before tax = A053RC1Q027SBEA, Federal Reserve Profits = B397RC1Q027SBEA, Federal Corporate Taxes = B075RC1Q027SBEA, Federal Reserve Bank Taxes = B677RC1Q027SBEA, US Nominal GDP = GDP).

the average effective corporate tax rate is about 15%. What this means is that the top tax rate does not drive business investment decisions, and so, expectations of increased capital spending from a cut in the top marginal tax rate are not easily justified.

Despite our pessimism on the linkage of tax-rate reductions to economic growth, tax cuts do have a market impact. Tax cuts are bullish for stocks. A meaningful corporate tax cut provides money for share buybacks, higher dividend payouts and strategic acquisitions — all of which have the potential to lead to higher share prices — just not higher economic growth.

Chapter 4

Yield Curve: Predicting Recessions

Erik Norland & Blu Putnam[1]

Editor's Note: When yield curves flatten, that is short-term rates rise toward the level of long-term bond yields or even higher, equity volatility and eventually recessions often follow. This research explores feedback loops between monetary policy and the economy that help us understand why economic expansions end — and it is not from old age. – KT

One of the rarely stated but nevertheless implied tenants of most schools of economic thought, including monetarism and Keynesianism, is that economic downturns are unpredictable and arrive randomly. In this chapter, we present evidence that this is not the case. Rather, the economy moves in cycles that are governed by a feedback loop in which monetary policy both drives changes in unemployment, credit spreads and equity index volatility and, in turn, reacts to those same three variables.

Our measure of the easiness or tightness of monetary policy is the yield curve, the difference between long-term and short-term interest rates. When the yield curve is steep, long-term interest rates are above short-term interest rates. This is great for banks, which make money, in part, by borrowing inexpensively short-term from depositors or other financial institutions, including the central bank, and lending long-term for a higher rate of interest.

---

[1] **Disclaimer:** All examples are hypothetical interpretations of situations and are used for explanation purposes only. The views expressed here reflect solely those of the authors and not necessarily those of their employer, CME Group or its affiliated institutions. The information herein should not be considered investment advice or the results of actual market experience.

Steep yield curves suggest easy monetary policy. They are both a sign that the central bank is keeping short-term interest rates below the long-term equilibrium level at which banks and other financial institutions will extend credit to the public and private sectors. This tends to lower unemployment, narrow credit spreads, and lower equity market volatility.

By contrast, when the yield curve becomes flat or even inverts, it reduces the profits of lenders. They can no longer make money by borrowing short-term and lending long-term. It also indicates that the central bank has raised interest rates near or above their long-term equilibrium level and is intent on restraining credit expansion and slowing the economy. Tight monetary policy eventually translates into rising unemployment, widening credit spreads and increasing equity market volatility.

The feedback loop between yield curve versus unemployment, credit spreads and equity market volatility manifests itself in a four-part cycle. Like any cycle, where it begins and ends is arbitrary, so we will start at the bottom of the economic cycle and loop around through the expansion back to the next low point in economic activity.

> **Recession:** Flat or inverted yield curves were a prelude to the recessions in 1990, 2001 and 2008. After a couple of years of flat yield curves, credit spreads began to widen, equity index volatility shot higher and unemployment rates rose.

> **Early stage recovery:** In each case, as credit spreads widened, equity volatility and unemployment rose, the central bank lowered rates, steepening the yield curve. Early stage recoveries typically feel miserable. Markets remain disjointed, the job market remains weak etc.

> **Mid-Stage recovery:** By this time easy monetary policy is showing results. Credit spreads are narrowing. Equity markets have calmed down. Unemployment is falling. This gives the central bank the confidence to begin tightening monetary policy which, in turn, begins the process of taking the yield curve from being extremely steep, to being rather flat.

> **Late stage economic expansion:** By this time the policy tightening cycle is well underway. Faced with low unemployment, narrow credit spreads and a still not volatile equity market, the central bank has allowed the yield curve to become rather flat or even inverted. This eventually translates into an explosion of credit spreads and equity market volatility, followed shortly by a rise in unemployment and another recession. Wash. Rinse. Repeat.

To better visualize how this works, let's break this down by variable and by economic cycle. Let's begin with unemployment and then move on to credit spreads and the VIX, an index of options of the S&P 500.

The Yield Curve Unemployment Feedback Loop

In 1979, President Jimmy Carter appointed Paul Volcker to head the Fed and entrusted him with the thankless task of killing inflation. Volcker succeeded. After he raised rates to 20% and put the economy into a double-dip recession that drove unemployment above 10% by 1982, inflation never returned to its previous levels. By 1982, the Fed was busy cutting rates. From 1982 until 1988, 30-year US Treasuries yielded about 200–250 basis points (bps) more, on average, than three-month T-Bills. The economy boomed. Unemployment fell. (Figure 4-1.) In 1988 and 1989, his successor, Alan Greenspan, began raising rates to prevent the economy from overheating. By 1989, the yield curve was flat, savings and loans institutions were going belly up and in 1990 the investment bank Drexel Burnham Lambert failed, creating chaos in the high-yield debt market.

As the US economy entered a recession in late 1990 and early 1991, the Fed vigorously cut rates as unemployment rose from 5.4% to 7.8%. By 1992, the US had a steep yield curve and unemployment peaked in July of that year and began falling once again. The Fed maintained easy monetary policy through early 1994 when it began tightening again. By 1995, the Fed had achieved something rare: a soft landing.

Unemployment stopped falling for a while but to the Fed's astonishment, productivity was booming and there was little in the way of wage pressures. So, the Fed eased up slightly.

Figure 4-1: The 1980s Cycle

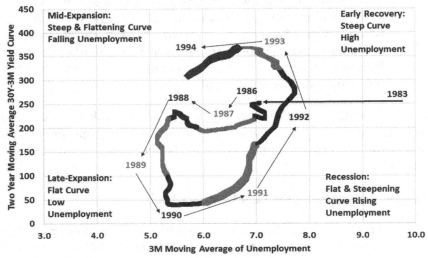

Source: Bloomberg Professional (USGG30Y, GB3 and USURTOT)

Figure 4-2: The 1990s Boom Extended With a Productivity Revolution

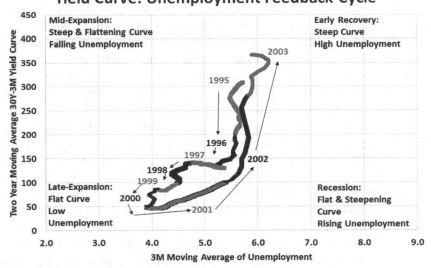

Source: Bloomberg Professional (USGG30Y, GB3 and USURTOT)

As a result of the Fed's easing up, the Fed did not bring the yield curve all the way to flat, instead leaving around 140bps of steepness between 3M T-Bills and 30Y Long Bond yields. Unemployment started falling again in 1997 and dropped all the way to 3.9% by the time the Fed flattened the yield curve in early 2000 (Figure 4-2).

The flat yield curve helped to trigger a collapse in business investment and a rise in unemployment in 2001 to which the Fed responded by slashing rates to 1.75% by the end of 2001. When the economy failed to revive, the Fed eventually set rates at 1.25% by the end of 2002 and to 1% in June of 2003. The low rates set off a massive housing boom and a consumer-borrowing binge. With a steeper yield curve, the labor market finally began to recover in the second half of 2003.

Figure 4-3: Yield Curve — 2004–2018

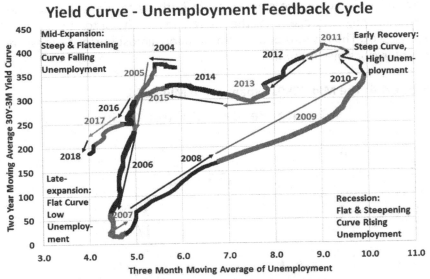

Source: Bloomberg Professional (USGG30Y, GB3 and USURTOT)

Confident that it had things under control, the Fed began raising rates in June 2004. After 17 consecutive rate hikes, it had Fed Funds back at 5.25% by June 2006 and the yield curve back to being flat. The economy continued to grow until spring 2007 when unemployment bottomed at 4.4% and began rising, slowly at first. As the subprime mortgage crisis spun out of control, unemployment soared in 2008 and 2009. By the end of 2008, the Fed had rates close to zero. One year later, unemployment peaked at 10% and began slowly falling by about 0.7% per year (Figure 4-3). After having hiked rates once each in 2015 and 2016, the Fed began tightening policy more vigorously in 2017 with three rate hikes and a reduction in the size of its balance sheet.

Yield curve versus credit spread feedback loop

A very similar cycle exists between the yield curve and credit spreads. Credit spreads and yield curves are both somewhat choppy on a day-to-day and month-to-month basis. What we are interested here is not so much the exact state of the market on any given day but rather the overall climate. As such, to see the relationship between credit spreads and the yield curve, we smooth them both by taking a 500-day (two year) moving average and then put the results into an "X to Y" scatterplot. The result is quite extraordinary: almost perfectly consistent counter-clockwise motion.

Figure 4-4: The Mid-1990s Expansion to Mid-2000s

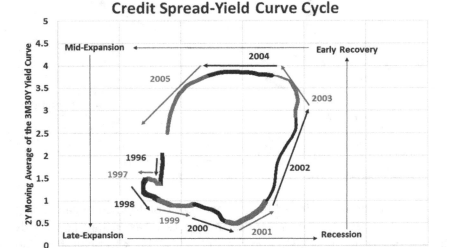

Source: Bloomberg Professional (GB3, USGG30YR, LF98OAS), CME Economics Research Calculations

Since we don't have a long time series for credit spreads as we have with the VIX or unemployment, we will examine two full cycles from the middle of the 1990s expansion to the middle of the 2000s expansion (Figure 4-4), and then from the middle of the 2000s expansion to now (Figure 4-5). Currently, we appear to be in the mid-to-late stages of an economic expansion.

Figure 4-4 picks up in the midst of the 1990s economic expansion. The S&L Crisis and the collapse of Drexel Burnham Lambert were distant memories. The Fed's easy monetary policy gave way to a narrowing of credit spreads beginning in late 1991 that carried on through the Fed tightening cycle in 1994.

It is in this period that Figure 4-4 begins. By 1996, credit spreads were as narrow as ever. The yield curve still had some steepness but was on a flattening trajectory. In March 1997, the Fed hiked rates once to 5.5% and shortly thereafter the first signs of trouble appeared. In June 1997, the Thai baht fell off its peg to the US dollar, triggering a crisis that quickly sent most of Asia, excluding China, into a downturn that culminated in 1998 with the Russian debt default and the subsequent collapse of large hedge fund Long-Term Capital Management (LTCM). The Fed staved off a US recession by lowering rates to 4.75% in the late summer and fall of 1998 but began raising rates again in June 1999, with the Fed Funds rate reaching 6.5% in March of 2000. During this time credit spreads widened considerably.

By 2001 the economy was in a recession, now remembered as the Tech Wreck and notable for a collapse in business investment. The NASDAQ 100 fell over 80%. Credit spreads were extremely wide. The Fed began slashing rates in January 2001, and by November 2001 the Fed Funds rate was at 1.75%. The Fed lowered rates to 1.25% by the end of 2002 and to 1% in June 2003. Dramatic cuts in the interest rates helped to isolate the recession to the business investment component of the gross domestic product while consumer spending grew slowly and housing boomed, spurred by low rates.

By late 2001 the yield curve was steep and remained so for three years. In the spring of 2003, credit spreads began narrowing and had tightened considerably by 2004. With credit spreads narrow, equity markets calm, economy growing and unemployment falling, the Fed, in June 2004, embarked on a series of interest rate increases that took rates from 1% to 5.25% by June 2006.

By late 2006 the yield curve was flat and credit spreads remained narrow, but not for long. The first signs of crisis emerged in February 2007 when some investors began to worry in earnest about subprime housing loans. In July and August 2007 credit spreads began to explode, eventually reaching far wider levels than in 1990 or in 2001. Our credit spreads-yield curve graph began making a sharp right turn across the bottom of the graph, signaling a coming end to the expansion.

Figure 4-5: The 2006–2018 Cycle

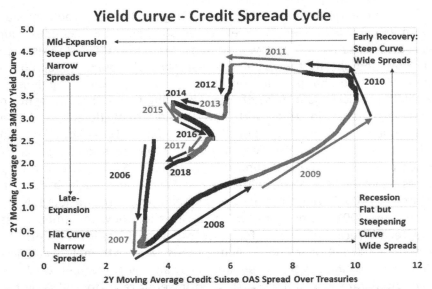

Yield Curve - Credit Spread Cycle

Source: Bloomberg Professional (GB3, USGG30YR, LF98OAS), CME Economic Research Calculations

The Fed cut rates slowly at first, but when the financial panic hit hard in September 2008 with the poorly managed bankruptcy of Lehman Brothers and the bailout of AIG, the Fed accelerated the pace until they reached 0.125% by the end of 2008. The Fed also in Q4/2008 created three special purpose vehicles and lent them a trillion US dollars to purchase "toxic" exposures from the financial system and remove a large part of the problem from the balance sheets of US banks allowing them to start their recovery much faster than otherwise.[2] [See Chapter 15, for an in-depth analysis of why the Fed's approach to the 2008 financial panic allowed for a much faster recovery of the banking sector compared to the approach taken by the European Central Bank.]

The Fed's rate cuts worked their magic. By 2009 the yield curve was steep, credit spreads began narrowing in March of that year and by 2011 had tightened considerably. Since then, however, a few factors have made our yield curve-credit spread cycle less smooth than in its previous iteration.

Three rounds of quantitative easing (QE) put some kinks in the yield curve. When the Fed could no longer lower rates, even as the economic recovery was taking hold and the economy was creating jobs again, the Fed began to buy bonds further up this curve (aka, Maturity Extension Program). This might have led to a yield curve that was less steep than it would otherwise have been. Moreover, there is no clear evidence to suggest that QE implemented once the economic recovery had clearly begun had any benefit in terms of encouraging more growth or inflation. [See Chapter 14 on how to evaluate the Fed's QE programs.]

When the Fed embarked on QE3 in early 2012, growth did not accelerate, but the yield curve did flatten and credit spreads, for a time, stopped narrowing. When the Fed announced the tapering of QE3 in May 2013, credit spreads began narrowing again and by the end of 2014 had fallen considerably.

Credit spreads blew out again in 2015 as the price of oil collapsed from US$90 to below US$50 per barrel, falling as low as US$26 by February 2016. During this time, the Fed worked up the courage to hike rates once in December 2015, without having much impact upon the yield curve.

By late 2016 oil prices had rebounded. Fears of an energy sector credit meltdown faded. With spreads narrowing again, the Fed embarked on a more aggressive pace of rate hikes, with one rate hike in December 2016 and subsequent hikes coming more or less every other FOMC meeting through 2018. In addition, the Fed began unwinding QE, contracting its balance sheet, by allowing a run-off of maturing assets

---

[2] Putnam, B. H., July 2014, "Evaluating different approaches to quantitative easing: lessons for the future of central banking", *The Journal of Financial Perspectives* 2(2): 109–119.

instead of re-investing the proceeds. This resulted in some yield curve flattening that brought the credit spread-yield curve cycle to the point that it closely resembled where the US was in 2005 on the chart but with important differences.

In 2018, economic imbalances were not as apparent as they were in 2005. There was no housing bubble. Although the S&P 500® had soared from 666 in March 2009 to around 2,600 in early 2018, it did not appear that there was an equity market bubble. (Of course, bubbles are always clear only in hindsight.) Certain valuation ratios did seem elevated even as long-term interest rates used to discount those future earnings remained low relative to the prevailing core inflation rate. In short, by early 2018, the yield curve was leaving the mid-stage recovery phase and entering the late-stage part of the cycle; however, the yield curve had not inverted and was not yet suggesting a recession was in sight.

Yield Curve — Equity Index Volatility Cycle

The VIX is the index of implied volatility on S&P 500® options and its daily time series is extraordinarily choppy. To see its relationship with the yield curve, we smooth them both by taking a two-year (500 business day) moving average and then put the results into an "X to Y" scatterplot.

The result is quite extraordinary: consistent counter-clockwise motion. From our arbitrary starting point in a recession, the Federal Reserve (Fed) has responded to the economic downturn with much lower short-term rates. Steep, upward sloping yield curves with short-term rates much lower than long-term bond yields eventually are associated with an economic recovery and lower equity-market volatility. A sustained economic expansion, with relatively low equity-market volatility, makes the Fed feel comfortable about removing monetary policy accommodation and flattening the yield curve (i.e., short-term rates moving higher with stable bond yields). A tight monetary policy, flat yield-curve environment finally is associated with an economic downturn and massive correction in the equity and credit markets which sends volatility soaring. High volatility and a crashing economy force the Fed to lower short-term rates and ease policy in order to assist in generating an economic recovery. Wash. Rinse. Repeat. (Figures 4-6 – 4-8).

Figure 4-6: Equity Volatility and Yield Curve Cycle — 1990–1999

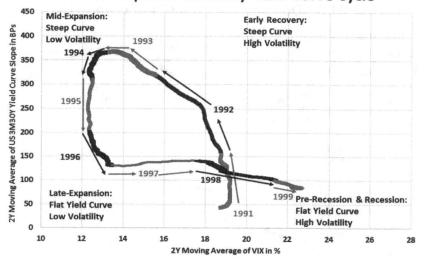

Source: Bloomberg Professional (GB3, USGG30YR and VIX), CME Economic Research Calculations

Figure 4-7: Equity Volatility and Yield Curve Cycle — 2000–2008

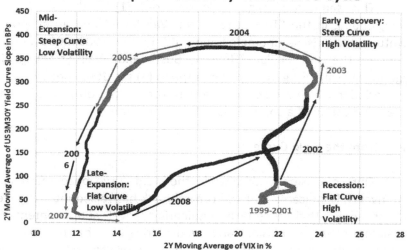

Source: Bloomberg Professional (GB3, USGG30YR and VIX), CME Economic Research Calculations

Figure 4-8: Equity Volatility and Yield Curve Cycle — 2009–2018

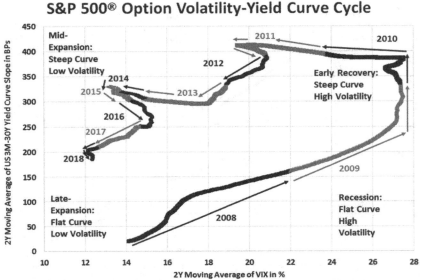

Source: Bloomberg Professional (GB3, USGG30YR and VIX), CME Economic Research Calculations

This same four-stage cycle occurred (1) in the 1990–1999 period, ending in the "Tech Wreck" on Wall Street and an economic downturn with rising unemployment; (2) in the 2000–2008 period, ending in the spectacular "Housing Bust" and Wall Street panic, triggering sharply rising unemployment; and (3) the 2009–ongoing as of 2018 period in which the economy entered stage four only in 2018 with no clear indication of a coming recession at the time.

Lesson from the Yield Curve

Our conclusion is that when the yield curve becomes flat or even inverts, it indicates that the central bank has raised interest rates near or above their long-term equilibrium level and is intent on restraining credit expansion and wants to slow the economy. If monetary policy gets too tight then it can eventually translate into rising unemployment, widening credit spreads and increasing equity market volatility. Our research suggests that the feedback loop between yield curve versus unemployment, credit spreads and equity market volatility manifests itself in a four-part cycle. To recap the four stages of the cycle:

> **Recession:** Flat or inverted yield curves are often a prelude to recessions.

> **Early stage recovery:** Credit spreads have widened, equity volatility and unemployment is elevated, and in response the central bank has lowered rates, steepening the yield curve.

> **Mid-Stage recovery:** Credit spreads are narrowing. Equity markets have calmed down. Unemployment is falling. This gives the central bank the confidence to begin tightening monetary policy which, in turn, begins the process of taking the yield curve from being extremely steep, to moving to a flatter shape.

> **Late stage economic expansion.** The policy tightening cycle is well underway. Faced with low unemployment and narrow credit spreads, the central bank pushes short-term rates even higher and allows the yield curve to become rather flat or even inverted. This last stage has the potential, eventually, to translate into an explosion of credit spreads and equity market volatility, followed shortly by a rise in unemployment and another recession. Wash. Rinse. Repeat.

Chapter 5

Demographics:
Appreciating Economic Growth
Potential

D. Sykes Wilford[1] & Blu Putnam[2]

Editor's Note: Often in the economic literature since the 1950s, demographic patterns are assumed to be stable. Demographic patterns may shift ever so slowly — like watching paint dry — so demographic factors are rarely picked up in monthly or quarterly time frame statistical analysis. But, ignoring these slow-moving demographic patterns is a prescription for poor policy and bad economic forecasts. – KT

Demographic patterns are one of the more important drivers of economic growth potential, ranking right up there with the type of economic system, the degree of political stability, property rights and viability of the rule of law. Economists in the 1800s paid plenty of attention to demographics. Witness the debates ignited by the economist and cleric, Reverend Thomas Robert Malthus[3], around

---

[1] Hipp Professor of Finance, Graduate School of Business, The Citadel, Charleston, South Carolina, USA.

[2] **Disclaimer:** All examples are hypothetical interpretations of situations and are used for explanation purposes only. The views expressed here reflect solely those of the authors and not necessarily those of their employer, CME Group or its affiliated institutions. The information herein should not be considered investment advice or the results of actual market experience.

[3] Malthus T.R., 1798, *An Essay on the Principle of Population* (reprinted by Oxford World Classics). Malthus' famous quote from Chapter VII, "... That the increase of population is necessarily limited by the means of subsistence, that population does invariably increase when the means of subsistence increase, and, that the superior power of population is repressed by moral restraint, vice and misery."

whether population growth might outstrip the ability of the planet to feed all the people. In the post-war era of modern economics, however, demographic patterns have often taken a back seat, at least until recently. Basic economics textbooks tend to downplay demographic patterns and macro-economic growth models may simply assume a constant age distribution of the population and steady growth of the labor force. These assumptions make for truly bad economics and very poor long-term macro-economic forecasting.

Implying no causality, the arithmetic is that the growth of an economy is the sum of its labor force growth and its growth in labor productivity. While a wide variety of factors can drive labor productivity, labor force growth is dominated by demographic patterns. Countries with rapidly expanding labor forces will, at least, have the potential to expand at a relatively fast pace, compared to countries with little to no labor force growth. Let's examine the US specifically, and then make some general comments related to how demographic patterns have influenced economic growth over the decades in Japan, China, Russia, India and Brazil.

United States: Boomers and Millennials

Since the 1960s, the pace of US real GDP growth has been decelerating, regardless of the tax structure, interest rate policies, which party held the Presidency, or stock market activity (Figure 5-1). If one removes the recession quarters and just looks at the pace of economic growth during the expansion periods, the pattern of deceleration becomes even clearer (Figure 5-2). The culprit lies in the demographic patterns.[4] After WWII, the soldiers came home and had babies — lots of them. The baby boomer generation, more or less people born after WWII and through the early 1960s, comprises some 75 million people. As this generation has matured, it has impacted the economy and culture in powerful ways.

---

[4] Population data for the US and most countries around the world are available in the US Census' International database: https://www.census.gov/data-tools/demo/idb/informationGateway.php

Figure 5-1: US real GDP — 1952 through 2017

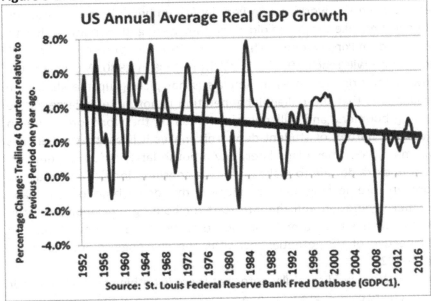

Figure 5-2. US Expansion periods

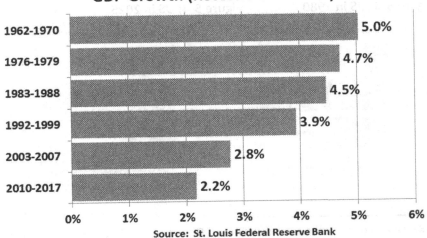

In the period commencing around 2015, baby boomers are retiring from the workforce in very large numbers. Retirees simply do not consume like they once did when they were getting married, having kids, and making money. The age 65 and up percent of the US population will reach 19% by 2025, from 11% in 1980. Moreover, the new generation known as millennials is not picking up the slack. The challenge is that the millennial generation is not quite as large as the retiring boomers, and millennials are entering the work force with an awesome burden of student debt. This makes it likely that millennials will marry later, have kids later, buy a house later, etc., and generally take an extra decade to make up for the consumption demand that the boomers are leaving behind. Indeed, the downsizing of the baby boomer generation and the late start for housing formation from the millennials has been a major influence on the US economy.[5] From the perspective of US potential real GDP, the challenge is greatest from 2015–2025.

We should carefully note that there is nothing to say that labor productivity cannot grow faster and make up some of the ground left by the retiring boomers. It is just that the demographic headwinds will be quite strong into the 2020s before reversing.

Figure 5-3: US in 1980   **Figure 5-4: US in 2025**

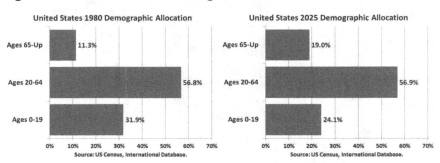

---

[5] Karagiannidis, Iordanis, and Wilford, D. Sykes, April 2018, "Household deformation trumps demand management policy in the 21st century", *The Capco Institute Journal of Financial Transformation*, 47: 67–78.

Comments on Long-Term Growth Patterns around the World

Japan is one of the oldest countries in the world based on average age. Population growth and labor force growth have been close to zero for several decades, and the pattern of economic growth mirrors the demographic picture.

Figure 5-5: Japan in 1980   **Figure 5-6: Japan in 2025**

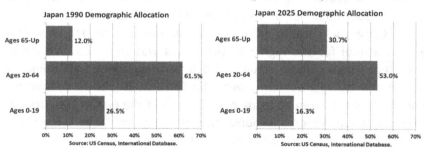

Figure 5-7. Japan Real GDP since the 1950s

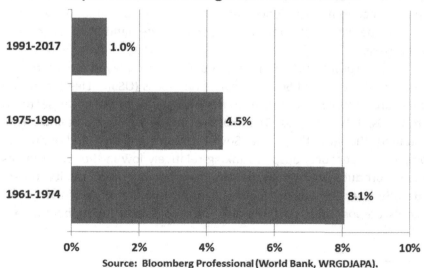

Many analysts like to refer to the 1991–2000 and 2001–2010 years as the lost decades, implying that the country never recovered from its stock market and real estate crash of 1989–1990. When one considers demographic patterns, though, there is a totally different explanation for the decades of slow growth. The major feature of Japanese demographics in the 1950s and 1960s was a transformation from a rural economy to an urban economy. After the war, as people left the rural sector and moved to urban centers, the growth of the industrial labor force helped to accelerate real GDP growth.

Once the rural-to-urban migration ran out of people in the 1980s, the fuel for the high real GDP rates was removed. We would argue that "Japan, Inc." actually did a terrific job of maintaining a modern and thriving economy over the 1991–2020 period despite the strong headwinds from an aging population and the end of the rural-to-urban migration. When the population is aging and labor force is not growing, sustaining real GDP growth in the 1% to 2% range is actually an excellent performance.

The over-65 population cohort was 12% in 1990, headed toward 30% by 2025. As noted, economic growth slowed dramatically with an aging population and zero labor force growth. Over 1991–2018 the Japanese economy experienced mild deflation or zero inflation, which is totally to be expected given the slowdown in demand from the retired generations.

The rural-to-urban migration pattern also played a huge role in the fall of the Union of Soviet Socialist Republics (USSR). Like Japan, the Soviet Union moved workers from the rural sector to the urban sector in the 1950s, 60s, and 70s. The massive inflow of new urban workers sustained the growth of the Soviet Union's military and industrial complex for decades, despite ranking relatively low in the world tables of labor productivity.[6] When the rural-to-urban migration ran its course, a decade later the Soviet Union collapsed. But the story of the Soviet Union's demographic patterns also encompasses a failing health care

---

[6] The common saying in the Soviet Union regarding labor productivity was, "They pretend to pay us and we pretend to work."

system and rising mortality rates.[7] The population peak was hit around 1991, further exacerbating growth challenges for Russia in the post-Soviet era. Population growth has only resumed since 2012 or so.

China is another country whose high growth rates have been bolstered in part by a strong rural-to-urban migration, which has been an offset to the country's lack of total population growth. Because of the one-child policy and its low fertility rates, China also set in motion a process of aging. The over-65 demographic cohort is set to grow from 7.7% in 1990 to 14.2% in 2025, a doubling of the percentage in 35 years. The challenge of a rapidly aging population will coincide in the 2020s with the slowing of the rural-urban migration. In short, in the 2020s, China will face unprecedented headwinds regarding its desire to maintain a robust pace of economic growth.

Note that China's one-child policy began in 1979 and has been credited with preventing over 400 million births. Phasing out of the one-child policy started in late 2015, but it will make little difference for decades, since it takes 25 years to grow a 25-year old new worker. And, it is not at all clear if fertility rates will rise much at all, since most young adults grew up in one child families and may simply prefer that choice as they form their own families.

Figure 5-8: China in 1990   **Figure 5-9: China in 2025**

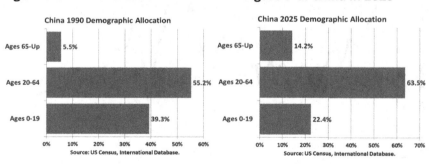

Figure 5-10: China Employment Growth

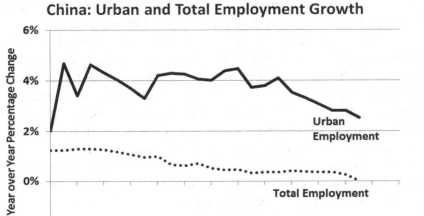

Figure 5-11: China Real GDP

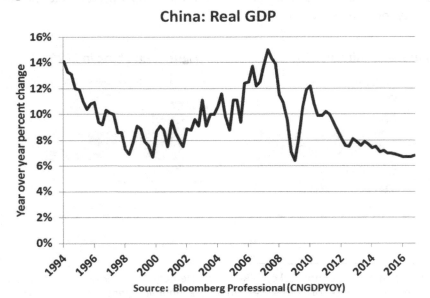

Figure 5-12: India in 2025   **Figure 5-13: Brazil in 2025**

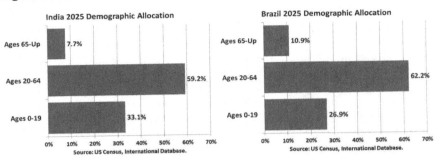

Our last observation about demographic patterns in the 2020s is the growing divide between the rich, mature, and aging countries, such as the US, Europe, Japan, and China, and the younger nations of India, Brazil, Indonesia, Nigeria, and Kenya. These younger nations typically have over half the population under 30 years of age and around 30% under 20. If they can provide a stable economic and political environment, their best growth decades are ahead of them. Of course, this is a big "if", yet if one is looking for growth potential, one needs to look to the younger, emerging economies.

Chapter 6

Wages and Productivity: Structural Changes are Crucial to Understand

Natalie Denby & Blu Putnam[1]

Editor's Note: Many economic models and theories of labor productivity and wage growth often assume a stable mix of jobs in the economy. This research argues that structural changes in the labor market and shifting demographic patterns are keys to understanding the sluggish wage growth in the US and limited gains in labor productivity over the 2007–2017 period. – KT

Despite a tight labor market, wage and productivity growth remained low in the US in the post-Great Recession decade. Nominal hourly average wages rose by 2.6% in the US between 2016 and 2017, on par with post-Recession performance. Labor productivity growth averaged only 1.1% between 2007 and 2016. Between 1995 and 2007, by contrast, the average growth rate was 2.5%. Although cyclical factors may be partially to blame, there are several key structural features of the US economy contributing to diminished growth. Wage and productivity growth have been held back by persistently low inflation expectations, workforce demographics, and the shift in the payrolls distribution in the economy in favor of lower-wage sectors.

---

[1] **Disclaimer:** All examples are hypothetical interpretations of situations and are used for explanation purposes only. The views expressed here reflect solely those of the authors and not necessarily those of their employer, CME Group or its affiliated institutions. The information herein should not be considered investment advice or the results of actual market experience.

By way of example, the Federal Open Markets Committee's (FOMC) minutes of the July 25–26, 2017, meeting underscored its concern with wage and productivity data. The committee noted there was "tightness in the labor market, but... little evidence of wage pressures." Some FOMC participants speculated whether the "hiring of less experienced workers at lower wages" was a contributing factor. Others pointed out that low wage growth is in line with what productivity growth and the inflation rate (both sluggish of late) would suggest. As the economic expansion continued at a steady pace and job growth was strong, the Fed struggled to understand why wage and productivity growth did not show stronger performance.

The FOMC's unease with wage and productivity growth is hardly unique. Analysts and academics alike have advanced a spate of theories to explain the low numbers. Favorite suspects include lingering weakness in the labor market not captured in the headline unemployment number; downward nominal wage rigidity; output mismeasurement, particularly in services and tech-related sectors; a drought of productivity-boosting, technological advancements; a slowdown in capital growth; and the deteriorating quality of public education.

Although many of these factors may play a role in limiting wage and productivity growth, the US economy has also undergone several key structural changes: 1) persistently low inflation expectations, 2) shifts in workforce demographics, as Baby Boomers exit and Millennials enter the workforce, and 3) the changing distribution of payrolls by industry favoring lower-pay sectors. Our view is that structural changes are largely responsible for the modest growth in wages and productivity in the economic expansion after the Great Recession of 2008–2009. By implication, there is nothing the Federal Reserve can do with monetary policy to address structural changes related to demographics and shifts in the distribution of jobs among sectors.

Low Inflation Expectations

Because inflation (along with productivity growth) is a key component in wage growth, inflation expectations play a role in determining wage growth. As measured by the University of Michigan survey, inflation expectations have declined sharply from a peak of over 10% in 1980.

Inflation expectations did rise at the very beginning of the economic recovery from the Great Recession, reaching 4.6% in March of 2011 — when a consensus anticipated a quick recovery. These hopes proved to be misplaced; the economy's real GDP grew at a steady but modest pace of 2%. Inflationary pressures have been largely absent. As early views were gradually revised, inflation expectations dropped, averaging 2.6% in 2017; still above the sub-2% trend in inflation in early 2018. The post-2011 decline in inflation expectations may have held back subsequent wage growth. Employees and employers increasingly expected lower inflation — and with it, lower raises.

Figure 6-1: US Inflation Expectations

Source: St. Louis Federal Reserve Bank,
FRED Database (MICH)

Demographic Shifts

As inflation expectations declined, the composition of the US workforce also underwent significant changes. The US has three major working-age generations: Baby Boomers (born post-WWII through 1965, per Pew Research Center), Generation X (1965–1980), and Millennials (1981–1997). Boomers comprise an unusually large generation, with 76 million born between 1946 and 1965, compared to 55 million for Generation Xers and 65 million for Millennials. The Boomers' ranks, however, have begun to fall in recent years as mortality outpaces immigration. In 2015, Pew found that Millennials had surpassed Boomers to become the largest generation, with 75.4 million Millennials, 74.9 million Boomers, and 66 million Generation Xers.

This generational distribution is changing the workforce. In the past few years, the large and aging Boomer cohort saw an increased number of retirements. Millennials, on the other hand, are still entering the workforce.

Figure 6-2: US Population over 65

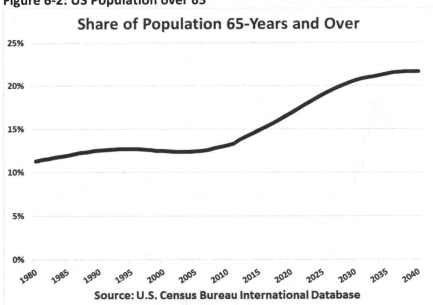

The ramifications for productivity and wage growth are significant. Boomers are more likely to be high-wage, high-experience workers. Their retirement from the workforce is a critical element for wage and productivity growth. The new entrants to the workforce, Millennials, are less experienced and earn lower wages. Their entrance to the workforce has the same effect as the Boomers' exit — wage and productivity growth are dragged down.

Graphing the share of the US population over the age of 65 reveals a post-recession retirement hike. There is a clear and dramatic spike in the 65-years and over population picking up after 2007 as the Baby Boomer retirement era commenced. The retirement-age population increased from 12.6% of the total population in 2007 to 15.6% in 2017, and will continue to increase until the 2030s.

Figure 6-3: US Working Age Population

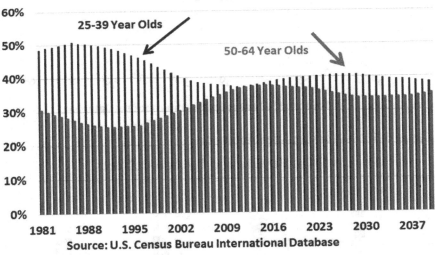

25-39 Year-Olds vs 50-64 Year-Olds, as a % of the Working-Age Population

Source: U.S. Census Bureau International Database

The generational composition of the working-age population itself can also be measured (the working-age population is defined here as 25–64 years). The oldest segment of the workforce (50–64-year-olds) increased as a share of the working-age population between 1992 and 2015, rising from 25.19% to 37.45% before declining slightly to 37.2% in 2017 as older workers retired. The youngest segment of the workforce (25–39-year-olds) increased to 39% from a low of 37.16% in 2011. As a share of the workforce, younger Millennials have come to the fore, while older Boomers are gradually retiring out.

Figure 6-4: US Workers — Younger vs Older

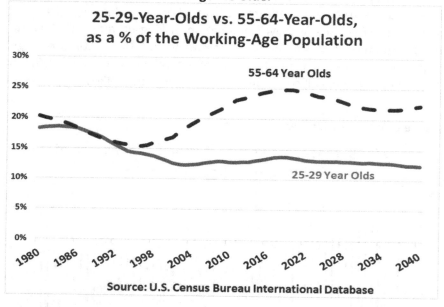

Source: U.S. Census Bureau International Database

Figure 6-5: US Working Age Population

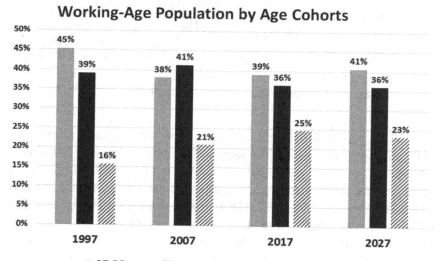

Source: U.S. Census Bureau International Database

The 25–29-year-old segment of the population, which provides a snapshot of very new workers, has increased as well. The 25–29 age cohort reached 13.72% in 2017 from 12.33% in 2003, reversing a decline that spanned the mid-1980s through early 2000s. The 55–64-year-old cohort, which provides a metric for older, near-retirement workers, has leveled out at around 24.66%, and will soon decline.

The result of these demographic shifts is a workforce adding an increasing number of young workers, while shedding an increasing number of older ones. This generational change is dampening wage and productivity growth.

Sector Shifts

The US is also undergoing a change in payrolls distribution. Much has been made of the transition toward a service-based economy — services accounted for around 70% of total nonfarm payrolls in 2017, compared to 55% in 1980. Manufacturing, meanwhile, fell from 20% of nonfarm payrolls in 1980 to 8% in 2017.

Figure 6-6: US Jobs by Sector

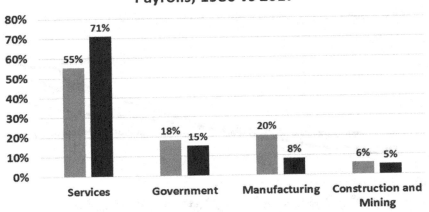

General Sectors, as a % of Total Nonfarm Payrolls, 1980 vs 2017

■ 1980 ■ 2017

Source: St. Louis Federal Reserve Bank, FRED Database

Three service sectors benefited tremendously from the shift toward a service-based economy: education and health services, professional and business services, and leisure and hospitality. These sectors have grown rapidly as a share of total nonfarm payrolls, representing 41% of total nonfarm payrolls in 2017, up from 37% before the recession, and 24% in 1980. The largest service sector (trade, transportation, and utilities) lost some ground as a share of payrolls, while still adding a considerable number of jobs; government, on the other hand, fell precipitously following the Great Recession, as state and local authorities aggressively shed jobs in the 2010–2013 period.

These shifts have proven significant in the tight labor market following the recession. The US added 2 million jobs in 2017. In total, over 16.6 million jobs were added to total nonfarm payrolls between the end of the recession in June of 2009 and 2017. If the allocation of payrolls is shifting as the labor market continues to add jobs at a breakneck pace, wage and productivity growth may be affected.

Figure 6-7: US Service Sector

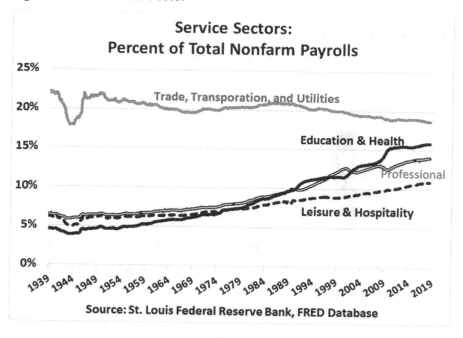

The post-recession payrolls expansion has benefited mostly lower-paying private service sectors. These include leisure and hospitality; trade, transportation, and utilities; and education and health services. Only one high-paying sector has seen considerable expansion — professional and business services. Low-pay growth has slightly outpaced high-pay growth; but the growth in both high- and low-paying sectors has surpassed that of mid-paying sectors. These expansion trends may also be contributing to sluggish wage and productivity growth.

The government sector is excluded here because hourly earnings data is not available. However, the government sector contracted considerably during the recovery from the Great Recession (losing 850,000 jobs in the early days of the recovery, and recouping only partially). This sector is usually higher-paying with excellent benefits; its contraction had a negative impact on wage and productivity growth.

Figure 6-8: US Jobs by Pay Scales

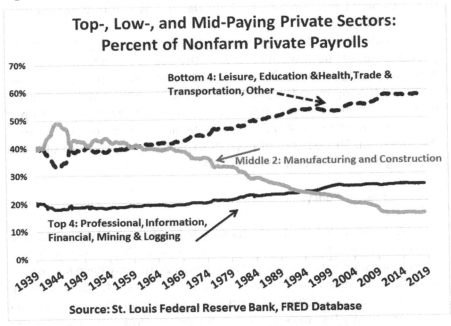

Source: St. Louis Federal Reserve Bank, FRED Database

In total, the three lowest-paying private sectors (leisure and hospitality; trade, transportation and utilities; and other services) contributed 38% of nonfarm jobs growth in the post-recession period. These jobs all pay below the "all employees" average; their expansion detracts from wage growth. With education and health services added (the fourth lowest pay sector, at around average pay), the four lowest paying sectors account for 60% of post-recession jobs growth.

The three highest paying sectors (financial activities, mining and logging, and information services) added only 4% of post-recession jobs growth. With the fourth-highest pay sector (professional and business services), that measure soars to 30%. Expansion in these sectors, which all pay above average, has contributed to wage growth.

The two mid-paying sectors (manufacturing and construction, both of which are at above-average pay) added only 10% of the post-recession jobs expansion.

This post-recession expansion paints a picture of an increasingly polarized jobs market, with jobs going largely to low-paying sectors and high-paying sectors. Expansion within low-paying sectors slightly outpaces high-paying sectors; both, however, have far outstripped mid-paying sectors.

Polarization by pay can be observed by graphing the share of private nonfarm payrolls allocated to the top-four, bottom-four, and mid-two paying sectors. Growth in the lowest four pay sectors has outpaced the top four. The gap between the two stood at 32% in 2017, up from 25% in 1980 and 29% at the start of the recession. Mid-pay sectors, meanwhile, have plummeted, stabilizing at around 15.5% after the recession. This pattern of payrolls expansion may pose an obstacle to strong wage and productivity growth.

Implications for Policy

The US economy's structural changes indicate that lower wage and productivity growth could linger for some time. First, lower inflation expectations, falling from the 1990s through 2016, may have influenced workplace decisions about raises. Second, the dual effects of retiring Boomers and new Millennial workers has left the US with a slightly younger, slightly less experienced, and modestly lower-paid workforce.

This trend will reverse — after Baby Boomers retire in the 2015–2025 period. Third, the reallocation of payrolls toward service sectors on either end of the pay spectrum is also a limiting factor, as a large share of new jobs are added to very low-paying sectors (such as leisure and hospitality).

In terms of policy implications, the Federal Reserve may worry about wage growth and productivity, but there is little monetary policy can do. Fiscal policy is a different story. Infrastructure spending and investment in education could make a difference over time as it builds both physical and human capital. The US Republican Administration, however, decided to prioritize a permanent corporate tax cut passed in late 2017, which is not likely to have any impact on wages or productivity. [See Chapter 3 for our analysis of tax cuts and economic growth.]

Chapter 7

Bitcoin Economics

Erik Norland & Blu Putnam[1]

Editor's Note: A version of this chapter was published in **The Journal of Financial Transformation, Fall 2018.** *Bitcoin has led the way for crypto-currencies and the economics are complex. To appreciate the economics of Bitcoin, one has to examine everything from demand and supply elasticities, to the rising difficulty of mining, to transaction costs. – KT*

What is most striking about the economics of bitcoin is the juxtaposition of the certainty of supply and the uncertainty of demand. The rate at which bitcoin is mined has been highly predictable and, unlike almost any other asset, currency or commodity, its ultimate supply is a known quantity, fixed in advance. There will never be more than 21 million coins. This feature makes bitcoin supply almost perfectly inelastic. No matter how high the price rises, miners will not ultimately produce any more than the prescribed amount. Moreover, price rises will not even necessarily incentivize a more rapid mining of bitcoin. Even if they did, it would mean miners create more bitcoin today at the expense of creating less of it in the future since the total supply will reach a hard, asymptotic limit of 21 million coins, expected to be reached by 2040 or so, based on the mining algorithms.

We analyze the economics of the bitcoin marketplace by finding parallels in the world of commodities to understand what it means to have an inelastic supply. Then, we move to the relatively more difficult task of demand analysis to complete the bitcoin economics picture.

---

[1] **Disclaimer:** All examples are hypothetical interpretations of situations and are used for explanation purposes only. The views expressed here reflect solely those of the authors and not necessarily those of their employer, CME Group or its affiliated institutions. The information herein should not be considered investment advice or the results of actual market experience.

Economics of Supply Inelasticity

The supply inelasticity explains in large part why bitcoin is so volatile. Items with inelastic supply show a greater response to demand shifts than items with elastic supply. The same is true of demand: the more inelastic the demand, the greater the price changes in response to small fluctuations in either supply or demand. In the abstract example below, we show the relatively modest price response to an upward shift in demand for a market with flexible supply elasticity on the left and contrast it with the much bigger price response from the same demand shift in a constrained supply market on the right.

Figure 7-1: Elastic Supply (Left) is Less Price Volatile Than Inelastic Supply Markets (Right)

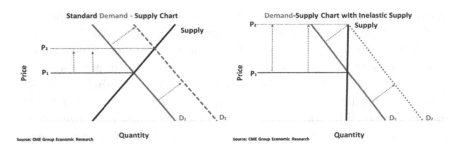

Take as an illustration the case of natural gas. Natural gas is a classic example of a market with highly inelastic supply and demand. If prices soar today, consumers will still need natural gas to generate electricity, heating and to fuel industrial processes; and they will be willing to pay up for it, at least in the short term. Natural gas demand is therefore highly inelastic.

The same is true of natural gas supply. If prices double, which for natural gas is not all that uncharacteristic, producers will likely not be able to supply a great deal more of it in the short term. Similar relationships hold for crude oil, although are less dramatic. What differentiates the analysis of commodities like natural gas and crude oil from bitcoin is that their long-term supply and demand shows a meaningful degree of elasticity, even if the short-term supply is more about inventory swings than production adjustments. If natural gas or crude oil prices experience a sustained rise, producers can and will find ways of producing more of them — or at least they have so far in history. Meanwhile, consumers will find ways to use them more efficiently in response to higher prices. This is not the case for bitcoin directly, although rising prices might increase the probability of "forks" that split bitcoin into the original and a spinout currency such as Bitcoin Cash (August 1, 2017), Bitcoin Gold (October 24, 2017), and Bitcoin Private (February 28, 2018).

Figure 7-2: Inelastic Expansion and Slowing Growth of Bitcoin Supply

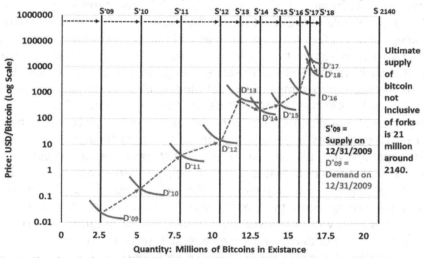

Source: Bloomberg Professional (XBT), Blockchain.Info (supply), CME Economic Research Calculations

Bitcoin's limited and highly inelastic supply is also a major factor driving its price appreciation, a rise so spectacular that it can only be appreciated when seen on a log scale. In bitcoin's first four years, supply grew by roughly 2.5 million coins per year. Even then prices were rising as the user community grew. Since then supply has continued to grow but the pace has slowed substantially while demand has occasionally dipped, even on a year-on-year basis.

Bitcoin's limited supply and soaring price make it difficult to be used as a medium of exchange outside of the crypto currency space. Imagine one's regret if one uses bitcoin to purchase a mundane item such as a cup of coffee only to find that the bitcoin spent on a cup of coffee would have been worth millions of dollars a few years later. As such, investors treat bitcoin as a highly unreliable store of value — a bit like gold on steroids.

One often asked question is: will bitcoin replace fiat currencies such as the US dollar? We think that the answer is a resounding no. Bitcoin's price is too unstable to compete as a store of value; Bitcoin's transaction costs are too high and too variable for it to be used as a medium of exchange.

Most importantly, for an asset to function economically as a medium of exchange, it must depreciate slowly over time — something that is impossible with a fixed supply. That loss of value is precisely what makes them useful. Without the fear of inflation, holders of currency tend to hoard rather than spend it. This is why most major central banks, such as the Federal Reserve, European Central Bank, and the Bank of Japan, for example, have set modest inflation targets of 2%, as suggested back in the 1960s by Professor Milton Friedman. The inflation target creates a dis-incentive to hoard the currency, since hoarding a currency depresses economic growth and creates financial instability. The Japanese yen, the one fiat currency that has experienced deflation over the past few decades, is a case in point. Far from being a virtuous store of value, the Japanese deflation produced a depressed, underperforming economy that the Bank of Japan is desperately trying to turn around with a colossal quantitative easing program four times bigger than that undertaken by the Federal Reserve or European Central Bank, relative to the size of the Japanese economy.

A Deep Dive into Bitcoin Supply through a Study of the Economics of Commodities

Bitcoin is "mined" by computers solving cryptographic math problems. In exchange for solving the problems, miners receive bitcoin. Those math problems grow in difficulty over time, increasing the required computational power required to solve them. This in turn drives up the equipment and especially the electricity cost of producing bitcoins. One needs more and more computers and to make them run at peak speeds, they must be kept cool.

This makes the economic analysis of bitcoin a bit like energy and metals. For example, as of late 2017, the swing producers of crude oil in the US were probably profitable at around US$40 per barrel. Above that price, there are incentives to add to production. Below that price, the incentives are to curtail production. Also like bitcoin, the difficulty of extracting energy from the earth has increased substantially over time.

Figure 7-3: The Cost of Mining Gold

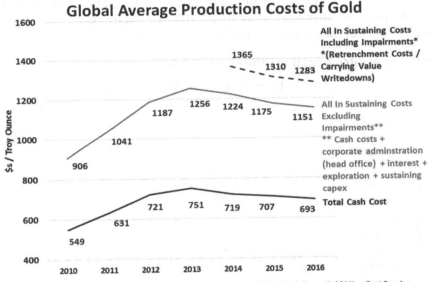

Source: GFMS Gold Survey 2016 & 2017, Metals Focus: Gold Focus 2015, Metals Focus Gold Mine Cost Service

For instance, humanity went through the easiest oil supplies located near the surface many decades ago. Now marginal supply increases come mostly from fracking deep under the ground, from offshore drilling or from oil in remote, difficult to access locations. In the second half of the 19th century, when oil was first produced in large quantities, one unit of energy invested in oil extraction produced around 150 units of energy. By the 1970s that was down to around 30 units of energy for each one invested and that ratio fell to around 15 by 2000 and by 2020 will have probably dipped below 10. This has been a factor in driving oil prices higher. In the energy industry, it is widely assumed that the marginal producers have a cost of production near US$40 per barrel. It bears mentioning that oil prices rarely traded at US$40 until about 2005, when they rose above that level and have only occasionally looked back.

For metals like copper, gold and silver, there are two numbers to watch: the cash cost and all-in sustaining costs. Cash costs give one a sense of price levels at which producers will maintain current production. All-in sustaining costs give one a sense of what current and anticipated future price levels will be necessary to incentivize additional investment in future production. For example, for gold, cash-cost for mine operators averages around US$700 per ounce while the all-in sustaining costs are around US$1,250 per ounce (Figure 7-3).

Figure 7-4: Bitcoin Mining Difficulty and Price

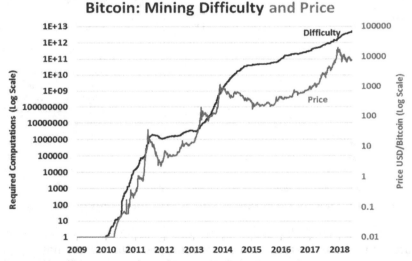

Source: https://blockchain.info/charts/market-price?timespan=all and
https://blockchain.info/charts/difficulty?timespan=all

What is interesting for gold, silver and copper is that after their prices began to fall in 2011, it squeezed the profit margins of operators, who in turn found ways to streamline their businesses and cut their production costs. The same is true of the 2014–16 collapse in energy prices which may have lowered the marginal cost of production from

US$50 to US$40 per barrel of crude. Like mining metals and extracting fossil fuels, mining bitcoin is also a competitive business. Not surprisingly we see a similar feedback loop between the bitcoin price and mining-supply difficulty — in this case "difficulty" is measured in terms of the number of calculations required to solve the crypto-algorithm to unlock a few more bitcoins in the mining process.

Glancing at Figure 7-4, it is obvious that as the required number of computations ("difficulty") has risen, producing bitcoin has become more expensive. It is not a stretch of the imagination to hypothesize that the exponential rise in the difficulty of mining bitcoin has contributed to the exponential rise in price. True, perhaps, but not the complete story. There is another side to this feedback loop. Notice what happened to "difficulty" after the first bitcoin bear market (a 93% drop) in 2010–11. Its inexorable rise came to a two-year long halt until prices recovered. It was only when the next price bull market began in 2013 that "difficulty" began increasing again. A similar phenomenon occurred in the aftermath of the 2013–15 bitcoin bear market (an 84% decline). There too "difficulty" stagnated until prices began their next bull market. Curiously "difficulty" did not stagnate in early 2018 despite a more than 50% drop in bitcoin prices from their December 2017 highs, but there are always lags to be studied and examined in future research.

Our conclusion is that bitcoin supply appears to have at least one similarity with that of energy and metals. When prices fall producers must take measures that cause production costs to stagnate or even fall. While "difficulty" never appears to decline, the cost of computing power has fallen over time by as much as 25% per year. As such, if "difficulty" goes sideways for a year, the actual cost of production probably falls as the amount of energy needed to perform the same number of calculations declines. Just as metals and energy producers find ways to reduce cost after bear markets, the bitcoin mining community appears to do the same.

One last comment on supply before we move on to demand: it has long been rumored that the founding community of bitcoin controls something in the order of 3–5 million coins. If this is true, in theory, higher prices could (and probably would) encourage them to part with their coins in exchange for fiat currencies or other assets. When one takes this into account, bitcoin supply might not be perfectly inelastic in the very short term. A similar phenomenon exists in precious metals. When prices rise, we see an increase in the recycling of gold and silver (secondary supply). What is interesting, however, is that recycling appears to respond to price but does not drive prices. For gold and silver, the only supply that appears to drive price is mining supply. Likewise, if an existing holder of bitcoin liquidates some or all of her holdings, this increases its short-term availability but does nothing to influence its total long-run supply, and in that sense, is more like a temporary inventory adjustment.

Demand Drivers are Not So Transparent

While bitcoin supply is extremely transparent, bitcoin demand is rather opaque. That said, there are a few quantifiable items that we do know about bitcoin demand. First, we have a pretty good idea of the number of bitcoin transactions performed each day. Second, and more importantly, it appears that fluctuations in bitcoin transaction costs play a major role in determining price corrections.

Figure 7-5: Does Bitcoin Volume Drive Price?

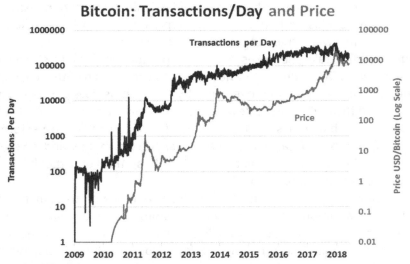

Source: https://blockchain.info/charts/market-price?timespan=all **and**
https://blockchain.info/charts/n-transactions?timespan=all

There appears to be a loose relationship between the growth rate of transactions and the rise/decline in price. For example, the number of transactions stopped growing in 2012, about one year before bitcoin's 2013 peak and bear market. It began to rise again in 2014 before bitcoin prices began to recover in earnest but has been stagnating since the end of 2016 (Figures 7-5 and 7-6), perhaps foreshadowing the correction in early 2018. What is particularly striking about this correction is that the number of transactions did not rise as prices fell, as they did during the December 2013–January 2015 bear market. During the two previous bull markets, the number of transactions began rising well in advance of the actual rally in bitcoin prices. Towards the end of the two previous bull markets, prices soared as the number of transactions stopped rising.

Figure 7-6: Relation Between Prices and Transactions

Source: blockchain.info/charts (Price, Transactions Per Day), CME Economic Research Calculations.

The relationship between bitcoin prices and transaction costs is even more compelling. Trading costs spiked from US$2 to around US$30 per transaction in late 2010 just before bitcoin prices suffered a 93% collapse. As bitcoin transaction costs subsequently fell, another bull market developed. Transaction costs edged higher in 2012 and then soared to over US$80 by early 2013 which coincided with another collapse in bitcoin prices. By 2015, transaction costs eased towards US$8 and another bull market began. Starting in late 2016, they began to rise again and by early 2018 were up towards US$100–US$150 per transaction (Figures 7-7 and 7-8). This third spike in transaction costs may be closely related to the early 2018 correction in bitcoin prices as high transaction costs may have played a role in causing demand for the cryptocurrency to wither at the time.

Figure 7-7: What Level of Bitcoin Transaction Costs Can the Market Sustain?

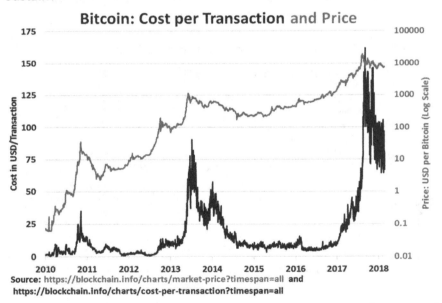

Source: https://blockchain.info/charts/market-price?timespan=all and
https://blockchain.info/charts/cost-per-transaction?timespan=all

We are not suggesting that bitcoin prices are a function of trading costs or vice versa; however, there is an association between the two with mutual feedback loops. When bitcoin prices rise, eventually transaction costs appear to rise as well. When transaction costs reach levels that market participants can no longer bear, the price of bitcoin often corrects. A decline in prices puts downward pressure on transaction costs which, at least in the past, allowed for another bitcoin bull market once they had corrected to lower levels.

If stagnating numbers of trades and rising transaction do in fact play a role in provoking bitcoin price corrections, then one might hypothesize that a given correction might last until transaction costs fall and the number of transactions begins to rise again. The spike in transaction costs in early 2018 and the sharp (more than 50%) decline in the number of transactions being recorded in bitcoin during the same period led to successive rounds of bitcoin price drops.

Figure 7-8: Relation of Prices to Transactions Costs

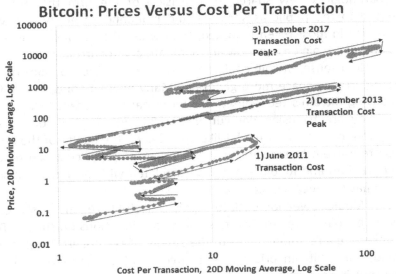

Source: blockchain.info/charts (Price, Cost Per Transaction), CME Economic Research Calculations

Incentives, Bitcoin Forks and Alternative Cryptocurrencies

When one thinks of incentives and reward structures, one might want to analyze some parallels with how shareholder value is created. This is tricky with bitcoin. Bitcoin certainly does not fit the definition of a company. It has no board of directors, no balance sheet, no income statement and no cash flow statement. That said, bitcoin does have a couple of features which need to be understood in the context of incentive structures. And, this adds a little more complexity to the supply analysis as well.

Miners and transaction validators receive rewards in bitcoin. One can see a corporation's shares as an internal currency used to compensate and motivate employees, aligning their interests with those of the organization. To that end, the number of bitcoins in existence is comparable to the "float" of a corporation — the number of shares issued to the public.

When bitcoin forks into a new currency, such as Bitcoin Cash, the move can be analyzed in a manner comparable to a corporate action, such as a spin out. In a spin out, a corporation can give each of its shareholders new shares in a division of the firm that is being released to the public as separate and independent entity. Likewise, when bitcoin most recently forked, the owner of each bitcoin received one unit of Bitcoin Cash, a new and separate cryptocurrency.

In a sense, bitcoin could be viewed as a reference index on the crypto-currency space more generally. Many new alt-coins, in addition to copying bitcoin's technology, are more easily purchased via bitcoin than they are by using fiat currencies. Bitcoin's central role in this ecosystem makes its price a bit like an index on the health of the entire ecosystem itself. Not surprisingly, the prices of other cryptocurrencies like Ethereum and Ripple are highly correlated with bitcoin when seen from a fiat currency perspective.

A quick diversion back to supply is useful here. The existence of forks in bitcoin serves to modify some of our intuitions on supply. That is, while bitcoin's supply is fixed, the supply of cryptocurrencies is not. Indeed, rising bitcoin prices incent bitcoin forks. This makes a lot of sense but it does complicate the analysis as it is a reminder that one should not look at bitcoin in isolation but as an anchor for the whole cryptocurrency space.

Economic Destiny of Bitcoin

Even if bitcoin fails to replace fiat currencies, it will not necessarily be without long-term economic impact. One possible result of the development of cryptocurrencies is that central banks may one day decide to issue their own distributed ledger currencies as Venezuela is struggling to attempt to do today with the launch of the "petro." Former Fed Chairman Alan Greenspan once compared making monetary policy to driving a car guided only by a cracked rearview mirror. Even now, important policy decisions must be based upon imperfectly estimated economic numbers that are weeks or months old by the time they become available. In 2018, economic policy making is still a vestige of the 20th century.

Blockchain technology has the potential to allow policy makers to issue their own cryptocurrencies that will give them real time information on inflation, nominal and real GDP. It will not allow them to peer through the front windshield into the future but at least they can look into the rearview mirror with much greater clarity and see out the side windows of the monetary policy vehicle. This could allow them to create the amount of money and credit necessary to keep the economy growing at a smooth pace more easily than they do today. Switching off the gold standard vastly reduced economic volatility and improved per capita economic growth. Moving to blockchain-enhanced fiat currencies could further reduce economic volatility and, ironically, enable further leveraging of the already highly indebted global economy as people find ways to use capital more efficiently. More broadly, crypto-inspired investments could bring about new technologies that we cannot yet imagine.

Investors who are buying bitcoin are presumably hoping to find someone to sell to at a higher price. That said, there is more to bitcoin economically than just the theory of the greater fool. As more people bid up the price, the difficulty of solving bitcoin's cryptographic algorithms increases. This in turn is driving up investment in more powerful and faster computing technology of both a traditional integrated circuit and non-traditional variety. Indeed, solving cryptographic problems may be one of the first tests facing quantum computers. Finally, we note that investors in bitcoin and its peers are mainly out to make profits and not to finance or subsidize the development of distributed ledgers nor more powerful computers. As such, we caution against linking topics such as the future of blockchain to performance of Bitcoin.

Bottom line:

> ➤ Bitcoin supply is highly inelastic; and as with commodities, inelastic supply increases volatility.

> ➤ "Difficulty" of mining bitcoin math problems and its price are in a feedback loop, where "difficulty" is a major driver of price, and price also influences "difficulty".

> ➤ Transaction volume may influence price trends, and rising transaction costs are a risk indicator for bitcoin.

Chapter 8

Market Regulation: Origins and Cultural Perspectives

Susan M. Phillips[1] & Blu Putnam[2]

Editor's Note: An earlier version of this chapter was originally published in **The Capco Institute Journal of Financial Transformation,** *May 2016,* **Volume 43.** *There are varying objectives and cultural differences among the major regulators of derivative markets in the US. The unique perspective presented here is that to understand the regulatory ecosystem in the US, one has to appreciate the implications of the different priorities of each regulator and, critically, whether its original focus was on market integrity, investor protections, or systemic risk. In short, the DNA of a regulator comes from the crisis that begat its birth. – KT*

The regulation of derivative markets in the US focuses on protecting individual investors from fraud and criminal activity, assuring the integrity of markets and safeguarding the economy against systematic risk emanating from the financial sector. These three critical objectives are not embedded in one regulatory authority, but are instead distributed across several institutions with very different origins and priorities, based in no small way on the historical context that led to their creation. That is, to appreciate the sources of different regulatory

---

[1] Susan M. Phillips, retired as Dean Emeritus of the George Washington University School of Business. Susan has considerable regulatory experience, including SEC Economic Fellow, 1976–1978, CFTC Commissioner, then Chairman, 1981–1987, and Governor, Federal Reserve Board, 1991–1998.
[2] **Disclaimer:** All examples are hypothetical interpretations of situations and are used for explanation purposes only. The views expressed here reflect solely those of the authors and not necessarily those of their employer, CME Group or its affiliated institutions. The information herein should not be considered investment advice or the results of actual market experience.

philosophies among the major regulators of derivative markets in the US, one has to examine why each institution was brought into existence and how that shaped its specific regulatory style and priorities.

Toward that end, this paper first succinctly summarizes the origins, mission, and policy focus of the three major institutions regulating financial derivatives in the US; namely, the Commodity Futures Trading Commission (CFTC), the Securities and Exchange Commission (SEC), and the Federal Reserve Board (Fed). We also include an analysis of how the Dodd–Frank Wall Street Reform and Consumer Protection Act of 2010 (Dodd–Frank Act) added powers and responsibilities to each of these regulatory institutions.

With the historical context as our foundation, we provide a set of observations about how their different birth stories and missions have affected the regulatory ecosystem in the US Our analysis is intended to shed light on why the CFTC, SEC, and the Fed may approach apparently similar challenges with different philosophical approaches.[3] In addition, we provide critical perspectives on such issues as transparency, self-regulatory organizations, too big to fail (TBTF), capital adequacy, and the unintended consequences of macro-prudential regulation on the effectiveness of monetary policy.

Historical Background: CFTC

Establishment. While not created in its present form until 1974, the CFTC has its origins in the Cotton Futures Act 1914/16.[4] The Cotton Futures Act was specifically focused on the issue of the terms and standards for the physical delivery process when a futures contract is held to maturity. The delivery process is viewed as having the potential for fraud and manipulation, which is why futures and options have long been regulated, first by exchanges, then by governments. In addition, federal pre-emptive regulation has allowed a distinction from state

---

[3] Kindly note that we are not covering all aspects of the three agencies' responsibilities; rather, we will focus on market regulation responsibilities.

[4] The Cotton Futures Act was originally passed in 1914, but it was deemed by the courts as revenue-raising legislation, which constitutionally must originate in the US House of Representatives. Since the 1914 version originated in the Senate, it was declared void, and the 1916 version was then passed in the proper sequence from House to Senate.

gambling regulations, preventing states from attempting to regulate futures and options exchanges under local gambling laws. Since its establishment in 1974, the CFTC has been given broad authority over named commodities "...and all services, rights and interests, ... all other goods and articles except onions and motion picture box office receipts."[5]

Mission. Quoting from the CFTC's official website, "the CFTC's mission is to protect market participants and the public from fraud, manipulation, abusive practices and systemic risk related to derivatives — both futures and options — and to foster transparent, competitive and financially sound markets."[6]

Market Integrity. The actions, rules, and regulations initiated by the CFTC have a clear focus on how markets work, and ensuring the integrity of the market place. Trading must be on exchanges (designated contract markets), although there have been some exceptions granted since 2001. Market professionals must be registered. Margin requirements are enforced.[7] Capital requirements are set to assure that exchange traded contracts will be honored. There are a variety of anti-manipulation initiatives, including speculative limits, delivery oversight, and daily settlement. Large trader reports are provided to exchanges and the CFTC to assist in market regulation, but not generally publicly disclosed except in aggregated form. The role of central clearing houses is primary to how futures and options exchanges function, and the CFTC has relied in part on clearinghouse oversight as well as embraced self-regulatory organizations (SROs) such as the National Futures Association (NFA) and the exchanges themselves.

Dodd–Frank. The Dodd–Frank Act gave the CFTC more authority to supervise and regulate over-the-counter (OTC) markets in swap transactions, and also in particular, swap dealers. Among many other

---

[5] See 7 U.S.C. § 13-1; CEA § 9–1.
[6] CFTC, www.cftc.gov/About/MissionResponsibilities/index.htm
[7] Margin requirements are established by CFTC regulations and delegated to exchanges with oversight by the CFTC. By law, the Fed was given powers related to margin requirements, however, it chose to delegate its role in setting margins to the CFTC and the SEC.

things, clearing and trade execution for standardized derivative products, including certain swap agreements, were mandated to move to exchanges or swap execution facilities and be centrally settled in clearing houses. In keeping with the CFTC's tradition of focusing on the integrity of markets, the additional powers given to the CFTC in the Dodd–Frank legislation were generally aimed at strengthening the infrastructure of derivative markets to ensure their integrity.

Historical Background: SEC

Establishment. The SEC was created by the Securities Exchange Act of 1934 (as a result of the stock market crash of 1929 that preceded the Great Depression) and charged with enforcing the Securities Act of 1933. The focus was aimed directly at providing stronger investor protections. In the years and decades that followed, the SEC was also given responsibility for enforcing a number of other investor protection legislation passed by the US Congress, including the Trust Indenture Act of 1939, the Investment Company Act of 1940, the Investment Advisers Act of 1940, and the Sarbanes–Oxley Act of 2002.

Mission. "The mission of the US Securities and Exchange Commission is to protect investors, maintain fair, orderly and efficient markets, and facilitate capital formation."[8] Investor protections are critical to the SEC's approach to market regulation including transparency and disclosure (e.g., financial data by firms, stock ownership by management, market transaction data, etc.). Insider trading rules play an important role to level the trading field so that insiders cannot benefit by having an informational advantage over the general public. As with the CFTC, there are requirements for the registration of securities market professionals — brokers and dealers.

Unlike the CFTC, which views exchange-traded derivative markets as focused on risk management and is neutral on the direction of markets, the SEC has specific restrictions on short- selling of stocks. Remember that part of the SEC's mission is to encourage capital

---

[8] SEC, www.sec.gov/About/WhatWeDo.shtml

formation, and it has accepted the view that in certain circumstances short-selling may cause harm to the capital formation process.

As with the CFTC, the SEC has embraced reliance on SROs to implement and enforce regulations (e.g., FINRA — Financial Institutions Regulatory Authority, as well as the securities exchanges).

Dodd–Frank. The Dodd–Frank Act gave the SEC more powers related to robust record-keeping and real-time reporting regimes including audit trails. Provisions of the Act also focused on giving the SEC anti-disruptive trading initiatives and increased securities exchange oversight to be implemented as a result of the "Flash Crash" in May 2010 and the Wall Street bailouts associated with the financial panic of 2008 and the subsequent Great Recession. In keeping with the SEC's focus on investor protections, the Act included new governance, capital and reporting requirements for individual firms. The role of the credit rating agencies in the lead-up to the 2008 financial crisis came under severe criticism and the SEC gained powers in this realm as well to better protect investors.

Historical Background: Federal Reserve

Establishment. After a series of banking panics in the late 1800s and early 1900s, the Federal Reserve Act of 1913 established the Fed to promote banking system stability.

Mission. The Federal Reserve Act of 1913 was all about the safety and soundness of the banking and financial system (i.e., systematic risk) and created an institution with powers of lender of last resort. The dual objectives of encouraging full employment and maintaining price stability were added after the Great Depression, an episode in which, by many counts and assessments, the Fed failed to use its lender-of-last-resort powers to limit the damage from the stock market crash of 1929 and to potentially avoid the downward spiral into deflation and the Great Depression.[9]

---

[9] For example, see Bernanke, B. S., 1983, "Non-monetary effects of the financial crisis in the propagation of the Great Depression," *NBER Working Paper No. 1054*. Also, Bernanke, B. S., 2000, *Essays on the Great Depression*, New Jersey: Princeton University Press.

Stabilizing the banking system, then managing the Economy. The Fed is the central bank of the US[10] It was founded by Congress in 1913 to provide the nation with a safer, more flexible, and more stable monetary and financial system. Over the years, its role in banking and the economy has expanded.[11] Today, the Fed's duties fall into several general areas: 1) implementing the nation's monetary policy by influencing the monetary and credit conditions in the economy in pursuit of maximum employment, stable prices, and moderate long-term rates; 2) supervising and regulating banking institutions to ensure the safety and soundness of the nation's banking and financial system to contain systemic risk that may arise in financial markets; 3) providing financial services to depository institutions, the US government, and foreign official institutions, including playing a major role in operating the nation's payments system. Until the financial panic of 2008, the primary tools of the Fed included bank reserve requirements, discount window (elastic currency, lender of last resort), and open market operations (T-bills). With the advent of the financial panic of 2008 and the Great Recession, the Fed expanded its toolkit, expanding its balance sheet and engaging in transactions involving a wider range of securities and derivatives (e.g., increased direct purchases of US Treasury securities and mortgage-backed securities, as well as creating and lending to special purpose vehicles holding a variety of credit and derivative exposures).

Dodd–Frank. The Dodd–Frank Act gave the Fed expanded authority over the financial system. New powers included the ability to regulate compensation practices of financial institutions. The Fed was also responsible for enforcing resolution regimes for systemically important financial institutions (SIFIs) in the event they had to be wound down.

---

[10] The US had been without a central bank since 1836 when the charter of the US Bank was allowed to expire. In 1832, Congress passed an act to extend the charter of the US Bank beyond its expiration date, and President Andrew Jackson vetoed the charter extension. The role of the central bank became a major issue in the 1832 Presidential election, and when President Jackson won a second term, the issue was settled and the charter was allowed to expire.

[11] Federal Reserve System, www.FederalReserve.gov/AbouttheFed/Mission.htm

There was an expanded emphasis on a much broader definition of financial firms, well beyond banks, with emphasis on governance, risk management, capital and liquidity. In effect, the Fed was empowered to address regulatory and systematic risk challenges in the "shadow banking system." The Fed also became the central regulatory institution for international coordination of financial system supervision, which includes the negotiations for reciprocal recognition of comparable institutions, such as exchanges or clearing houses, with foreign governments and regulatory bodies.

Observations on the Regulatory Challenges of Different Missions

How do these three regulatory regimes differ? What affects their ability to work together on regulatory reform or impacts the compliance structures required of regulated financial institutions?

Our perspective is that the different historical contexts and varying focuses of regulation that were incorporated into the creation of each of the major derivative regulatory institutions has shaped their style and approach to market supervision. That is, the CFTC's primary emphasis on market integrity contrasts with the SEC's central focus on investor protections and the Fed's mission regarding the containment of systematic risks.

Transparency. Take transparency as an example. The SEC puts transparency on a pedestal in attempts to protect investors and level the trading playing field. Mutual funds and asset managers have to report positions quarterly, which are made available publicly by the SEC. By contrast, the CFTC has tended to preserve the confidentiality of trading positions. The CFTC's commitment-of-traders report gives an aggregated sense of the positioning of large groups of specific types of traders, but there is no ability to back into the positions of any one trading firm. Individual business strategies involving price hedging are kept confidential in the CFTC regulatory structure in contrast to the SEC's requirement to disclose ownership positions in public companies.

The inherent differences between risk management instruments, such as exchange-traded futures and options, compared to capital formation instruments, such as stocks and bonds, underlie the contrasting approaches of the CFTC and SEC and help explain why their philosophical approaches to transparency policies are also different. We also note that the Fed focuses on financial confidentiality, although not nearly to the degree that the transparency issue challenges the different instruments regulated by the CFTC and the SEC.

Market Direction.   Then, there is the embedded view on market direction. The CFTC, with a focus on risk management tools, is neutral — price protection (hedging) in both directions is actively desired and derivative markets are considered a zero-sum game. The SEC has a distinct emphasis on promoting economic growth through capital formation and this is reflected in specific restrictions on short selling. The Fed also seeks to promote economic growth, which can lead to a bias in favor of equity bull markets, although the latter has been occasionally tempered by fears of systematic risk coming from "exuberant" markets.

SROs. There are also significant differences in the approach to financial oversight through the use of SROs. With the CFTC's emphasis on market integrity and SEC's focus on investor protections, both regulators have embraced SROs. By contrast, the Fed's role in the banking system and focus on systematic risk has kept its attention on individual financial institutions. We may be stretching the point here, however, we believe that these differences in approaches to SROs may be more related to budgets than to mission and focus.

The Fed has a very different budget structure than either the CFTC or SEC. While the Fed receives user fees for its financial institution supervision and bank payments system services, in a manner not dissimilar to the fees generated by the CFTC and SEC, the Fed also has a very large net income coming from its asset-liability structure. That is, the Fed has a large portfolio of interest-bearing securities funded by virtue of its powers to issue zero- interest currency as well as to set the interest rates it pays on required and excess reserves. As a result, the Fed generates substantial portfolio earnings and is typically able to return a considerable portion of its net interest income to the US

Treasury.[12] Thus, while the Fed sends an annual report to Congress every year, unlike the SEC and CFTC, the Fed does not need to get its budget approved, giving it considerably more independence than enjoyed by the SEC and CFTC.

Both the CFTC and the SEC examined their use of SROs after the 2008 financial crisis and passing of the Dodd–Frank Act. The SEC previously viewed SROs as partners but recently has been bringing enforcement actions against them. This raises the question of whether SROs continue to be effective if they are placed in an adversarial position with their primary regulating agency. In addition, as exchanges have gone public, the regulatory authorities have had to assess the unavoidable conflict of interest between the business side of the exchange and its traditional self-regulatory responsibilities. While these conflicts appear manageable, the need to clarify roles is critical.

Trade-offs between containing systematic risk and encouraging market liquidity and efficiency. There are inherent philosophical debates that are becoming more obvious depending on whether the focus is on systematic risk or the efficient functioning of markets. For example, the Volcker Rule, which seeks to limit proprietary trading by certain types of financial institutions, especially banks, is part of an attempt to reduce the risk of failure leading to systematic problems. The unintended side-effect, however, is to reduce the amount of risk capital and trading activity in certain markets, potentially adversely impacting market liquidity and the costs of trading and capital formation for users of the markets.

Also, the Dodd–Frank legislation appears to have made regulatory compliance tasks more complex for financial companies.

---

[12] Prior to the 2008 financial crisis and the expansion of the Fed's balance sheet through asset purchases (i.e., quantitative easing), the Fed typically returned around US$20 billion per year to the US Treasury from its net earnings. In the 2012–2014 period for example, with a much larger balance sheet, the Fed provided the US Treasury with US$80–US$100 billion dollars annually from its net earnings.

The SEC and the CFTC both have an interest in the regulation of securities and related derivative products, often with different missions and objectives that are not always easily compatible.

For example, index-based contracts trade on futures exchanges, while index-linked exchange traded funds (ETFs) trade on securities exchanges, yet often utilize futures contracts to track their benchmarks. Further, the SEC and CFTC often find themselves with challenging overlapping market concerns with the Fed regarding trading in US Treasury securities and on bank trading practices involving securities and futures contracts.

Capital adequacy and too big to fail (TBTF). TBTF will be an issue as long as economies of scale exist. Moreover, different approaches to managing the systematic risks of large institutions are likely to create considerable debate, even among the various regulators. For example, to mitigate the systematic risk of the failure of one large institution spreading through the financial network, the Dodd–Frank Act mandated that many OTC swaps now be settled through a central counterparty clearing facility. By mutualizing risk, that is, putting the clearing house in between buyers and sellers, the Act reduced the risk of a domino effect from the bankruptcy of a large institution while making clearing houses more critical to the functioning of the system. This required intermediation may reduce swap participants' contract flexibility while possibly improving liquidity, especially for exiting swap contracts.

In addition, TBTF issues spillover into capital adequacy questions. The Fed has traditionally been a regulator of banks, which are leveraged lending institutions, and capital requirements are a key part of the Fed's supervision and oversight. As the Fed's jurisdiction has expanded to non-bank institutions, with containing systematic risk as the key focus, there has been a tendency to apply bank type rules to institutions that have little in common with banks, such as insurance companies. Moreover, some clearing houses are designated as systematically important institutions for certain purposes, and, thus, the Fed may weigh in on issues impacting clearing house capital requirements, and not necessarily from the same regulatory perspective as the CFTC or SEC. If the various regulatory requirements become too onerous or costly, we may see financial institutions move offshore.

Internationally, we also observe that the Bank of England is moving in this direction of using heightened capital requirements for a variety of non-bank institutions in very different types of businesses.

Impact of macro-prudential regulation on the effectiveness of monetary policy. Indeed, the focus on additional capital charges for the largest banks proposed by the US bank regulators and risk-based capital charges (equity or debt) for Global Systemically Important Banks (GSIFI) proposed by the Basel Committee for Banking Supervision (BCBS) are designed to mitigate the challenges of systematic risk. But a reliance on capital ratios and charges by a central bank can raise new issues with regards to the unintended side effects related to the interaction of the conduct of monetary policy aimed at managing economic risks and regulatory activities focused on macro-prudential systematic risks. We would broadly define macro-prudential regulation as using supervisory tools to control perceived financial bubbles or asset price movements that are considered by the regulator as undeserved. These types of actions can have the unintended effect of rendering traditional monetary policy considerably less effective.

For example, in the aftermath of the Great Recession, the Fed, the European Central Bank (ECB), and the Bank of Japan (BoJ) all expressed concerns, to varying degrees, about the potential for deflation. Neither zero short-term interest rates nor massive asset purchases (i.e., quantitative easing) had any observed ability to encourage inflation.[13] One very powerful reason for the inability of extraordinary monetary policy measures to promote an increase in inflation pressures is that the link between the credit creation process and both short-term interest rate policy and the size of the central bank's balance sheet has been severed by more stringent capital controls and macro-prudential regulation.

That is, if a central bank buys the government debt of its country it may put some limited downward pressure on bond yields, as it did in the US during 2012 and early 2013, but it is not clear at all if

---

[13] Putnam, B. H., 2013, "Essential concepts necessary to consider when evaluating the efficacy of quantitative easing," *Review of Financial Economics*, 22: 1–7. Also, reprinted here as Chapter 14.

such actions impact the decision by capital-constrained financial institutions to increase lending. What seems to matter much more for the credit creation process are the expectations of financial institutions about the state of the economy and the perceived risk of extending new loans with a careful eye on capital preservation and capital ratios. On net, in the era of expanded central bank balance sheets, central banks will own a much higher percentage of their country's outstanding government debt while the private sector will own a smaller proportion. One could even see credit agencies viewing this development as a positive factor for their sovereign credit ratings, but central bank asset purchases will not have made any difference in creating inflation. Similarly, zero short-term rates have not ignited the kind of lending boom necessary to fuel inflation pressures, because banks are much more worried about their own profitability and risks. In short, at low rates, the link between central bank policies and credit expansion is very loose if almost non-existent.

We are not arguing against expanded macro-prudential regulation. What we are observing, however, is that one form of regulation designed to mitigate systematic risk may well render other policy tools used for managing the economy less effective. And, there is the plausible scenario that relying more heavily on macro-prudential regulations, such as very large mandated capital ratios, may curtail risk capital allocated to trading activities and potentially make markets used for risk management purposes less liquid and not as efficient. These types of trade-offs are often at the heart of regulatory debates, especially when the focus of the regulators differs. The Fed's focus on economic management and systematic risk, in this sense, places it in a different philosophical position compared to the CFTC's focus on market integrity and efficiency as well as with the SEC's primary emphasis on investor protections.

Concluding Thoughts on the Culture and Origin of Regulatory Institutions and the Need to be Wary of Unintended Consequences

The types of unintended consequences from the multi-institutional regulatory structure in the US seem bound to become more challenging as regulators seek to achieve different objectives, ranging from improving market integrity, to enhancing investor protections, to containing systematic risk. In essence, we are brought back to two important strands of market structure and regulatory theory — namely, 1) the causes of market failure and 2) the public choice theories of why any political system creates the regulatory system that it does. Each market failure, whether the banking panics of the 1800s, or the old-style delivery squeezes in futures markets, or the stock market crash of 1929 and the Great Depression, tend to give way to new legislation and new regulatory powers specific to the last crisis or market failure. Viewed in this historical light, it is not so surprising that the US has one of the more complex financial regulatory systems leading to regulatory institutions approaching similar market challenges from different philosophical approaches based on their birth stories and missions.

Chapter 9

Volatility and Uncertainty

Katina Stefanova[1] & Blu Putnam[2]

*Editor's Note: This chapter is an adaptation of an article originally published in **The Hedge Fund Journal, Q4/2017.** There is a rather pervasive confusion in the financial world between uncertainty and volatility. They are not the same thing at all. Rising uncertainty is a psychological concept, involves behavioral feedback loops, and is nearly impossible to measure. Volatility is most often represented as an observed statistical calculation, such as the standard deviation, or an expectational metric such as implied volatility derived from options prices. This research explains how rising uncertainty and low volatility can co-exist, and what are the triggers for higher volatility. – KT*

Volatility in equities, bonds, and other asset classes remained at very low levels compared to historical norms in 2017, as measured by the standard deviation of daily market price movements. Yet, at the same time, uncertainty was exceptionally high concerning a wide-ranging array of potentially market-moving events which were often in the daily news and getting considerable attention. The co-existence during 2017 of relatively low volatility and high uncertainty presented an interesting conundrum.

The list of potential volatility-inducing questions was quite long during the year 2017. And, even if they did not produce volatility in

---

[1] Chief Executive Officer & Chief Investment Officer, Marto Capital.
[2] **Disclaimer:** All examples are hypothetical interpretations of situations and are used for explanation purposes only. The views expressed here reflect solely those of the authors and not necessarily those of their employer, CME Group or its affiliated institutions. The information herein should not be considered investment advice or the results of actual market experience.

2017, 2018 would be a different story, given the significance of the list of uncertainties. Would the future course of fiscal policy in the US involve a big corporate tax cut or not? Would this involve fears of heightened inflation resulting in higher bond yields and more equity volatility? How would trade relationships around the world change as the US pulled back from its world leadership role? Would the Brexit negotiations hang over the UK economy like Damocles' sword for years to come? The Federal Reserve embarked on incremental plans to shrink its balance sheet and the European Central Bank followed with small adjustments to its asset buying programs. How would asset classes that positively benefited from QE respond to the unwinding? Diplomatic tensions with potential military implications abounded, especially in the Middle East as Iran and Saudi Arabia sparred with each other.

Figure 9-1: Stock and Bond Volatility

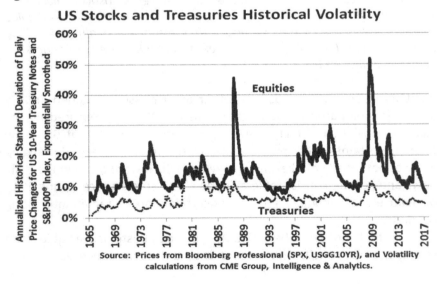

Source: Prices from Bloomberg Professional (SPX, USGG10YR), and Volatility calculations from CME Group, Intelligence & Analytics.

Essentially, 2016 and 2017 highlighted that the world faced serious economic and political challenges with the likelihood of binary outcomes. That is, not only was the environment experiencing rising uncertainty, the probability distributions of potential market outcomes were decidedly not normal, often highly skewed, and sometimes even bi-modal, which meant that generating returns had gotten markedly more difficult for investors.

And, it was not just about the short-term questions that worried market participants. Context mattered and demanded attention be paid to major long-term drivers such as the trend of anti-globalization, demographic changes, migration and societal transformation. The net was that global markets in the "binary age" were impacted by greater exposure to social and political risks than in the 1950–2015 post WWII environment. Particularly, the rise of social populism had caused uncertainty across the markets. In 2016, we witnessed both Brexit and the US election adding tremendous volatility across the markets, with a boom in banking and energy sector equities and added volatility for the Mexican peso.

One might think all of these uncertainties would have been associated with increased market volatility, especially in equity and bond prices, but it did not happen in 2017, although equity volatility did arrive in 2018 as certain catalysts triggered an end to the complacency. To appreciate what events would actually trigger volatility, we need to examine the complex relationship between uncertainty and volatility.

The Long-term Drivers of Uncertainties

While we typically cite current events and various policy issues that are in the news as sources of uncertainties, our perspective is that it is even more important to look deeper into the often overlooked, long-term drivers of the uncertainties. We need to appreciate that a trend that takes decades to develop may manifest itself quite suddenly and in very powerful ways. What happens is that perceptions of reality tend to be inertia driven, even though virtually everyone is aware that long-term changes are afoot. Then, a catalyst suddenly changes the consensus view of reality. Let's take a few examples — from bond markets, technology, social perceptions, and corporate change — to illustrate the analytical challenge.

Tailwinds from falling bond yields reversing. For over 30 years from 1982 into 2016, investors benefited from falling interest rates. From 2018 forward, more observers believed that time may have ended. As 2017 closed, industrial commodities appeared to have exited

their bear market — a necessary condition for inflation pressures to re-
emerge. The US passed a massive, permanent corporate tax cut (See
Chapter 3) which greatly expanded the debt of the country (See Chapter
2) and increased the size of US Treasury auctions by a significant degree.
The US Treasury 10-Year Note yield responded by moving from 2.4% at
end-2017 to touching 3% in Q2/2018.

Figure 9-2: Government Bond Yield Comparisons

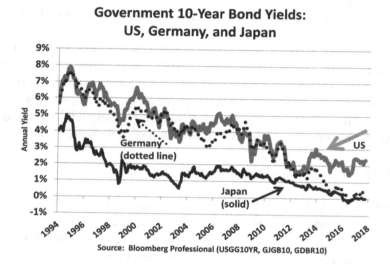

Source: Bloomberg Professional (USGG10YR, GJGB10, GDBR10)

Technological innovation has disrupted employment patterns.
Innovation provides kinetic energy that makes disruption possible in all
industries. It is no secret that most workers in manual, routine jobs have
a high probability of seeing their jobs automated during the 2020s and
2030s. Indeed, in the US, percentage growth rates of jobs termed as
non-routine cognitive (i.e., problem solving jobs) have grown more
rapidly than manual routine jobs.

Figure 9-3: Job Growth by Category

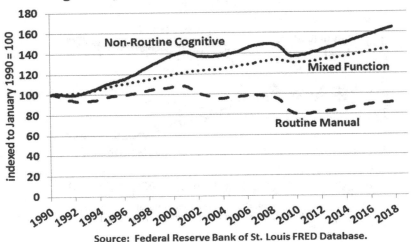

Growth of Routine Manual, Non-Routine Cognitive, and Mixed Function Jobs in the US

Source: Federal Reserve Bank of St. Louis FRED Database.

Technological innovation has also dramatically changed the world of oil production. From the demand-side in the last decade, the emergence of hydraulic fracturing methods of energy extraction dramatically altered production patterns. With the changing role of US shale oil production, it is unlikely that OPEC will have the same ability as in the 1970–2010 period to independently manipulate oil prices. By 2018, it was clear that the US had joined Saudi Arabia and Russia as the three largest oil producers in the world, diminishing OPEC's power, since Russia and the US are not OPEC members, even though they do negotiate with each other over oil policies.

In the 2020s, the disruptive change may appear from the demand side of the equation. Oil is about three-quarters used in its refined state as a transportation fuel. Technological change may dampen demand for oil as transportation fuel efficiency makes great leaps forward. And, further technological innovations in alternative energy sources are likely to put continuous pressure on global oil prices and make traditional oil valuation models unreliable. It is obvious that underlying fundamentals have changed. It is not so obvious when and how risk management approaches will adjust.

Figure 9-4: Major Country Oil Production

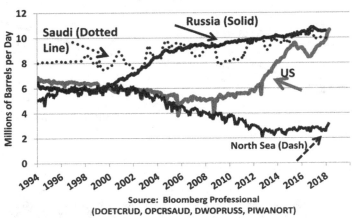

US, Russian, Saudi Arabian, and North Sea Oil Production

Source: Bloomberg Professional
(DOETCRUD, OPCRSAUD, DWOPRUSS, PIWANORT)

Figure 9-5: US Oil Consumption

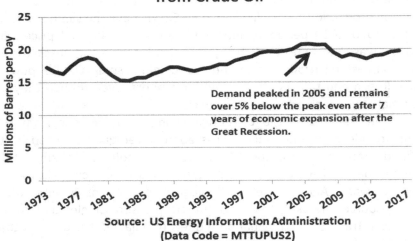

US Consumption of Refined Product from Crude Oil

Demand peaked in 2005 and remains over 5% below the peak even after 7 years of economic expansion after the Great Recession.

Source: US Energy Information Administration
(Data Code = MTTUPUS2)

The developed world is a major contributor to global instability. In the mature, industrial economies, the widening income gap creates large social impacts, resulting in the potential for resource misallocation. In the long term, a substantial segment of the population will lose confidence in government, eroding social cohesion. With positive growth and low unemployment rate statistics, analysts will often neglect the depths of the divisions that occur underneath the average numbers. Wealth and income gaps are widening at an accelerating pace, which can become substantial fuel for social volatility.[3] Unfortunately, there is little monetary policy can do to narrow the wealth and opportunity gap.

Additionally, aging populations are a source of social change in the developed world. For example, the population in the US is aging rapidly with about 73 million Americans, or approximately 22% of the US population, turning 62 or older by 2020 (www.census.gov). An aging population entering retirement in the US, Europe, and Japan desires predictable income from their nest egg. Growth is still a must for underfunded pension funds and retirees who have not saved enough.

Finally, we note that the number of displaced persons around the world reached record high levels in 2017. The refugee crisis from Syria, the rest of the Middle East and Africa adds a new variable and increased level of tension — economically and culturally. Germany's Chancellor Merkel's belief that the refugees will provide a much-needed source of low cost labor when the European population is declining and aging at the same time is unlikely to pan out in the short run. Instead, Germany is bursting at the seams trying to effectively integrate the more than a million refugees who crossed into Europe since 2014, making the recent migration the largest global refugee crisis since WWII.

The speed of corporate destruction has added to the sense of uncertainty, if not equity volatility. The average public company lifespan has declined sharply from the 1950s when the lifetime of an

---

[3] The income equality challenges in the US are extensively documented in a Federal Reserve study by Jesse Bricker, et al., September 2014, "Changes in U.S. Family Finances from 2010 to 2013: Evidence from the Survey of Consumer Finances", *Federal Reserve Bulletin*, 100(4).

S&P500® company was about 60 years, before it was acquired, failed, or otherwise dropped from the horizon. In the 2010s, corporate lifespans in the US had declined to about 20 years, reflecting the powerful forces of economic disruption.[4] And, Sante Fe Institute faculty member, Geofrey West, in a book entitled *Scale*, takes a look at the maximize size and length of life of companies and cities from the perspective of a natural scientist, adding extra depth to the changes impacting the economic behavior of corporations.

Why Rising Uncertainties Co-Exist with Low Volatility

When you place the current long list of market worries into the context of the long-term drivers of uncertainty, one may be confused as to why rising uncertainties were able to co-exist with low volatility during 2017. Essentially, we need both to appreciate the drivers of uncertainty as well as to examine the behavioral patterns related to reacting to uncertainty. The science of fear often sees patterns of behavior that bear a strong resemblance to chaos theory[5], and these observations may help explain the conundrum of why it is possible for elevated levels of uncertainty to co-exist with relatively low levels of market volatility.

Pretend you find yourself walking down a deserted road late at night, and you are more than a little concerned about your safety. You hear footsteps behind you. You keep on walking. The footsteps are getting closer. Your fear level is rising, and yet you keep on walking. As the footsteps get ever-nearer, perhaps you hear a sound or some catalyst, your fear reaches a point where you face a decision to turn and confront the challenge (if there is one) or run away. Once you choose, there will be no going back.

These are among the types of decisions analyzed by chaos theory. Rising fears, or uncertainties, do not trigger a change in behavior. A reaction to the rising fears takes a catalyst; fear or

---

[4] As reported by ValueWalk (www.valuewalk.com/2017/08/disruptive-forces/) in its report of August 29, 2017, titled: "Disruption has cut company life-span by 66%", based on research provided by Eugene Klerk of Credit Suisse in an August 24, 2017, report titled: "Disruptive forces in Europe: A Primer".
[5] James Gleick, 1987, *Chaos: Making a New Science*, New York: Viking Books.

uncertainty alone is not a cause of volatility. In our example, the footsteps get so close as to force a decision about what action to take. And, once the decision is made, you are committed to the new path. By way of another illustration, the same thing happens on a ski slope. You are at the mountain top and resting on your skis peering down the steep expert slope. You could take the bunny slope down or you could push off on a wild ride. Once the decision is made to tackle the steep slope, there will be no turning back.

What we observe is that the uncertainties are well appreciated, from technology, demographics, social change, as well as from the current policy issues such as taxes, trade, and monetary policy. The catalyst only arrives when something actually happens that changes the consensus view from worrying about uncertainties to taking actions to manage the risks associated with the potential market-moving events.

In 2017, despite the uncertainties, the global economy moved forward. The US remained on a path of +2% real GDP growth. Europe and Japan gained a little economic momentum. The real improvement in the global economy came from the developing world. China may have added to its massive debt loads; however, the economy kept on growing. Inflation in the major countries remained subdued. Brazil exited a deep recession. Higher oil prices helped the Russian economy. With economic activity moving forward and without a catalyst, market participants during 2017 ignored the uncertainties, kept on walking, and volatility was relatively low.

Risk Management Implications

Low volatility by historical standards, relatively benign markets, and our general inability to estimate the timing, magnitude or even the nature of a coming catalytic event, however, does not mean that risk management should be passive. There was considerable evidence that risk managers were actively involved in addressing the challenges they faced. Indeed, in 2017, open interest in a number of CME Group products, from Treasury bonds to oil to copper and cattle shot to record highs. The Commodity Futures Trading Commission's (CFTC's) commitment of traders' reports showed heightened short open interest activity from commercials and producers as they hedge risks in commodity production. Cash levels at many major corporations were extremely high, suggesting a cautious approach to new ventures. Investors for some time had moved in the direction of passive, index-based securities, rather than taking aggressive stock-picking risks. Volatility may have been low in 2017, but market participants were on the alert.

Here is our summary of potential risk management solutions for managing heightened uncertainty regardless of whether observed volatility is low or high.

More sophisticated use of options can help mitigate event risks. On a basic level, options strategies are especially well-suited for managing the risks of uncertainty even when volatility is low. As uncertainty rises, so does the risk, even if the probability is low, of a large, quick change in market prices. This price gap risk (up or down) is not the same as volatility. Traditional, simple options pricing models, such as the original Black-Scholes options pricing model, assume price gap risk does not exist — allowing for a clean interpretation of implied volatility. This approach does not work well in rising uncertainty conditions when event risk generates more highly skewed and sometimes bi-modal probability distributions.

Traditional models do not adequately account for uncertainty because markets exhibit exogenous characteristics. Taking investment analysis as an example, the traditional model focuses on the valuation and the growth analysis of companies and industries. But, other social political factors, such as financial regulations, and military conflict, could be the main drivers for certain periods, and cause extreme and frequent tail risks. Uncertainty in the global environment makes traditional valuation models unreliable.

Dangers of ignoring context in a world of rising uncertainty should not be ignored. The underlying causes of structural change may take a long time for markets to accept the new reality. Asset managers cannot afford to ignore exogenous risks, because the game-changing catalyst could appear at any time. Flush global liquidity suppressed market volatility, even with global uncertainty at heightened levels. This is a prescription for rising probabilities related to event risk.

Static correlations do not provide diversification. When "black swan" types of events occur, intra-asset class correlations spike, which illustrates the interconnectedness of securities with similar risk characteristics even if their cash flow sources are strikingly different. A recent example from 2016 is Brexit. The pound crashed leading to an emerging market FX sell-off. Meanwhile, the dollar rally impacted the ability of emerging markets to pay off US dollar-denominated debt. In this case, for a short period of time, uncertainty led to risk aversion, with a larger proportion of investors seeking a flight to safety.

There is a strong case for thematic portfolio construction and risk management. All of these challenges and ideas coming from the co-existence of rising uncertainty and low volatility point to the need for thematic-based financial engineering. The long-term drivers of uncertainty provide the context. These themes generate the economic and political conflicts that create short-term, event risk probability distributions that may be highly skewed or even bi-modal and may dramatically shift correlation structures under certain scenarios. Working with themes instead of assets is not a new idea; it is just more important than ever because of the risks of price gaps, shifting correlations, and binary outcomes.

Chapter 10

Machine Learning: Challenges for Financial Market Predictive Analytics Suggest a Bayesian Solution

Blu Putnam[1]

Editor's Note: Machine learning and artificial intelligence have made awesome progress in the last few decades. Using these methods, computers can win at chess and "Jeopardy", recognize faces, drive cars, make medical diagnoses from radiology images, assist in identifying what chemical structures might inhibit cancer, and develop encryption techniques, among other uses. And some quantitatively oriented hedge funds have explored using the latest machine learning and artificial intelligence methods to help predict market behavior and manage investment portfolios. While remaining optimistic, the research here suggests that predicting economic outcomes and financial market behavior has some serious challenges not faced in many other applications of machine learning and artificial intelligence. – KT

In the age of Hollywood's *Moneyball*, big data, machine learning and artificial intelligence (AI), it seems only natural to apply our new and evolving statistical tools to predicting outcomes in financial markets.

Given the difficulties in predicting market behavior, the bar seems low, and open to dreams of making significant improvements in predictive analytics as applied to financial markets.

Not to throw a wet blanket over dreams of achieving financial genius and wealth through machine learning and AI, but perhaps one should start with an exploration of the challenges before moving on to some useful rules to guide one's efforts in predictive analytics as applied to financial markets.

Just to be clear, we are optimists. And, we are fully engaged in using the new tools, especially machine learning, in a wide variety of research and operational tasks — it is just that the financial markets long ago taught us to look both ways before crossing the street; to be cautious and not to over-promise.

Challenges of Predicting Financial Market Behavior

If you think about the progression of machine learning and AI, the achievements over just the last few decades have been amazing and impressive. Take facial recognition. Computers can do this extremely well these days. Of course, the basic structure of faces has not changed in tens of thousands of years, so part of the achievement has been made possible by advances in image storage and search functionality — not just machine learning. Computers beating humans in "Jeopardy" is similar to advances in facial recognition. As computer algorithms improved and their memory enhanced through huge advances in storage and search capabilities, they were eventually able to win at "Jeopardy".

Winning at chess was a little harder for computers. Chess has feedback loops. The computer makes a move; the human makes a move; and so forth. Again, with enough memory to store a zillion possible games, a great search engine, and a deep machine-learning algorithm, computers finally broke through and were able to defeat the world's top chess player.

Financial market prediction, however, is going to be much, much harder than chess, although to be sure, algorithms are already doing pretty well in some aspects of financial markets, with some major success stories and more than a few failures.[2]

Let's think a little bit, though, about the comparison of financial markets with the game of chess. In chess, the rules are known, fixed, and do not change. The definition of winning is clear — capture the opponent's king. Not so with financial markets. Different market participants can have strikingly different objectives. Economists are fond of assuming that market participants, on average and over time, are rational in how they go about maximizing their utility — often expressed as a clear trade-off between financial gain and risk. Even if humans behaved this way, which is not so clear, market participants often have very different risk-return trade-offs, and they may change the nature of these trade-offs over time.

Then, there are organizations that are huge players in markets that have totally different goals. Take central banks. They have a different view of winning. They are not looking to maximize profits relative to the risks or anything like that. After the Great Recession of 2008, central banks held short-term interest rates near zero and bought assets (i.e. Quantitative Easing or QE) in hopes of stimulating inflation and encouraging above-average economic growth. Inflation remained subdued and growth was modest at best. Central banks failed in their primary mission. Nevertheless, central banks were able to create asset-price inflation — with bond yields lower (prices higher) and equity values higher than they almost certainly otherwise would have been. Then one major central bank, the Federal Reserve, changed direction. Since 2016, the Federal Reserve has raised short-term rates and allowed some of its assets to mature and not be replaced. Not only do central banks have different definitions of winning, they can change their level, direction, and motivation for market participation over time.

With financial markets and economies, there can be big changes in the rules. The Dodd–Frank legislation of 2010 literally changed the parameters of the playing field. In 2018, some of the Dodd–Frank rules were rolled back. There can also be important but smaller changes in

---

[2] Heaton, J. B., April 2018, "Quantitative Investing and the Limits of (Deep) Learning from Financial Data", *The Capco Institute Journal of Financial Transformation*, 47: 117–122.

how rules are interpreted. If you do not like a Securities and Exchange Commission (SEC) rule, you can apply for an exemption or a "No-Action letter." You might or might not get it.

And then, different players in the market interpret the rules differently. And, of course, there are some players who do not follow the rules — such as during the sub-prime mortgage scandals in 2006–2008, LIBOR reporting scandals of 2008–2010, exchange rate scandals, etc. All of this makes the feedback loop from action to response very, very tricky to predict.

Financial markets also have to contend with non-linear behavior from market participants.[3] Economists' typical assumptions of what constitutes rational behavior do not reflect so many of the important asymmetric aspects of human behavior.

For one thing, humans typically treat losses and gains quite differently. Humans like to make money; but they really hate losing it — displaying asymmetric risk preferences.

Humans also tend to set their reference points based on the recent past. The financial panic of September 2008 and meltdown of financial markets influenced market participants for many years. The success of equity strategies in the 2013–2017 period, such as buy the dips, was a recognition of the persistence of the rally with few setbacks, and became the reference point — until it wasn't in early 2018. Behavior is heavily influenced by the recent past regardless of whether the future is cloudy or relatively clear.

Humans are often not very good at appreciating statistics — they typically give small sample sizes undue influence — which gives machines an edge, although the human reliance on intuition makes the human action and response feedback loop even harder for machines to understand, anticipate and predict.

The dynamic, ever-changing nature of markets is a big challenge. When rules change, participants' motives and risk/reward trade-offs change, technology changes, tastes and fashion change, and so on; the predictive challenges grow exponentially.

---

[3] See Akerlof, George, and Shiller, Robert J., 2009, *Animal Spirits: How Human Psychology Drives the Economy, and Why It Matters for Global Capitalism*, New Jersey: Princeton University Press.

The Reverend Thomas Bayes, Machine Learning and AI

The dynamic nature of markets and ever-changing feedback loops and structural changes due to technology or regulation suggests that error-learning and other methods of statistical analysis have the potential to work better in financial prediction than methods anchored in fixed periods in the past. That is, if one had trained a machine learning algorithm to identify patterns in the post-Great Recession period of 2010–2016 with near-zero short-term interest and aggressive asset purchases from non-profit maximizing central banks, then applied the algorithms to 2017–2018, some severe problems may have occurred, given the shift to rising interest rates and a shrinking of the balance sheet of the Federal Reserve.

Figure 10-1: The Reverend Thomas Bayes (a common rendering, although no one knows if it is accurate)

As the above example indicates, the dynamic nature of markets suggests the need for regular updating of AI and machine learning algorithms. While there are many types of dynamic updating techniques, we would like to take as a case study the work of The Reverend Thomas Bayes (c. 1701–1761). Whether or not one chooses to adopt Bayesian Inference — using Bayes' Theorem to refresh the probability of a hypothesis as more information becomes available — and embed it into the machine learning and AI processes, one can gain many insights from considering the approach. In essence, our perspective is that Bayesian Inference has a lot to tell us about how to develop successful prediction systems using big data, machine learning, and AI processes. So, bear with us as we digress for a few minutes into the mind of Thomas Bayes, an English Presbyterian Minister, at around 1750.

It is interesting to note that back in 1750, Presbyterianism incorporated a belief in Predestination. That is, the Presbyterian God had a plan for your life (Predestination), but that plan was not conveyed to you. Perhaps, the Reverend Bayes was motivated to study probability and statistics to determine his life plan?

Also of note is that The Reverend Bayes was buried in Bunhill Fields — a burial ground for Nonconformists, which back in the day meant not accepting the Book of Common Prayer of the Anglican Church. Bunhill Fields is home to the graves of many notable people, including John Bunyan (died 1688), author of The Pilgrim's Progress; Daniel Defoe (died 1731), author of Robinson Crusoe; William Blake (died 1827), artist, poet, and mystic; Susanna Wesley (died 1742), known as the "Mother of Methodism" through her education of sons John and Charles; and Thomas Bayes (died 1761), statistician and philosopher. Bayes was clearly an innovative thinker and more than willing to challenge received wisdom and customs.

Moving back to our discussion of Bayesian Inference, one starts with view and a level of confidence. One takes in a piece of new information; and then one reviews both one's view of the future and the level of confidence in that view.

This is what happens in financial markets. Market participants have a view (or a set of positions or a portfolio), and they have an assessment of the risk. Participants get new information all the time, most of which is 'noise,' and occasionally they get a new piece of information that makes them change their positions or adjust their portfolio as well as alter their assessment of the risks.

Bayes wrote down his ideas and he provided illustrations — even using a billiard table to explain the dynamic probabilistic process. The equations were not documented until after his death by French mathematician Pierre-Simon Marquis de Laplace. Laplace was quite famous for work in mathematics and physics. He was an early thinker about the existence of black holes and gravitational collapse. He was an examiner when Napoleon Bonaparte attended the Ecole Militaire in Paris in 1784, and gave him high marks. Laplace also read Bayes' work and translated it into a set of three elegant equations obeying the laws of probability. What is truly amazing is that he named his work Bayes' Theorem — Frenchmen do not always give the English due credit, and well, mathematicians are quite competitive.

One of the neat things about Bayesian Inference is its ability to take in expert information in a seamless manner with data-driven insights — so long as both come with views and confidence assessments. The importance of expert advice is controversial in these days of big data and artificial intelligence.

One huge challenge is that even a sequence of random numbers can generate interesting patterns — but they just do not persist. One has to train a machine not to be fooled by patterns from random data. A case can be made that experts may be able to help — especially when the rules were just changed, or when a big new player enters the market with a different objective function, such as central banks and QE, or when technology makes a great leap, such as in shale oil production or fuel efficiency.

Importantly, all of these events greatly devalue historical data for predictive purposes, and that means the data used to train a machine learning algorithm may not be appropriate for the objectives of the project. Big structural changes in markets essentially create a period when the new data sets reflecting the change are small and still evolving. This is a great time to use Bayesian methods to add expert advice. With a Bayesian system, if the expert is wrong too often, the system can continue to take in the advice — but it just ignores it by assigning little to no value.

And with dynamic Bayesian systems, one can decide how rapidly to decay the information value of older data. That is, all data points are definitely not created equal. Decaying the value of older information is very tricky. Some economic or market processes might see the value of historical data decay much faster than others. Moreover, these different time decay processes can be observed in the same economic system. And, humans may see the same data patterns differently, implying different rates of historical data decay.

Figure 10-2. Bayes' Billiard Table Example

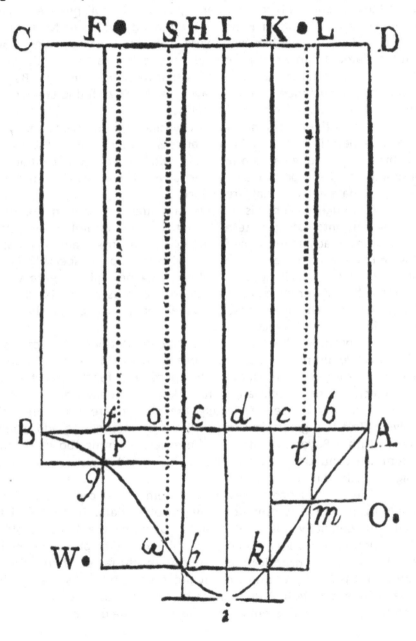

For example, economists are often wedded to their regression techniques — which goes a long way to explaining their inability to predict. In a regression, all data points are of equal value. Often in hypothesis testing, new information mixes with old, while in predictive analysis it is critical to make sure only available information is used at any given time period in a simulated history. And, regressions assume that estimated parameters are fixed over the study period, when financial market experience clearly reveals that parameters are moving targets, dynamically evolving, and time-varying. Why choose a technique that assumes the challenge does not exist?

By the way, this happens all the time. In the world of options, the Black-Scholes-Merton basic pricing models assume there are no price jumps or gaps — trading and price evolution progress in a smooth, continuous fashion. Not so, of course, in the real world — especially as in 2016 when event risk, such as the Brexit vote or the US elections, took center stage. Teasing out market fears of event risk and price gaps with an implied volatility model of option prices that assumes price gaps cannot happen is probably not the right analytical approach.

For example, if one studies the oil market, one must capture the development and continued improvement in shale drilling methods, or one will never get it right. With interest rates, the panic of 2008 there was the move to zero rates, then the move to QE, and then in 2016 and 2017 the withdrawal of QE commenced by the Federal Reserve along with slowly rising rates. These were big dynamic shifts.

In studying GDP, demographics may be more important than Federal Reserve policy, but demographic patterns change so slowly that they are very easily ignored. (See Chapter 5.) Yet the retirement of baby boomers and the entry of student-debt-laden millennials into the labor force is much more explanatory of today's modest real GDP growth pattern than anything going on with monetary or fiscal policy.

So, the conclusion is that time-varying, dynamic processes are critical to financial market prediction. Machine learning and AI can incorporate these observations if you are willing to tackle the complexity and take the time to set up the system to do it. It will not be easy.

Machine Learning and AI Processes

The lessons we have learned from Bayesian Inference when applied to machine learning and artificial intelligence can summarized rather briefly:

> ➢ Start with unsupervised learning. See what the data says — even if one might not believe it.

> ➢ Add analysis and always be probabilistic.

> ➢ Include expert information and various stress-testing of simulations (see Chapter 13).

> ➢ Do not just focus on confirming evidence (how well the system seems to work) — focus even more on when/what does not work, what does not fit, understand why.

> ➢ Make the whole process dynamic, take in new information and recalibrate. Refresh the "learning periods" way more often than you might think is necessary.

> ➢ And lastly, do not get too confident in your "best" historical simulations. Remember, the "best" simulations are the ones which probably contain the most "luck." Dampen your research expectations with an appreciation for random patterns and the role of luck.[4]

---

[4] For a lay version, see Markowitz, H., Xu, G. L., Putnam, B. H., 2000, "Deflating Research Expectations", in *Integrating Risk Management into Asset Allocation* by Blu Putnam, published by Global Investor, London. For the mathematical explanation of potential biases in data mining, see Markowitz, Harry and Xu, Gan Lin, Fall 1994, "Data Mining Corrections", *Journal of Portfolio Management*, 21(1): 60–69. DOI: https://doi.org/10.3905/jpm.1994.409494.

Chapter 11

Portfolio Optimization: Revolutionizing Risk Assessment Systems

Blu Putnam[1], Graham McDannel, and Veenit Shah

Editor's Note: This chapter was originally published as an essay in **The Capco Institute Journal of Financial Transformation,** *Volume 44,* **November 2016.** *The efficacy of portfolio optimization and risk assessment systems depends critically on the embedded assumptions underlying the models. Unfortunately, many model builders are very sloppy with their assumptions and lean heavily on a belief that the world displays normal or log-normal probability distributions. This research argues that assumptions of normality are a prescription for disaster. – KT*

Challenges to optimization abound in the world of portfolio construction and financial risk assessment. While financial optimization theory is highly sophisticated, with detailed attention paid to model construction and critical assumptions, the current state of practice leaves much to be desired, and may best be described as a patchwork quilt held together by band aids or the ubiquitous duct tape. On the horizon, however, are some potential improvements in the analytical techniques underpinning how optimization methods are used in both

---

[1] **Disclaimer:** All examples are hypothetical interpretations of situations and are used for explanation purposes only. The views expressed here reflect solely those of the authors and not necessarily those of their employer, CME Group or its affiliated institutions. The information herein should not be considered investment advice or the results of actual market experience.

portfolio construction and financial risk management. From the promise of exhaustive searches using quantum computers to the advances in pattern recognition available through structured machine learning, financial optimization methods are about to get a major makeover. Change may be coming, and it's about time!

To understand the importance and promise of the new developments in technology for financial optimization, however, it is imperative to appreciate the state of current practice faced by portfolio managers and risk officers. Critical challenges exist in the internal consistency of volatility and correlation estimates given the mixed methods used in many quantitative practices. With the heightened occurrence of event risk coming from politics, policy, and disruptive innovation, common assumptions concerning the stability of volatility regimes and correlation estimates are in question. Moreover, event risk can create short periods when bimodal expected return distributions dominate, often resulting in underestimation of the potential for pricing gaps and volatility regime shifts. Future progress with exhaustive search optimization using quantum computers and structured machine learning offers the possibility of a much deeper assessment of the probabilities surrounding event risk, improved analysis of the potential presence of bimodal and other non-normal return distributions, and the construction of more robust portfolios to handle the extreme (or fat-tailed) risks that seem to be happening more and more often than traditional approaches tend to predict.

Our research is divided into three sections. First, we go back to the father of Modern Portfolio Theory (MPT), Professor Harry Markowitz, and provide some perspective on his contributions. Second, we take a closer look at a few of the all too common practical approaches to financial optimization that fly in the face of critical assumptions embedded in the Markowitz approach. In our analysis of the common challenges to financial optimization that often lead to vast underestimations of risk and the construction of highly sub-optimal portfolios, we draw heavily from examples and illustrations taken from the U.K.'s June 2016 referendum to leave the European Union or "Brexit." Lastly, we come back to our key themes of how two major technical advances — quantum computing and machine learning — are likely to change financial optimization practices for the better.

Harry Markowitz and the Assumptions Underlying Mean-Variance Optimization

The pioneer of modern financial optimization for portfolio construction and risk assessment is without a doubt Professor Harry Markowitz, winner of the Nobel Prize in Economics in 1990. What is amazing is that over 65 years after the Markowitz mean-variance optimization came into the financial world back in the early 1950s, most practically applied financial optimization problems are addressed with the creative use of band-aids and duct tape (including some especially sophisticated mathematical methods) to handle known challenges that were embedded in the key assumptions chosen by Professor Markowitz in his doctoral dissertation at the University of Chicago to make the optimization problem tractable and available for real world use.

While there is a large and highly sophisticated body of literature involving the use of mean-variance optimization in finance, we will spare the reader both the mathematics and a recitation of the academic literature in favor of an intuitive review of some of the key challenges that scholars and practitioners have spent decades addressing. Our perspective is that an appreciation of the challenges of working with optimization methods in the real world effectively makes the case as to why a revolution in optimization methods is finally on the horizon.

The brilliance of Professor Markowitz's seminal work[2] in the early 1950s was to recognize the role played by risk assessment in valuing stock and analyzing portfolios, since investors were effectively constructing portfolios with considerable uncertainty about the future. Indeed, MPT effectively embraced the approach set forth by Professor Markowitz as a key element in security analysis.

As Professor D. Sykes Wilford noted in his insightful review of the contribution of Professor Markowitz to Modern Portfolio Theory (MPT)[3] [Wilford (2012)]: "In fact, MPT is ubiquitous to all financial theory and practice. By the same token, often the implementations of MPT break many of the basic assumptions behind MPT (and Markowitz),

---

[2] Markowitz, H. M., March 1952, "Portfolio Selection", *The Journal of Finance*, 7(1): 77–91.

[3] Wilford, D. S., 2012, "True Markowitz or assumptions we break and why it matters," *Review of Financial Economics*, 21(3): 93–101.

thereby making the conclusions derived from these actions extremely misleading, and in many cases completely incorrect."

Professor Wilford's contribution was to underscore the need to take a challenging look at how practical applications of financial optimization techniques handle the sometimes heroic assumptions embedded in the basic theory. This will be our approach here as well, and in so doing, we hope to set the stage for an appreciation of how quantum computing and machine learning are going to change the practice of portfolio construction and risk assessment — taking the real world closer to the theoretical world of Professor Markowitz.

Theory to Practice with Financial Optimization Techniques

While less appreciated, one of the more important research philosophies of Professor Markowitz was his focus on practical, applicable versions of portfolio optimization. There was in the 1950s and 1960s a controversy in academic circles over whether economics should be seeking precise and general solutions or whether good approximations were acceptable. In his Nobel Lecture in 1990, Professor Markowitz commented on his approach and this debate:

> "We seek a set of rules which investors can follow in fact — at least investors with sufficient computational resources. Thus, *we prefer an approximate method which is computationally feasible to a precise one which cannot be computed.* I believe that this is the point at which Kenneth Arrow's work on the economics of uncertainty diverges from mine. He sought a precise and general solution. I sought as good an approximation as could be implemented. I believe that both lines of inquiry are valuable" (italics added).[4]

The practical approach of Professor Markowitz is where we start in our intuitive analysis of the challenges of portfolio optimization. We will focus on just a few critical assumptions commonly used in the

---

[4] Markowitz, H. M., June 1991, "Foundations of Portfolio Theory", *The Journal of Finance*, 46(2): 469–477.

current state of practice as we set up the case for the advances that will follow from quantum computing and machine learning. The critical assumptions we will review here include: 1) use of historical data to compute estimates for expected volatility and correlations while using a forward-looking method of creating expected returns; 2) use of the standard deviation as the common measurement for volatility; and 3) instability of the correlation matrix and existence of non-normal expected return distributions. All of these challenges are exposed in rather dramatic fashion with the presence of event risk. These intuitive discussions then lead us to illustrate our analysis with examples taken from the study of the "Brexit" referendum in June 2016.

Dangers and challenges of relying on history. To implement a Markowitz mean-variance optimization system, one needs expected values — that is, expected returns, expected volatilities, and expected correlations — that are used to describe aspects of the subjective probability distribution representing the risks faced by investors. When it comes to expected returns, there is no shortage of forward-looking quantitative and qualitative approaches. When turning to the expected volatilities and correlations, however, history is often used as a guide. There is a rarely used yet profound comment by Professor Markowitz on using history as a guide that bears remembering:

> "The calculations . . . are the same as historical returns. *It is not that we recommend this as a way of forming beliefs; rather, we use this as an example of distributions of returns which occur in fact."* (italics added).[5]

Using history as a guide for expected volatilities and correlations absolves the risk manager of any forecasting duties, yet subjects the owners of the underlying portfolio to very large error risk. There are good empirical reasons why many financial regulators require the disclaimer that "past performance is not necessarily a guide to future performance." History is always informative, however, every episode is different, so history is simply not always a good guide for developing expectations. There are serious questions about what period of history to use, how far back to look, to what degree is it appropriate to give

---

[5] Ibid.

older observations less weight and recent observations more weight. These are all quantitative questions on the surface that require subjective analysis, and they are beyond the scope of this research. We chose to place the focus on another challenge that is less well appreciated and yet potentially very dangerous. That is, the optimization problems get worse and the likelihood of risk underestimation gets much larger when the use of a forward-looking expected return method is attached to using history for volatility and correlation estimations.

A common refrain in the computer world is "GIGO" or "garbage in, garbage out." With optimization, the so-called garbage coming into the method bounces around the system in a highly networked manner determined by the expected correlation matrix, and one is quite likely to observe "garbage in, and a landfill of waste coming out the other end" — in effect, mean-variance optimization takes GIGO to an exponentially higher power. The problem is the inconsistencies involving three types of inputs — expected returns, expected volatilities, and expected correlations.

For example, if one has an aggressive expected return assumption for a given security, coupled with a historical set of data that do not reflect very much volatility, then this is asking for trouble in the mean-variance optimization space. The challenge arises from an interesting attribute of mean-variance computer systems — they actually believe what one tells them about expectations. Hence, if one provides an aggressive expected return with an expectation of little volatility, the mean-variance optimizer is going to produce a very large recommended exposure for the security. And then, the portfolio manager or risk officer will look at the output of the mean-variance optimization, remark that the output fails the real-world smell test, and either discount the method or add a set of constraints designed to create a more reasonable looking output.

This latter idea of adding constraints to optimization systems to achieve reasonable looking results is a very bad approach. Effectively, the unreasonable output has been caused by the inconsistency in the expected return and expected volatilities input into the optimizer. Rather than fix the inputs by adjusting expectations to make them more internally consistent, the common solution is to add constraints until the portfolio output passes the real world smell test.

This is like diagnosing the patient as a crazy man, and then resorting to putting the patient in a straitjacket to get the desired behavior. The much better approach, in psychoanalysis and in optimization, is to address the source of the problems directly.

One approach is to use the implied volatility in options pricing. However, efficient and useful options markets may well not exist, and some options-pricing models have built-in assumptions related to stable or flat future returns. Another, simpler band-aid is to incorporate information from the return expectations into the expected volatilities. That is, start with a measure of expected volatility, and then augment the volatility expectation based on the degree of aggressiveness of the expected return. With this approach, the mean-variance optimizer will see the aggressive return forecast, yet it will be coupled to a much larger expected volatility, so the exposure that is recommended in the optimized output will be much smaller and make more sense to the portfolio manager and risk officer.

Figure 11-1: The Impact of Brexit on the USD-GBP Exchange Rate

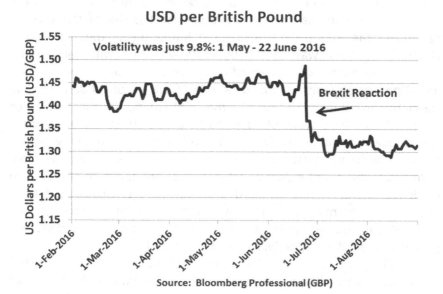

Source: Bloomberg Professional (GBP)

Take the case of the U.K.'s June 2016 referendum on remaining in the European Union (E.U.) or leaving, known as "Brexit" (Figure 11-1). Prior to the vote on 23 June, the US dollar (USD) was trading at around 1.42 against the British pound (GBP). If one thought the U.K. was going to vote to "leave," a typical forecast for the USD per GBP was 1.32 or even lower. By contrast, the "remain" camp expected a relief rally and a rise in the pound toward 1.52 (USD per GBP) or higher.

The historical volatility in the three weeks before the vote was only an annualized 9.8% (standard deviation), even though market participants were looking for a one-day 7% or so move in one direction or the other depending on the outcome of the vote (i.e., a 5+ standard deviation event, one in a million event). As this case illustrates, and as the aggressiveness of the expected moves in the pound given the outcome of the vote suggested, a risk system or a portfolio construction system needed to augment the recent historical volatility to capture the risks appropriately.

Standard deviation may underestimate volatility and potential skewness. The previous intuition, augmenting expected volatilities with information from the expected returns, raises another challenge. Is the standard deviation the appropriate proxy for the risk of the security returns in the first place? Again, and interestingly, the use of the standard deviation was chosen by Professor Markowitz back in the 1950s to represent risk because of its practical attributes. The standard deviation was straightforward to calculate from historical data and the standard deviation fit neatly into the mathematics of mean-variance optimization. There were other important side-effects of this choice. The standard deviation easily leads to embedding into the closed-form mean-variance optimization method the assumption of a normal or log-normal distribution of expected returns. Thus, we focus on at least two challenges here, 1) the standard deviation as often calculated from historical data may underestimate future volatility, and 2) the probability distribution of returns may well have considerable skewness (that is, fat-tailed event or "black swan" potential).

There are a couple of duct tape solutions available. First, the risk officer can embrace the need to take a forward-looking view of potential risks and incorporate them into the quantitative inputs for expected volatility. That is, when the future looks especially risky, despite the current calm state of markets, risk managers may choose to qualitatively augment their estimates of future volatility. We highly recommend this approach, as risk officers should not be able to hide behind historical calculations when such approaches are well known to underestimate risk and to understate the probability and frequency of highly skewed market events.

Second, one can look at alternative approaches for volatility measurement, such as looking at intra-period swings in prices. For example, if one is willing to assume a normal distribution of returns, then there is a deterministic mathematical relationship between the intra-period high/low price spread and the period-to-period standard deviation based on work by Garman and Klass[6], as well as Parkinson[7]. If these two measures start to deviate in a meaningful way, then a market indicator can be constructed which incorporates the information from intra-period trading activity that may point to market participants worrying about more future volatility potential than the standard deviation suggests.

Again, by illustration, "Brexit" provides an interesting case study. In the weeks and months leading up to the "Brexit" referendum, as already noted, volatility, as measured by the standard deviation of daily percent changes in the USD:GBP exchange rate, suggested only modest risks more typical of "business as usual" activity.

By contrast, in the pre-vote period, the intra-day price swings, as measured by the daily high and lows recorded in the nearby British pound futures contract price as traded on CME Group's Globex® electronic platform, suggested much higher risk. And, when the adjusted intra-day high-low price spread[8] is well-above the volatility estimate given by the standard deviation of closing price changes, then one has an indication that market participants are worried about a skewed or fat-tailed event occurring.

---

[6] Garman, M. B., and M. J. Klass, 1980, "On the estimation of security price volatilities from historical data", *The Journal of Business*, 53(1): 67–78.

[7] Parkinson, M., 1980, "The extreme value method for estimating the variance of the rate of return", *The Journal of Business*, 53(1): 61–65.

[8] Adjusted for the difference in volatility measurement between standard deviation and high-low swings.

Figure 11-2. Market Worry Indicator: Before/After Brexit Referendum

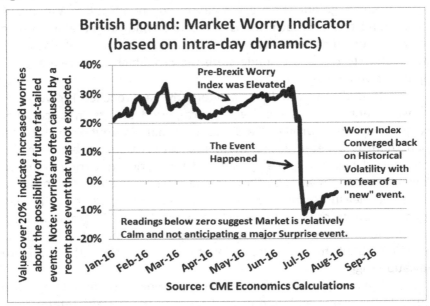

Once the vote occurred and the outcome was known, the difference in volatility measures from these two techniques disappeared. Essentially, market activity reflected the fact the event had occurred and that another similar event was not expected. That is, the storm was a big one, but once it had passed by, the "worry" indicator slipped into neutral.

Instability of correlations and possibility of non-normal return distributions. Market participants quite often have to deal with the prospects of event risk. For example, corporation A makes a bid to acquire corporation B. However, the bid, even after being accepted by corporation B, needs regulatory approval, which may well be quite controversial. The event of the regulatory decision may be binary and result in the termination or consummation of the announced deal. Before the regulatory decision is announced, the stock prices of corporations A and B will reflect the probabilities of the deal terminating or consummating, meaning that the market price of the stock before the deal will not fully reflect the announced deal price if the probability of termination is greater than zero. After the regulatory decision, the stock price moves instantly to reflect whether the deal is going through or ending. Political event risk can look much the same, as it did with the binary "Brexit" vote. What we are describing here is the likelihood that event risk creates the possibility of bimodal return probability distributions.[9] A distribution with two modes, where one mode is usually lower and far away from the higher mode, is a strikingly different subjective probability distribution than the normal distribution which is embedded in many risk assessment and portfolio construction systems.

During the pre-event stage, market prices of securities likely to be impacted by the event will move when expected probabilities of the binary outcomes shift. This means that the typical drivers of market prices, and thus observed correlations, may be highly distorted by the very different drivers of the shifts in subjective probabilities related to the event in question. That is, in more typical times, earnings expectations might drive the prices of stocks A and B. Once the acquisition is announced, the earnings matter much less, and the ebb and flow of news and views about the regulatory process that will approve or deny the acquisition take precedent.

As can be appreciated, the apparent increasing frequency of event risk, especially related to political events and policy decisions, is complicating the challenges of portfolio construction and risk assessment. A common practical solution, and one we endorse, is stress-testing with various scenarios reflecting the nature of the event risk about which one is worried. Critically though, the scenarios should be assigned subjective probabilities as suggest by the research of Karagiannidis and Wilford.[10] It is pathetically easy to ask 20 questions or develop some interesting scenarios, but stress-testing has no meaning or useful application if subjective probabilities are not attached to the scenarios. Again, we see that the risk officer has to be forward-looking and probabilistic.

In addition, some market participants may be drawn to adopt options strategies to manage risk related to upcoming events. Options are favored in this regard because they embed a view of volatility in

---

[9] Putnam, B. H., March 2012, "Volatility expectations in an era of dissonance," *Review of Futures Markets*, 20(2).

[10] Karagiannidis, I., and Wilford, D. S., "Modeling fund and portfolio risk: a bimodal approach to analyzing risk in turbulent markets," *Review of Financial Economics*, Volume 25 (April 2015): 19–26.

their price. We are strong supporters of options as a tool to manage event risk. However, we note that some additional sophistication may be required when event risk is present. Options behave differently when confronted with event risk than one might suspect if using an options pricing model derived from the basic Black-Scholes approach. We mention this because it highlights one of our key themes — namely, watch out for embedded assumptions. The Black-Scholes[11] options pricing method and the method by Merton[12], both from 1973, in their original and basic forms make a number of heroic assumptions designed to simplify the mathematics and allow one to use an options-replicating approach to value the option.

When event risk is present, two critical assumptions are likely to be violated and both have profound implications for the price of the option and the implied volatility expectation embedded in the option price. Event risk raises the prospect of both an instantaneous price jump and a major shift in the volatility regime after the event occurs. That is, one can sometimes observe deceptively calm markets as they wait on the event to happen, such as the release of an important piece of economic data, a merger-and-acquisition regulatory decision, a political election, or referendum. Once the outcome is known, though, the price jumps with no intervening trading to its new equilibrium, reflecting the new reality based on the event outcome, and the volatility regime also shifts to reflect the new post-event reality. Basic Black-Scholes assumes no price jumps (i.e., continuous trading) and no volatility shifts (i.e., homoscedasticity). When these two assumptions are violated, traditional delta hedging strategies will fail miserably and basic options models will underestimate volatility. Fortunately, there are many options pricing models available, although quite complex, that deal with these known challenges, such as those developed by Cox, Ross, and Rubenstein[13]. Unfortunately, many risk assessment systems do not use these complex options pricing models and instead embed assumptions of normal distributions, no price jumps, no volatility shifts, and stable

---

[11] Black, F. and Scholes, M., May–June 1973, "The pricing of options and corporate liabilities," *Journal of Political Economy*, 81(3): 637–654.

[12] Merton, R., Spring 1973, "Theory of rational option pricing," *Bell Journal of Economics and Management Science*, 4(1): 141–183.

[13] Cox, J. C., Ross, S. A., and Rubinstein, M., 1979, "Option pricing: a simplified approach," *Journal of Financial Economics*, 7(3): 229–263

correlation structures. No wonder these systems are "surprised" by how many "100-year" floods seem to occur in just one decade, instead of the expectation of one per century.

Figure 11-3: Hypothetical Risk-Return Probabilities Pre-Brexit

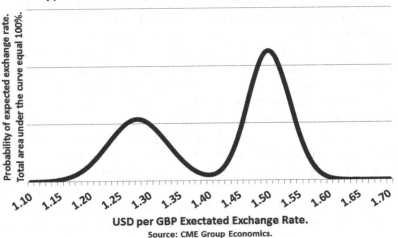

Pre-Brexit Vote: USD per GBP
Hypothetical Expected Probability Distribution

USD per GBP Exectated Exchange Rate.

Source: CME Group Economics.

As an aside, relating to previous discussions, price jumps are especially confusing for volatility measurement systems that only look backwards. The price jump creates a one or two-day period where the standard deviation calculation will be extreme; sometimes four or five standard deviations from previous history, and then it settles into a new, more subdued pattern that may or may not be elevated from previous history. From a behavioral finance perspective, what market participants appear to do is to start to discount the event – meaning that its impact on expectations of future volatility starts to diminish, and sometimes rather quickly unless there is good reason to think lightning will strike twice in the same place. Any historically based volatility measurement system needs to consider whether older data should be more-heavily discounted, or be given equal weight. For example, if one uses a fixed time period for the look-back, say three months, then there will be a spike upward when the event occurs in the volatility measure, followed by an "unexplained" reversal when the three-month period ends and the price-gap day drops out of the backward-looking volatility calculation. Bayesian techniques easily handle time decay parameters, as do exponentially-lagged time decay systems. We highly recommend them.

Back to considering bimodal distributions and their challenges, and again, "Brexit" is a good example of the potential for a bimodal expected return distribution prior to the vote date (Figure 11-3). As noted earlier, a "leave" vote was expected to weaken the British pound and "remain" vote was expected to lead to a relief rally and a strengthening pound. What market participants were trying to do was gauge the probabilities of one outcome versus the other. Since the range of probabilities ran more or less from a coin flip to about 60/40, this was a classic case of a bimodal expected return distribution. Of course, once the vote occurred and the outcome was known, the new expected return distribution collapsed almost instantly back into a typical single-mode probability distribution. [14]

Moreover, the process of collapsing back into a single-mode expected return probability distribution had the ability to disturb correlations for a few days. On the 24th and 27th of June 2016, the Friday and Monday after the UK's vote to leave the European Union, the British pound fell 7% and 2%, respectively, while other risky assets, such as equities, also declined, with even the US S&P500® Index falling 3% and 1%, respectively, while most European equity indexes had sharper falls on the 24th. In the weeks afterwards, though, US equities resumed their climb to new highs, while the British pound did not recover, although it stopped falling and traded in a relatively narrow range. In effect, during the disruption, correlations between the British pound and equity indexes were sharply positive, and then fell back toward zero in the weeks after the referendum. Portfolio construction or risk analysis that failed to consider the possibility of a bimodal expected return distribution collapsing back into a single-mode distribution after the event would have underestimated potential volatility, not necessarily have anticipated a gap or price jump as the outcome was announced, and would have missed some very critical correlation shifts.

---

[14] Putnam, B., McDannel, G., Ayikara, M., Peyyalamitta, L. S., February 2018, "Describing the dynamic nature of transactions costs during political event risk episodes", *High Frequency*, 1(1): 6-20. DOI: https://doi.org/10.1002/hf2.10018.

Future of Financial Optimization

Two evolving techniques for data analysis are likely to greatly improve risk assessment and portfolio construction – namely, exhaustive search using quantum computers and advances in pattern recognition available through structured machine learning. We will start with a discussion of optimization with quantum computers, although this approach is going to take another five years or so before the computers move from the experimentation phase to being large enough for operational use. Machine learning is already here and gaining ground fast on traditional risk assessment techniques.

Quantum computing is on the way. Quantum computers can be purpose built, and there are a number of experiments on-going in academic labs. To move from the lab to the real world, there is a commercially available quantum computer using an annealing process to solve optimization problems offered by D-Wave Systems of Vancouver, Canada. 1QBit, another Vancouver-based company, is creating software that allows one to utilize the new quantum computers without having to be a quantum computing expert to leverage the best known methods for interacting with quantum hardware. Their software development kit (SDK) enables the rapid and systematic development of higher-level applications that are compatible with both classical and quantum processors. In addition, major computing companies, such as Fujitsu, Google, Microsoft, and IBM, are known to be experimenting in various ways with quantum computing, including quantum simulators.

The difference in how quantum computers work compared to classical computing is quite amazing and fascinating. Classical computers have bytes that hold a zero or a one. Quantum computers have qubits that hold a zero or a one as well as a second piece of information that can be intuitively thought of as a probability that the information is a zero or a one. To solve an optimization problem, the quantum computer does not add, subtract, multiply, and divide like a classical computer; instead some types of quantum computer chips use a process known as quantum annealing to seek the lowest energy state based on how the information in the qubits is arranged. That is, the second piece of information in the qubits allows for quantum effects, including tunneling, not possible in classical computers. Tunneling is the concept in quantum physics of a particle moving through a barrier that would not be possible in a classical system. Suffice to say, explaining quantum computing is well past the scope of this research; however, for optimization, the demonstration of quantum effects represents a huge step forward.

Optimization with quantum computers offers the promise of solving certain problems that have traditionally been challenging for classical computers using a process that exhaustively searches problems known as "quadratic unconstrained binary optimizations," or qubos. In a classical computer, a complex optimization problem such as a qubo is solved by way of iteration to achieve a close, but estimated answer. In a quantum computer, exhaustive search finds the exact answer. For many uses, the estimated optimal solution from a classical computer may work fine, if the practitioner is artful in how the problem is set up and how the embedded assumptions are handled. However, the promise of quantum computing is to free the researcher from having to make some difficult and often wrong simplifying assumptions. In finance, these difficult optimization problems appear in areas such as asset clustering, cash flow modeling, taxation, and portfolio risk decomposition. We should caution, though, that appreciating the characteristics of the return distribution and how it changes will remain critical to developing robust, forward-looking risk assessments. Quantum computing is going to offer some incredibly important new tools for risk analysis and portfolio construction; however, it is unlikely to provide good answers without an expert at the helm.

Machine learning is here. Machine-learning techniques are essentially a highly sophisticated and advanced pattern recognition system. (See Chapter 10 for an in-depth analysis of the challenges and opportunities in applying machine learning to financial prediction problems.) They constitute methods that involve cleaning (harmonizing) the data, building the model on known data (also known as "training" phase), optimizing the model, and then applying the model on unseen data (often called "testing" phase). The beauty of these algorithms is that they need not be programmed for all the data out there. They learn as they see new datasets. All the machine learning algorithms are categorized into one of these two categories:

➢ **Supervised learning:** the datasets that belong to supervised learning techniques already have a "label" (outcome/prediction variable) attached to them. Most of the classification and regression problems are categorized as supervised learning techniques.

➢ **Unsupervised learning:** these algorithms aim at the descriptive nature of the data rather than classifying them. Data exhibits certain characteristics and patterns over a period of time (in case of time-series data) and techniques like clustering and association rules help identify them.

One can develop algorithms for machine learning that are unstructured or structured. The unstructured systems are essentially "frequentist" methods, where the data is asked to speak for itself without expert advice. The unstructured methods are likely to be most popular; simply because they are easy to use and open-source software is available. Unstructured machine learning is great for descriptive analytics; however, as one moves into the world of predictive systems, the unstructured methods are likely to appear extremely successful in back-testing and suffer from a myriad of problems in actual practice – not unlike the challenges facing current practices in financial optimization when history is not necessarily a good guide.

Machine learning has been heavily linked with "big data." Initially, much of the research in finance is aimed at discerning new trends and augmenting security returns forecasts with all kinds of new information not previously available – hence, the term "big data." Data is growing at an enormous rate. "Big data" is usually characterized by the three basic V's – volume, variety, and velocity. (There are of course other V's added over time – value, veracity, etc.) The datasets can be from different sources (i.e., variety), can be in motion (real-time data demonstrating velocity), can use different data architecture, and they can still inform a machine learning process. Apache has a lot of open-source projects that have gained popularity in recent years. Apache Spark, an in-memory distributed computing platform, is worth mentioning. Spark can scale financial modeling and optimization which includes calculating Value-at-Risk (VaR) to fit models, run simulations, store, and analyze results in the cloud.[15]

Structured machine learning methods allow for different types of expert information to guide the learning process. The combination of expert advice and sophisticated pattern recognition systems offers tremendous process for forecasting financial variables – from returns to volatilities to correlations and beyond. And, machine learning is not necessarily tied to the straitjacket of time series data, so pattern recognition processes can be much more creative in how the historical data is interpreted.

Pattern recognition with financial data does come with some special challenges, and one of the biggest is that the data is exceptionally noisy. With classical statistical regression techniques, one observes the noisy data by finding only relatively weak fits for the modeling of daily returns. With machine learning, the existence of relatively noisy data will put a greater premium on how one sets the various parameters that filter the pattern or how one adds expert advice to the system. This will be essential for the forward-looking results to add substantial value, and it will not be easy.

The advances from machine learning for quantitative finance are already making themselves felt in sales forecasting and marketing techniques; however, this is just the beginning of a revolution. For financial optimization, structured machine learning promises more robust forecasting tools, for expected returns, and using more diverse measures of volatility for risk assessment, while allowing for very creative assessments of stylized (structured) correlation patterns. The era of parallel and distributed computing is here, which makes it possible for computations to scale and provides the ability to make predictions at a granular level. Hence, financial optimization will look totally differently in just a few years as the new tools permeate the industry and change an age-old mindset about portfolio construction and risk assessment.

---

[15] Ryza, S., "Financial Modeling with Apache Spark: Calculating Value at Risk", *InfoQ*, published July 12 2015, https://www.infoq.com/presentations/spark-financial-modeling.

Chapter 12

Beyond Implied Volatility: Estimating Robust Risk-Return Probability Distributions

Blu Putnam[1]

Editor's Note: The financial crisis of 2008 may be over a decade old and a fading memory; nevertheless, we should not forget the failures of many risk management systems. Risk metrics in too many cases still do allow for the possibility of unusual probability distributions, especially those involving two credible scenarios that may be strikingly different. We now call this event risk, and it is critical that risk systems are capable of allowing for the possibilities much more extreme that the typical bell-shaped curves often driven by implied volatilities from options markets. We can do much better. — KT

We have observed in studying financial markets that 100-year floods occur quite often, maybe several every decade, so we know simple risk models can be inadequate and misleading. Many financial risk models start with a risk reading taken from the options markets — implied volatility. Implied volatility is a standard deviation based metric and, while not required, users typically embed the presumption of a bell-shaped curve. Starting with implied volatility, the risk manager or financial analyst then must work to augment the tails of the probability

---

[1] **Disclaimer:** All examples are hypothetical interpretations of situations and are used for explanation purposes only. The views expressed here reflect solely those of the authors and not necessarily those of their employer, CME Group or its affiliated institutions. The information herein should not be considered investment advice or the results of actual market experience.

distribution to increase the odds of extreme events actually happening to align more closely with historical experience. After all, it is the extreme events that can do the most financial damage, so it is critical that the expected probability distribution be augmented beyond a simple standard deviation analysis to properly account for the possibilities.

Our approach and perspective is quite different. We believe that starting points matter. Starting one's risk analysis with implied volatility introduces some hidden biases that may be surprisingly hard to overcome.

Volatility is Not Risk

To begin with, volatility is a poor measure of risk. Many analysts like volatility because the historical standard deviation is easy to calculate and fits nicely into basic risk systems and mean-variance portfolio models. The problem is that an investor, or a financial institution for that matter, may have asymmetrical risk preferences, preferring to avoid substantive losses rather than to make large gains. That is, if avoiding large losses is the primary risk, then a symmetrical standard deviation based metric that only looks at the average noise level and not the extremes is certainly not appropriate.

Another challenge is that implied volatilities are typically calculated from straightforward options pricing models that embed the heroic assumption that prices move up or down with continuous trading — that is, price breaks or price gaps are assumed never to occur. If market participants fear the possibility of price breaks or gaps, options prices will reflect this risk with a higher calculated implied volatility. But it will not be easily apparent that the implied volatility is reflecting price gap risk instead of an upward shift in the volatility regime. And, price gap risk is not the same risk as volatility regime shift risk. Depending on one's financial exposures, one of these risks could be much more important than the other. For those managing options portfolios, for example, the risk of an abrupt price break can do considerable damage to delta hedging strategies, while a volatility regime shift represents a different risk, commonly known as "vega" risk. **What one needs to create is a comprehensive view of the whole risk probability** distribution providing a robust perception of risks, allowing for decidedly different risk scenarios, and not being biased toward bell-shaped curves.

Starting Points Matter

To build a risk probability distribution that is not necessarily bell-shaped or even of a single mode and can capture the extremes in a robust manner, we prefer to start from a very different point of view. We start with the Bayesian prior of a very unusual distribution — in our case, a bi-modal distribution that might reflect a type of binary or two-scenario risk often associated with event risk. Then, we examine market data to see if the risks are actually more bell-shaped. While the implied volatility is one of the market metrics we examine, it does not necessarily have the primary influence it does when it is the starting point for the risk analysis.

Figure 12-1: Pavnuty Chebyshev (from Wikipedia)

Put another way, if we start from a prior of an extreme and unusual distribution, we know that it can exist and we have not assumed it away. Starting from a standard deviation approach, such as implied volatility, may inadvertently make it very hard to estimate when extreme and highly dangerous risk distributions are present. The math behind this observation is quite old and goes back to the Russian mathematician, Pafnuty Lvovich Chebyshev (1821–1894). What most people take away from Chebyshev's Inequality Theorem is that if you know only the standard deviation you have a very good idea of the typical ranges in which values will fall the vast majority of the time. **What we take away from the Inequality Theorem is that if you only know the standard deviation, you know absolutely nothing about the extremes of the distribution where the most dangerous risks reside.**

Event Risk

The motivation for our research was the observation that in financial markets, especially since 2016, we have been seeing important episodes of event risk associated with elections — UK Brexit Referendum of June 2016, US President election of November 2016, French and UK elections in 2017, Brazilian elections of October 2018, US Congressional elections of November 2018, etc.

Figure 12-2: UK Brexit Referendum

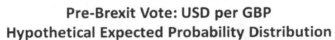

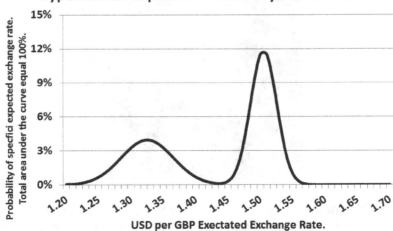

USD per GBP Exectated Exchange Rate.
Source: CME Group Economics.

This various event risk episodes led us to a study of how markets cope with two strikingly different scenarios. When there are two possible scenarios, then pre-event, the market is going to price the probability-weighted outcome, or the middle ground. So, post-event, when the outcome becomes known, the market immediately moves away from the middle ground to the "winning" scenario — a price break. For example, with Brexit, the "Leave" vote generated a sharp downward move in the British pound (vs USD), while a "Remain" vote would have presumably generated a sharp almost instantaneous rally in the pound — either way, the pound was no longer going to trade in the middle. **Even if they are extremely rare, if one's risk system cannot create the possibility of a bi-modal probability distribution, then price break risk and tail risk may be greatly underestimated.**

Expected Probability Distributions are Unobservable

From a practical perspective, starting with the prior of an abnormal, bi-modal risk probability distribution requires some creativity that might put off some risk managers. The challenge is that expected risk-return probability distributions cannot be directly observed. What we are able to do is to estimate some of their characteristics from looking at market behavior — prices, volumes, futures versus options, intra-day activity, etc.

While our research is still at early stages, we have found a few metrics that are especially enlightening relative to the shape of the probability distribution. Our three primary metrics are: 1) the evolving pattern of put option trading volume relative to call option volume, 2) intra-day market activity, especially high/low spreads, and 3) implied volatility from options prices relative to historical volatility.

Studying put/call volume patterns helps us understand if one side of the market is more at the center of the current debate than the other side. For example, immediately after former Federal Reserve (Fed) Chair Ben Bernanke threw his famous "Taper Tantrum" in May 2013, he set off a debate about if and when the Fed would withdraw quantitative easing (QE) and raise interest rates. Put volume on Treasury note and bond prices soared relative to call volume as an indicator that a two-scenario situation had developed. While there is a buyer and a seller for every trade; one side thought prices would fall (yields rise) and volatility might rise very soon (buyer of puts), while the other side thought the process of exiting QE would take a long time (seller of puts).

Intra-day market dynamics help us appreciate risk in a different way. The observed high price to low price intra-day trading spread is informative in helping us assess the degree to which fat-tails might be present. Mathematically, work by Mark B. Garmin and others back in the 1970s and 1980s has shown that if one assumes a normal distribution then there is a straightforward way to estimate the standard deviation of daily returns from the intra-day high-to-low spread. Put another way, if the relationship between intra-day dynamics and the day-to-day standard deviation diverge in a significant manner, then this is strong evidence that the risk probability distribution is not normally distributed.

To ascertain the risk of price breaks we track the evolving pattern of implied volatility relative to historical volatility. While it is usual for implied volatility to exceed recent historical standard deviations, a shift in the pattern toward a much higher implied volatility may indicate that expectations for the potential of a sharp price break are building in the market. And, if a price break occurs, scenarios resolve one way or the other, so we often see a quick decline in the implied volatility representing a shift back to a single-mode bell-shaped distribution.

To gather all our risk information and create a probability distribution, we use a probability mixture technique that is distribution independent — that is, it is not constrained to take on a given specified shape. Most of the time, bell-shaped curves are appropriate descriptions of the probability distributions — balanced risk distributions. Our method does, however, occasionally generate some especially tall distributions (i.e., high kurtosis and/or relatively lower volatility), which we classify as "complacent" and worthy of special study to see if the market may be underestimating risks. We also see on occasion some very flat distributions, not unlike the Wall Street maxim about the equity markets "climbing a wall of worry" which we call "anxious" risk distributions. And, finally, on rare occasions our metrics actually support the idea of a two-scenario, event risk, bi-modal distribution. That is, we classify expected risk distributions into four types: "Complacent" which are very tall and thin, "Balanced" risks with a typical bell-shape, "Anxious" reflecting a relatively flat bell-shape with very fat tails, and finally our bimodal or event risk distribution which are trying to anticipate what happens if one of two very divergent scenarios is the outcome.

When it comes to the most extreme distributions, the most likely source of event risk and bi-modal distributions are highly polarized elections, when the candidates are far apart, and the vote is closely contested. We classify these event risks as "known date, unknown outcome". We also see event risk around "unknown date, unknown outcome", which has shown up when the US-induced trade war evolves into a tit-for-tat tariff retaliation episode. This type of event risk, for example, hit soybeans, quite hard during 2018. Policy decisions taken at scheduled meetings, like a Fed interest rate decision or an OPEC oil production decision fall into the "known date, unknown outcome" category, but they almost always are associated with bell-shaped probability distributions, because the policy makers go out of their way to telegraph the decision ahead of time, reflected in the fact that our metrics pick up no unusual risks.

Case Studies

To illustrate our probability risk distributions, we will start be examining two examples from US equities, one involving a complacent distribution and one involving potential event risk. And, we will also examine an event risk distribution from the commodity markets, specifically in corn.

In late 2017, our probability risk distribution for US S&P500® (CME E-Mini Futures) shifted from "balanced" to "complacent". US stocks were being propelled higher in no small measure by the large and permanent US corporate tax cut which was increasingly likely to become law and, indeed, was passed by Congress and signed into law by the President in December 2017. Due to the corporate tax cut, market participants were expecting more stock buybacks and higher dividends, among other things. As it turned out, the complacency was somewhat misplaced. Early in 2018, the US-initiated trade wars, with China, the European Union, Canada, and Mexico, resulted in a sharp market selloff, temporarily higher volatility, and then a market that started to gain ground again with diminishing volatility.

In late October 2016, our probability risk distribution for US S&P500® shifted into the event risk state showing a bi-modal probability distribution. The cause was the upcoming US election, which was becoming increasingly polarizing and involved two candidates with strikingly different views on many issues, including a few of major interest to equity market participants, such as whether taxes would be cut or raises, or whether free trade deals would be scuttled or embraced. Once the election outcome was known, within a week the probability risk distribution shifted quickly to an anxious state and then a balanced risk state.

Figure 12-3: S&P500® Futures

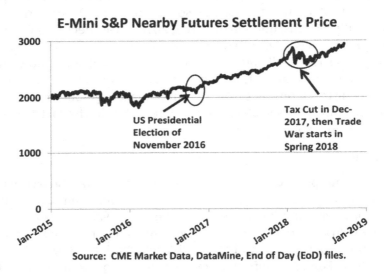

Source: CME Market Data, DataMine, End of Day (EoD) files.

These two polar opposite probability risk distributions of the US equities illustrate the method's ability to identity event risk (polarizing US Presidential and Congressional elections in November 2016) as well as to highlight a market state with a noticeable absence of fear, namely the "complacent" distribution, which occurred as the US corporate tax cut was being passed into law. Neither of these more extreme probability distributions lasted very long. Complacency in December 2017 and January 2018 gave way to fears related to the trade wars. And with the event risk from the US elections, the outcome resolved the debate about which scenario would be the winner, and the bi-modal distribution quickly resolved into a single-model distribution.

Figure 12-4: Drought Monitor for August 2012

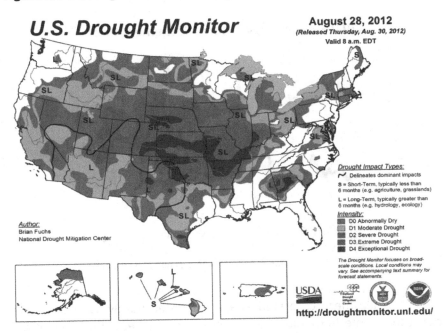

U.S. Drought Monitor

August 28, 2012
(Released Thursday, Aug. 30, 2012)
Valid 8 a.m. EDT

Drought Impact Types:
~ Delineates dominant impacts

S = Short-Term, typically less than
6 months (e.g. agriculture, grasslands)

L = Long-Term, typically greater than
6 months (e.g. hydrology, ecology)

Intensity:
D0 Abnormally Dry
D1 Moderate Drought
D2 Severe Drought
D3 Extreme Drought
D4 Exceptional Drought

The Drought Monitor focuses on broad-
scale conditions. Local conditions may
vary. See accompanying text summary for
forecast statements.

Author:
Brian Fuchs
National Drought Mitigation Center

USDA

http://droughtmonitor.unl.edu/

There was a very interesting evolution of our probability risk distributions in the corn market in late 2012 and into the first half of 2013. The summer of 2012 had seen large swaths of the US corn-belt experience severe drought. Late in 2012, after the harvest, market participants' thoughts turned to the 2013 crop, about which there was much disagreement. How much acreage would be planted after the drought year? Would 2013 see another drought or its disappearance? While not of the political version of event risk, corn market participants were worried about the drought and a two scenario market developed for a while in February 2013 as one side of the market took the view that the 2013 crop would be much better than 2012's drought constrained crop and other market participants worried about another poor crop. Our probability risk distribution was already in an "anxious" state late in 2012, shifted to "event risk" in February 2013, went back to "anxious" for most of the spring of 2013, before returning to the most common state, "balanced risks" in the summer of 2013.

Figure 12-5: Corn Futures Prices

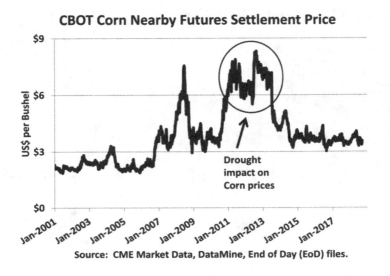

Source: CME Market Data, DataMine, End of Day (EoD) files.

While these case studies are presented purely as illustrations, our research methods allow for the most rare market state — event risk with a bi-modal probability distribution — to occur in all of the product classes we have studied so far, which includes US Treasury notes futures, equity index futures, Euro (versus USD), gold, oil, and corn. And, we believe it is important to monitor our risk states, especially when they shift from one category to the next. We do not expect the most common state — "balanced risks" occurring as much as two-thirds to three-quarters of the time, depending on the product, to provide any critical information that one would not acquire looking only at implied volatilities from options markets. We do think, however, that when the probability risk distribution shifts into a less typical state — "complacent", "anxious", or "event risk" — that risk managers should go on high alert.

We also warn that while our naming conventions describe the risk distributions, they may not describe what actually happens. "Complacent" states may well be followed by volatility when some new and unexpected risk factor takes priority. "Anxious" states may or may not overstate fears, as equity analysts talk about when the say "a market is climbing a wall of worry". "Event risk" states do not last long, as they tend to be resolved back to a one scenario, single mode distribution when the event occurs and the outcome becomes known or when market participants become more confident that a one scenario outlook with appropriate skepticism is more appropriate than a two scenario approach.

Chapter 13

Death by Simulation

Blu Putnam[1]

Editor's Note: The original version of this research was first published as an article in Global Investor magazine in March 1991, then updated and included as an essay in the book Integrating Risk Management into Asset Allocation *by Blu Putnam, published by Global Investor, London, 2000. While the examples are dated, the critical take-aways have lost none of their relevance. Essentially, when developing quantitative algorithms for investment management, the developers may be tempted to put forward simulations which look great in the past and may not perform well in the future. This research explains what not to do to avoid big financial losses in the future from methods that tested well with historical data. – KT*

Many fund managers offer investment programs or portfolio management services based on quantitative models. Model-driven investment strategies offer the promise of a disciplined approach that may enhance returns with only a minimal increase in risk, if any. Quantitative investment strategies typically are supported by an impressive amount of background research that can give the investor added confidence. But the reliable evidence of actual track records to evaluate these quantitative strategies is not always available, especially due to the severe survivorship bias present in investment performance

---

[1] **Disclaimer:** All examples are hypothetical interpretations of situations and are used for explanation purposes only. The views expressed here reflect solely those of the authors and not necessarily those of their employer, CME Group or its affiliated institutions. The information herein should not be considered investment advice or the results of actual market experience.

databases. Consequently, simulations of past performance take on special significance.

Simulations showing performance over five years or longer with absurdly high annual returns, only a handful of losing months, and no losing years occasionally are seen in the marketing pitches of fund managers who want to sell newly developed quantitative strategies. However, the anecdotal evidence of managers that have used quantitative strategies suggests that the promise of very high annual returns (with low volatility) is seldom delivered. Despite some impressive success stories, all too often returns are often below average or worse, and without the reduction in the volatility suggested in the simulations.[2] This means there are numerous losing months and an occasional losing year, if the new model attracts enough assets and is allowed to run that long.

The divergence of simulation performance and actual performance for many quantitative strategies should not be interpreted to mean that simulations do not contain useful information about potential future performance. One should pay attention to the risk/return characteristics displayed by simulated investment strategies. However, there are some important rules of analysis to remember if one wants to avoid quantitative strategies that look good on paper but perform poorly in action.

There are many ways in which a quantitative fund manager can boost simulation results without improving the eventual live performance of the model. Some simulations are enhanced by the genuine belief that improvements made to the strategy will carry through into improved live performance. Other improvements in simulations can be the result of beautification programs that are aimed at improving sales prospects and may inadvertently hurt actual performance.

In-Sample Versus Out-of-Sample Results

Quantitative fund managers have learned the hard way that they cannot adopt the standard statistical procedures used by academic

---

[2] Heaton, J.B. "Quantitative Investing and the Limits of (Deep) Learning from Financial Data", *Journal of Financial Transformation*, The Capco Institute, April 2018, Volume 47.

economists. Many academic economists test their theories over specified periods of time using in-sample statistical techniques. With in-sample statistical hypothesis testing, the typical regression analysis is conducted over the entire period so that accurate information about the end of the period is known along with information about the beginning of the period. This can lead to statistically high confidence.

Real-world investment does not work this way, however. Investment strategies are developed in an uncertain environment about what the future may bring. Out-of-sample techniques, such as one-step-ahead forecasts, offer an approach to replicate real-world decision-making. In the one-step-ahead approach, for example, the model is estimated using data from some past period, such as five years of daily or weekly data. Then, the model forecasts the next day or week beyond the sample period. This procedure is repeated for many times for all the available data. In this process, the quantitative model is provided with new data for the previous period and asked to forecast another period ahead.

One-step-ahead forecasts are much less precise, as gauged by standard statistical tests, than those from an in-sample exercise. This means that the simulations will not look as good, but they will conform more closely to real world conditions. Out-of-sample statistical techniques are an attempt to ensure against basing the model on future information that could not have been known at the time the forecasts were being made. The general rule is: out-of-sample research techniques are much more likely to provide reliable live investment performance than in-sample techniques. This is now well known and few quantitative fund managers now try to sell their investment products with in-sample simulations.

Avoiding Spurious Correlation

Both in-sample and out-of-sample statistical research procedures can be prone to bouts of spurious correlation. That is, an explanatory variable seems to perform well over the period investigated, thereby generating forecasts that appear to make money. Then, at some point, after the strategy has gone from the testing stage to live trials, the key explanatory variable loses its predictive power and the quantitative portfolio management strategy blows up, sometimes in spectacular fashion.

This can happen to fundamental or chart-driven variables as well as to more sophisticated or complex models. And there is no certain way of ridding quantitative models of explanatory variables with research period correlations that are spurious and do not hold up to live investment. However, there are a lot of good questions that should be asked by both the researcher and the prospective investor and that may allow managers to avoid the major disasters that spurious correlation may engender.

The Arizona effect is a good illustration of spurious correlation. Many people from all across the US have moved to Arizona to help cope with a variety of breathing problems. They are attracted by a lack of certain plant pollens in the Arizona air due to the dry climate. Consequently, on a statistical basis, living in Arizona would be highly positively correlated with an increased incidence of people with breathing difficulties. That is, the hypothesis that geography is a good predictor of one's coming down with a debilitating breathing disorder could be postulated and then supported by this statistical evidence.

Of course, Arizona is the solution, not the problem or the cause of breathing disorders. But statistical tests cannot discern causality, although some pretend to try. The most common source of spurious correlation is the failure to question why a variable should have a causal and explanatory relationship with a particular financial market. This failure occurs most often when the computer is allowed substantial discretion in mining the data and hence in choosing the explanatory variables. The computer will follow instructions and choose the variables that maximize a given set of statistical criteria, most often the best fit of the data.

The researcher then needs to look at the computer's choices of explanatory variables and see if they can be explained in terms of a reasonable financial market theory. Many quantitative researchers have neither the background, nor see the need, for completing this task. Yet, if the researcher cannot understand why a particular explanatory variable should be included in the model, then the researcher will not know when to take it out of the model - until it is too late.

Also, quantitative managers like to put only their best foot forward to prospective investors. Of the thousands of simulations that the model builder has run, published marketing materials contain only a few, and naturally these are the best. There is a real danger in using your very best simulations for live portfolio management or for marketing. As Professor Markowitz observed, the problem is that the "best" simulation, based on purely statistical criteria, is also the one that probably contains the most luck.[3]   One needs to evaluate simulation results holistically as well as statistically, using expert practical knowledge to determine which simulation should go into live production.

If the computer chooses an explanatory variable just because that variable has fortuitously and without apparent reason performed well over a particular sample period, then the future investment results are likely doomed. And if the researcher has run a thousand simulations, then it is not too difficult to find such lucky variables and simulations. The key is to reject models that are too good and that cannot be understood by market professionals. The general rule is: do not invest in lucky guesses. Understand why explanatory variables are included in the model.

A situation very similar to spurious correlation is when a structural change in the underlying financial and economic relationships has occurred after the estimation period has ended. In this case, it is all the more important for the researcher to understand the reasons why a particular variable exhibits explanatory power, so that when those reasons change or are reversed, the researcher can alter the model or close it down before it can severely damage a live portfolio. Structural shifts are so important and so poorly understood by most quantitative researchers that an example is needed to underscore the severity of the problem.

Suppose the time is the beginning of the 1980s and forecasting inflation is viewed as critical for predicting the future course of bond yields.   A monetarist economist is asked to develop a model for forecasting inflation that would then be used to predict bond market price developments.   First, the monetarist postulates a particular relationship between the growth of the money supply and future

---

[3] For layman's explanation, please see: Markowitz, Harry; Putnam, Bluford; Xu, Gan Lin. "Deflating Research Expectations" published in *Integrating Risk Management into Asset Allocation*, Global Investor, 2000, pp. 165-173, (which was reprinted from Global Investor magazine, September 1996).   For a mathematical treatment of the simulation challenge gauging how much luck is involved, please see Markowitz, Harry, and Xu, Gan Lin, *Journal of Portfolio Management*, Fall 1994, pp. 60-69.

inflation, selects a test period (in this case the 1970s), and performs a statistical regression analysis.

If the relationship appears statistically significant, based on a standard set of tests, then the typical academic economist will assert that money growth is a relatively good predictor of inflation, with the unstated implication being that this relationship is likely to hold in future periods.

Figure 13-1: Monetarism Worked in the 1970s

Source: St. Louis Federal Reserve Bank FRED Database
(PCEPILFE, M1SL)

Indeed, in the 1970s U.S. M1 (currency plus checkable deposits) money supply growth served as a good predictor of inflation two years into the future. So, if one believed that this relationship held in the 1970s, then one might assume that it would also hold in the 1980s. Unfortunately, the relationship broke down in the 1980s. Monetarist models spent the first half of the 1980s overestimating future inflation and betting that bond prices would fall rather than rise. The problem was that the world changed. The first half of the 1980s was a period of dramatic financial deregulation, and consequently, the traditional relationship between money supply growth and inflation in the U.S. was altered permanently.

Figure 13-2: Monetarism Failed in the 1980s and onward

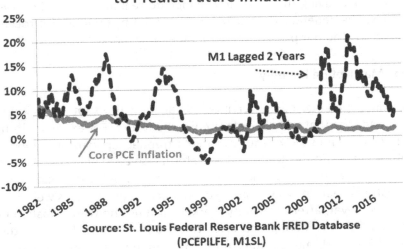

Monetarism Did Not Work after 1982 to Predict Future Inflation

Source: St. Louis Federal Reserve Bank FRED Database
(PCEPILFE, M1SL)

Many economists understood that financial deregulation was going to change how people viewed monetary aggregates, M1 and M2 (M1 plus savings accounts, small time deposits, and money market mutual funds). Some bank checking accounts now paid interest. Most forms of savings now paid market rates of interest, not the lower, regulated rate as before. Consumers began to hold more money in their savings (M2) and checking (M1) accounts. These extra funds were often intended as savings and represented money that consumers did not plan to spend, at least immediately.

The tight relationship between money supply growth and spending, and ultimately inflation, which had held in the 1970s, broke down in the 1980s. Anticipation of this breakdown went a long way to understanding the dramatic rise in bond prices during the '80s. (See Chapter 1 for an in-depth discussion of the money supply and inflation forecasting.)

A quantitative manager who understands why certain explanatory variables are included in his models and why they work has a big advantage over one who relies solely on some computer package to pick the explanatory variables. A quantitative manager with market knowledge will sometimes know when structural change, such as a policy shift or change in banking laws, will cause an explanatory variable to lose its predictive power. These market-wise managers can then take steps to avoid having the structural change do real damage to their live portfolios. The general rule is: avoid models built by quantitative rocket scientists who do not pay attention to underlying market structures.

Trends May Not Be Friendly

In trending markets, computer models can pick up a lot of spurious correspondence that will not help predict the future. For example, from mid-1982 until mid-1987, equity markets trended upward, and lots of variables mimicked this trend and therefore, displayed high correlations with equity market prices. Price-earnings ratios, even those constructed from historical earnings data, seemed to forecast equity prices well.

However, after the equity markets around the world crashed in October 1987, and during and after the economic slow-downs in the 1990-1992 period, many equity forecasting models performed poorly, especially those depending on trailing price-earnings ratios. The problem this reflected was that around turning points, markets are especially sensitive to forecasts of future earnings and may pay little attention to historical earnings.

Similarly, the spectacular collapse of IBM's share price occurred at the same time as the spectacular rise in the share price of Intel. On a trailing earnings basis, quantitative models would have been late getting out of IBM and late getting into Intel. The models that survived this change in fortunes had a more sophisticated structure based on forward-looking and structural adjustment variables, such as a measure of the growth of personal computers (Intel) relative to the market for mainframe computers (IBM).

Unfortunately, more forward-looking types of variables are often difficult to quantify or appear to predict less well during simulation periods dominated by trends. Their strength is at the turning points. Many researchers leave these variables out of their models because they can hurt simulation performance in a trending market even though they can save investors a small fortune when the trend changes.

The researcher and the investor must recognize explicitly how the choice of the time period in present simulations and in developing models can affect the choice of variables. Time periods dominated by major trends in the market are notorious for producing quantitative strategies that appear to be extremely successful. In reality, they are little more than trend-following systems that will fail to work when the trend reverses or when markets become trendless, yet remain volatile. Investors must insist that quantitative models be simulated over a sufficiently long period of time for trends to have developed and to be reversed.

Sometimes five years will be enough, but often, especially in the case of currencies, trends can easily last for many years and then reverse spectacularly. Thus, currency models require longer testing periods. The general rule is: the more cycles included in the testing period, the better. This is regardless of the length of time required for the cycles to complete their run.

Watch out for simultaneously determined variables. Correlations that can be supported by economic theory often occur between two financial market variables, and give the appearance that one "causes" the other. Such is the case in the relationship between long-term interest rates and exchange rates. Each of these variables is affected by inflation. When U.S. inflation was rising in the late 1970s, the dollar was weak and bond yields were rising. In the 1980s, however, this negative correlation between the dollar and bond yields weakened significantly and was often reversed.

When the Federal Reserve pushed short-term interest up to record highs to fight inflation in the beginning of the 1980s, the dollar reversed course and soared until it hit a peak in February 1985. Bond yields continued to rise and dip in a different pattern until they hit a peak in 1984 at 14%. Indeed, the bond yield and exchange rate correlation that had held in the 1977-1979 period weakened in 1980-84, and then reversed in 1985-88 because monetary policy, not the inflation trend, dominated both variables, but in very different ways.

Tight monetary policy supported the dollar, but caused bond-financing costs to rise. Not until the markets were convinced in the mid-1980s that inflation was beaten did bond yields begin to decline steadily. By then, however, the dollar was falling. Clearly, models based on the 1970s correlation between bond yields and the dollar took a beating in the 1980s.

The problem is that bond yields and the dollar are both affected by a similar set of variables, but not always in the same way. Inflation raises bond yields and hurts the dollar. An inflation-fighting central bank helps the home currency, but may still push bond yields higher in the first years of the tight policy. When policy is passive, inflation rules and one correlation works well. When policy is active, another correlation dominates. The rule is: be very careful with models that use explanatory variables that are themselves determined by more fundamental causes. The possibility of a sign reversal is very high during periods in which monetary or fiscal policy change direction.

To be sure, quantitative strategies are going to be an increasingly more important investment tool, as global market linkages become stronger and information technology opens up new frontiers. Model-driven investment strategies offer disciplined approaches that appear to offer favorable risk- return characteristics.

Unfortunately, the promise on paper has often turned into real-life disaster, because neither the fund manager nor the investor really understood the information being conveyed by the impressive simulations of investment performance. The ultimate rule is: to avoid death by simulation, investors must understand the flaws inherent in the simulation of investment returns.

Do not avoid quantitative strategies just because they do not have actual track records, but do investigate simulation results thoroughly. Make sure that the model builders understand both quantitative techniques and financial markets, and have integrated information from both sources into their approach to investing.

Chapter 14

Quantitative Easing:
Evaluating QE's Impact

Blu Putnam[1]

Editor's Note: This chapter was originally published in the **Review of Financial Economics, Volume 22, 2013**. *Many Ph.D. dissertations will no doubt be written on the topic of evaluating the non-traditional asset purchases, aka quantitative easing or QE, introduced by the Federal Reserve in the aftermath of the financial panic of September 2008. The essay discusses many of the key factors that will need to be considered and will greatly complicate the analysis of whether QE achieved its objectives or not.*
– KT

After the 2008 financial panic, central banks in the US, UK, Europe and Japan experimented with the aggressive use of their balance sheets to stabilize their financial markets and encourage a return to higher rates of economic activity. These activities have become known as quantitative easing or QE. This research focuses mostly on balance sheet activities employed by the US Federal Reserve (Fed), and distinguishes between the initial round of quantitative easing (QE1) in late 2008 with later rounds of balance sheet activity to purchase more US Treasury securities or mortgage-backed securities (QE2 & QE3) and to adopt the maturity extension program (i.e., Operation Twist). With respect to certain ideas presented here, in a few cases we also consider European Central Bank (ECB) activities that were relevant to the

---

[1] **Disclaimer:** All examples are hypothetical interpretations of situations and are used for explanation purposes only. The views expressed here reflect solely those of the authors and not necessarily those of their employer, CME Group or its affiliated institutions. The information herein should not be considered investment advice or the results of actual market experience.

discussion. [See Chapter 15 for an in-depth comparison of the effectiveness of the Fed's QE programs versus the approach utilized by the ECB.]

Our first priority is to present a generalized set of theoretical ideas to guide our assessment of quantitative easing and to identify the conditions under which it is likely to achieve the desired economic and financial market results. We recognize that some of these ideas may be controversial. There is considerable value, however, in explicitly recognizing the embedded assumptions in models designed to assess the impacts of quantitative easing. By making key assumptions explicit, we better understand why different quantitative models see QE and central bank balance sheet expansion in such varying lights, and we can better interpret their likely robustness as a tool to guide either policy decisions or market participant actions. Finally, as we link our theoretical ideas with the actual quantitative easing that occurred, we want to draw some tentative conclusions about when it is most appropriate to use QE and, in addition, to evaluate whether future QE policies are likely to achieve their objectives. To enhance the flow of the arguments made here and increase the value of this research as a road map for the evaluation of quantitative easing, relevant research from the academic literature is cited at the appropriate point in the discussion rather than in a separate review of the literature section.

To highlight and anticipate our conclusions, this research suggests the following:

➢ QE is a very effective tool for central banks to use when combating a failing banking system facing systematic solvency and liquidity challenges.

➢ Central bank purchases of high-risk or stressed securities held by a weakened or failing banking system may be more effective in encouraging a rapid return to economic growth than other forms of QE such as outright loans to the banking system.

➢ QE in the form of purchases of government securities with long-term maturities can have a meaningful effect in terms of lowering long-term interest rates.

➤ QE may have little positive impact on economic activity and job creation once the banking system has been recapitalized and returned to profitability.

➤ QE applied to an economy that has returned to positive growth, even with elevated unemployment, has the distinct potential to be counterproductive in terms of achieving the objectives of the central bank due to the fact that the use of QE in non-emergency situations sends a powerful signal from the central bank in terms of economic pessimism to market participants.

➤ Exit strategies from QE by central banks may be extremely challenging to implement and have the potential, if not the certainty, to delay a return to the normal conduct of monetary policy to the detriment of longer-term economic growth, currency values, and potential future inflation.

Quantitative Easing and the Case of a Failing Banking System

Virtually all equilibrium models of economic activity and market behavior start from the presumption that money is fungible and that the domestic money and credit markets, generally characterized as the banking system, are functioning normally, whether these models explicitly recognize the embedded assumption or not. What we mean by functioning normally is that banks are willing to pay and receive payments from each other and to make and take short-term loans from each other on essentially a no-name basis. This requirement is essential for payment systems to work properly and grease the wheels of commerce.

The financial panic of September 2008 was triggered by the bankruptcy of Lehman Brothers and the next day's relatively messy bailout of AIG. Bankers were so scared that they were afraid to take each other's credit risk, even overnight. The interbank market nearly froze, and spreads for interbank loans rose dramatically relative to similar maturity Treasury bills. That is, the sharp widening of the TED spread (i.e., LIBOR minus Treasury bill rates) was a reflection of a failing banking system. The spread between three-month US dollar denominated deposits (LIBOR) and three-month US Treasury bill rates averaged under 30 basis points over the period from 2002 to 2006, before the subprime crisis began and before the financial panic of 2008. In September 2008, with the failure of Lehman Brothers, the TED spread widened sharply and briefly to over 400 basis points as financial panic began (see Figure 14-1).

Figure 14-1: TED Spread

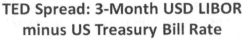

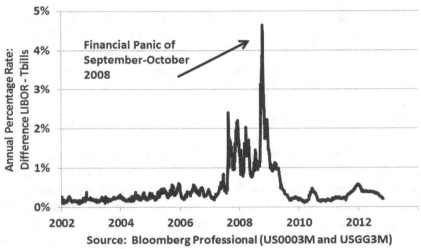

Source: Bloomberg Professional (US0003M and USGG3M)

As thoroughly examined by Reinhart and Rogoff (2009)[2], recessions triggered by a financial crisis are fundamentally different from cyclical recessions that do not involve a breakdown of the banking system. Recessions related to banking system breakdowns are characterized by a sharp drop in asset values which puts bank solvency into question and leads to extensive deleveraging by consumers, corporations, and local governments. Consumers seek to reduce their liabilities to better match the lower value of their assets. Corporations seek to rapidly shed costs, including workers, to better match future

---

[2] Reinhart, Carmen M., & Rogoff, Kenneth, 2009, *This Time is Different: Eight Centuries of Financial Folly*, New Jersey: Princeton University Press.

production with the likely lower demand. Local governments face a sharp drop in tax and fee revenue, and thus seek to cut costs by reducing services, laying off workers, and avoiding new projects that would require additional debt issuance.

In a financial crisis, the banking system faced liquidity and/or solvency challenges because it was widely perceived as being vastly over-extended. In the face of a failing banking system, central banks can use their balance sheets to make loans to banks to ease their liquidity issues or to purchase securities from banks which potentially allows for a smoother reduction in banking assets.

We note historically that the Federal Reserve System was established in 1913, following a series of financial panics of which the one in 1907 was especially severe. The Fed was specifically given extensive powers to use its balance sheet and serve as a lender of last resort to prevent financial panics turning into severe recessions or depressions. Virtually all central banks that control their own currencies have similar powers, even if they have been given different long-term economic objectives regarding inflation, currency stability, or economic growth and job creation. As an aside, the national central banks inside the Eurozone no longer control their own currencies and can lend to their domestic banking system only in so far as the ECB lends to them — which the ECB did in considerable size in the 2009–2012 period.

In terms of economic modeling, there are several points to consider here. Reinhart and Rogoff's (2009)[3] arguments can be interpreted in terms of a regime shift which depends on whether the banking system is functioning normally or breaking down. Economies with failing banking systems are likely to undergo severe deleveraging by all sectors during and immediately after the crisis period. During the period of deleveraging, interest rates largely do not matter to the decision process of consumers, corporations, and local governments (i.e., governments without access to a printing press). That is, the need for consumers to reduce liabilities, for corporations to reduce costs and shed workers, and for local government to cut services dominates any potential stimulatory effect implied by equilibrium macro-economic models from near-zero short-term interest rates. Decisions by consumers to spend, by corporations to invest in new plant and

---

[3] Ibid.

equipment or to hire new workers, by local governments to expand services, are no longer interest rate sensitive. The path back to a regime involving market equilibrium depends critically both on the banking system recovery and recapitalization as well as the time it takes for consumers, corporations, and local governments to deleverage.

Figure 14-2: Factors Supplying Reserves to the US Banking System

Federal Reserve Factors affecting Reserve Balances (US$Millions)				
	Averages of Daily Figures for Week Ended ($Millions)			
	17-Sep-2008	31-Dec-2008	29-Dec-2010	31-Oct-2012
US Treasury Securities	$479,818	$475,961	$1,010,285	$1,650,297
Mortgage-backed & agency securities	$0	$20,266	$1,148,892	$933,915
Repurchase agreements, term auction credit, and other loans	$322,469	$717,989	$45,112	$1,317
Special facilities	$29,333	$407,433	$92,945	$2,500
All other sources of credit	$151,721	$676,976	$170,310	$283,572
Total factors supplying reserve funds	$983,341	$2,298,625	$2,467,544	$2,871,601

Source: Federal Reserve Statistical Release H.4.1 - Table 1 - Factors affecting reserve balances of depository Institutions.

During QE1, most of the immediate balance sheet expansion by the Fed was concentrated in a very short period of time after September 17, 2008, with over US$1.3 trillion of troubled security purchases, loans, and other credit facilities implemented mostly in a matter of weeks and all before the end of 2008. In effect, during the emergency period when the financial panic first started, the Fed was plugging holes in the financial system wherever they found them, from AIG to money market funds, from the commercial paper market to troubled assets on bank balance sheets. Please note that QE1 did not involve the purchase of US Treasury securities. Subsequent programs were conducted in relative calm and focused solely on US Treasuries, as in QE2 and the maturity extension program, as well as more mortgaged-backed securities in QE3, while at the same time the emergency purchases during QE1 of troubled assets and special facility investments were cleaned-up (see Figure 14-2).

Analyzing the recovery of the banking system, interestingly, is one place where the different forms of QE as practiced by the Fed in the US and the ECB in Europe appear to have had varying impacts. The Fed bought assets from the banking system, and this did two things. It provided liquidity and it allowed the banks to shed assets without a fire sale into an imploding market. In turn, shedding assets reduced the banks need to raise new capital, so that the amounts of new capital required for the now smaller bank balance sheets were manageable in a reasonably rapid fashion. The US financial sector returned to profitability relatively quickly, as shown in Figure 14-3.

By contrast, initially as the financial panic developed in 2008 and in the first stages of the European sovereign debt crisis in 2010 and 2011, the ECB focused on long-term liquidity facilities rather than asset purchases, although there were some asset purchases. The loans from the ECB relieved the immediate liquidity issues, but did not assist in helping banks to shed assets and raise capital, so solvency challenges remained in play. The result was that the European banking system lagged far behind the US banking system in adjusting its capital ratios and returning to a reasonable level of profitability. Moreover, the use of bank loans rather than asset purchases kept the pressure on banks to sell assets to reduce their own balance sheets to meet required capital ratios.

Asset sales by banks, including sales of sovereign debt, tended to keep downward pressure on the prices (upward pressure on the yields), such that government fiscal solutions to the sovereign debt crisis were more complex, challenged, and drawn-out than might have been the case had the ECB aggressively purchased sovereign debt directly from banks from day one of the crisis. [See Chapter 15.]

Our conclusions about quantitative easing under conditions of banking system failure are that QE is extremely effective medicine, and secondarily that asset purchases may work better than direct loans to the banking system. While we are sure that academic economists and policy makers will try to put a number on the quantity of jobs saved, this will not be easy. We would argue that the balance sheet expansion from September 2008 through December 2008 by the Fed, known as QE1, stabilized a failing US banking system and prevented the recession from spiraling downward into a very deep depression. The US economy still had to go through a multi-year deleveraging phase, but at least the return to a normally functioning banking system was relatively rapid (see Figure 14-2).

Figure 14-3: US Financial Profits

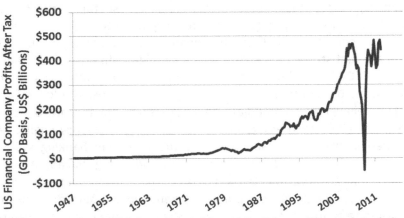

Source: U.S. Department of Commerce: Bureau of Economic Analysis
(Total After Tax Profits minus Non-Financial Sector After Tax Profits).

We would also argue that the ECB's bank lending approach tackled bank liquidity issues but not solvency challenges, and thus was not nearly as effective in containing the sovereign debt crisis as asset purchases would have been. Since the ECB decided in September 2012 to expand sovereign debt purchases, this hypothesis can be reevaluated in a few years after more experience has been gained.

Quantitative Easing When the Banking System is Functioning Normally

Once the banking system is back on its feet, by which we mean consistently profitable and well capitalized, then the analysis of quantitative easing shifts to the linkages from asset purchases by the central bank to questions of the impact on longer-term interest rates and to the interest rate sensitivity of the economy. The portfolio balance linkage from asset purchases (and later asset sales when QE is unwound) is relatively straightforward, while the macro-economic transmission process from interest rates to real GDP growth, job creation, and potential inflation is highly controversial.

As then Fed Chairman Ben Bernanke described in his speech and accompanying research paper, "Monetary Policy since the Onset of the Crisis", presented at the Federal Reserve Bank of Kansas City Economic Symposium, Jackson Hole, Wyoming, on 31 August 2012,[4] the mechanism from QE to market interest rates and also stock prices runs through the portfolio balance effect. As noted above, this is not the controversial part of QE. There is little doubt in anyone's mind that the Fed's purchases of trillions of dollars of US Treasuries and mortgage-backed securities raised debt prices, lowered yields and supported stock prices. Studies cited by Bernanke (2012) have attempted to quantify the interest rate effects.

These studies include Li and Wei (2012)[5], both economists at the Federal Reserve Board in Washington, and Christensen and Rudebusch (2012)[6], economists at the Federal Reserve Bank of San Francisco. The Li and Wei estimate is that the first and second large scale asset purchase programs had a combined effect of pushing the 10-

---

[4] Bernanke, Ben S., 2012, "Monetary policy since the onset of the crisis." Speech at the Federal Reserve Bank of Kansas City Economic Symposium, Jackson Hole, Wyoming, 31 August 2012.

[5] Li, Canlin, & Wei, Min (2012) "Term Structure Modeling with Supply Factors and the Federal Reserve's Large Scale Asset Purchase Programs", Preliminary and incomplete version: May 7, 2012, also presented at the 2012 FRBNY SOMA Portfolio Workshop.

[6] Christensen, Jens H. E., & Rudebusch, Glenn D., "The response of interest rates to U.S. and U.K. quantitative easing", *Federal Reserve Bank of San Francisco working paper series* (May 2012).

year Treasury yield about 100 basis points lower than it otherwise would have been.

What is interesting about the studies cited by Bernanke (2012) concerning the impact of quantitative easing on US long-term interest rates is that these empirical studies are US-centric and do not consider the potential effects coming from two international sources that were happening at the same time. First, many central banks around the world, especially emerging market central banks such as China, were purchasing large quantities of US Treasury securities as part of their policy to stabilize their exchange rates. Second, because of the worsening sovereign debt debacle within the European Union, US Treasuries were a popular flight-to-quality investment vehicle when fear gripped the financial markets. While difficult to quantify, both of these effects would have also lowered US Treasury yields. Thus, the Federal Reserve studies of the impact of quantitative easing probably overstate the case, even though the direction of the effect is not in question.

The next bit is the tricky part. Did the reduction in Treasury yields have any impact on economic activity or job creation? The asset purchases as part of QE1, as discussed in the section above, are definitely thought to have saved job losses and prevented a much worse recession or depression by the stabilization of the banking system. But did further asset purchases that occurred after the banking system was stabilized and had returned to substantial profitability have any further impact in terms of actually increasing job creation, as opposed to preventing job losses as in the QE1 phase of a failing banking system?

The answer to this question depends on assumptions about the interest rate sensitivity of various sectors of the economy, especially consumers and corporations in the aftermath of a financial crisis. There are several issues to address. First, if consumers and corporations are still in a deleveraging phase caused by the drop in asset values that also sunk the banking system, then it is highly unlikely that they are interest rate sensitive. That is, when deleveraging is the order of the day, near-zero short term rates and reduced long-term rates would probably not make any difference to economic decision making by consumers, corporations, and local governments.

Historically, the cyclical interest rate sensitivity of the US economy has depended in no small part on the housing sector. But in the aftermath of a financial crisis, housing prices can be severely depressed, and the route from lower rates to an expanding housing sector is completely short-circuited. In the US, there was no sign of life in the housing sector until the year 2012, four years after the crisis began.

Second, even after the deleveraging phase had ended (see Figure 14-3), if consumers and corporations have little confidence in the likelihood of future economic progress, regardless of the rationale for their lack of confidence, it is also likely that the lack of confidence would trump lower rates in any decision about future consumption or corporate expansion. Put another way, for there to be a material link between lower bond yields and economic activity, there needs to be a strong expectation that consumer and corporate decisions will be impacted by the lower rates, given the state of the economy, banking system, and confidence in the future. We saw no convincing evidence of a link between lower interest rates and consumer or corporate decision making during the deleveraging period from 2009 through approximately the middle of 2011 before consumer credit and bank commercial and industrial loans began to rise again.

Also, the continuation of zero short-term interest rates and expanded QE to lower long-term rates after the economy had started to grow again might have had a very depressing impact on certain segments of the population in terms of their savings and consumption behavior in the aftermath of a financial crisis. Demographically, the US is an aging country, and the role of retirement planning in the 45–65-year-old segment and the actual retirement situation of the over-65 segment puts the impact of an emergency low rate monetary policy into question.

Many retirees and pension funds depend in no small way on fixed income investments as a source of income. Reducing this source of income from the rates paid on short-term and cash equivalent investments can force current and future retirees into reducing consumption so as to increase savings, given the lower expected returns from their retirement portfolios. In essence, zero short-term rate policies coupled with QE to lower long-term rates imply a redistribution of wealth away from savers (current and future retirees) and in the direction of borrowers, including corporate borrowers, who are not likely to expand their businesses during periods of heightened uncertainty regardless of the low level of rates.

Figure 14-4: US Consumer and Commercial Credit

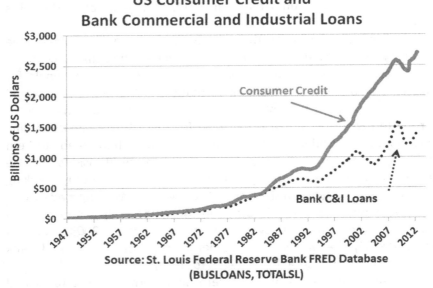

These challenges to traditional assumptions about the degree of interest rate sensitivity of the economy in the post-crisis recovery phase must be at the heart of any evaluation of the efficacy of quantitative easing. That is, we note that most domestic large country macro-economic equilibrium models are extremely comfortable with assuming a constant and material degree of interest rate sensitivity for consumers and corporations through all phases of the business cycle. This assumption is not nearly so obviously appropriate in the aftermath of a financial crisis with significant deleveraging activity. Tellingly, Bernanke[7] makes the cautionary statement: "If we are willing to take as a working assumption that the effects of easier financial conditions on the economy are similar to those observed historically, then econometric models can be used to estimate the effects of LSAPs (Large Scale Asset Purchases) on the economy." Bernanke displays his apparent willingness

---

[7] Specifically, see page 7 of Bernanke, Ben S., 2012, "Monetary policy since the onset of the crisis". Speech at the Federal Reserve Bank of Kansas City Economic Symposium, Jackson Hole, Wyoming, 31 August 2012.

to make this critical assumption since he goes on to cite several research studies that follow this path. There are many in the economic analysis fraternity, however, who would refer to Reinhart and Rogoff (2009), and emphatically assert that "this time is different"! Kiley (2012)[8], an economist at the Federal Reserve Board in Washington, DC, for example in a paper cited by Bernanke, notes in his research that "the analysis herein stops before" the period of zero rates "because it is likely that the binding zero-lower bound on nominal interest rates implies that the linear rational expectations structure of the model ... may be problematic."

Our suggestion and intuition is that there are four phases involved in analyzing a financial panic and the recovery process, and they are as follows:

> - **Phase one** is about **outright financial panic** involving a failing banking system (September 2008–March 2009), with the shift into recession coming abruptly and much more sharply than with typical business cycle recessions.

> - **Phase two** sees the **recovery of banking profitability** and return to normal functioning, but consumers, corporations, and local governments are still in a deleveraging phase brought on by the initial decline in asset values (April 2009–June 2011, perhaps).

> - **Phase three** (July 2011–ongoing as of 2018) involves a functioning banking system, but **economic growth remains constrained** because economic confidence is missing or there are long-lasting changes to risk preferences from the shock of the earlier financial panic.

> - **Phase four** completes the return to some form of economic equilibrium in which the standard macro-economic assumptions about interest rate sensitivity might begin to apply again.

---

[8] See page 4, last paragraph. Kiley, Michael T., 2012, "The aggregate demand effects of short- and long-term interest rates", *Federal Reserve Board, Finance and Economics discussion series.*

That is, even if an economy has arrived at phase three with deleveraging being completed and the banking system functioning normally, this is only a necessary and not a sufficient condition to re-apply assumptions about the interest rate sensitivity of consumption and investment. The reason involves confidence or the potential lack of it. We have to remember that financial panics, even those that do not spiral into depression, can leave a lasting and negative impression on confidence that is not necessarily easily or quickly restored. If long-term return expectation is reduced, then risk-taking will also be reduced, and this could last for a decade or more if the lasting effects from the Great Depression of the 1930s or the Inflationary 1970s are any guide.

Take corporations for example, if they are unsure about tax policies, fiscal spending policies, new regulations, etc., coming out of a financial crisis, they may well hold back on expansion and hiring plans due to their lack of confidence in the future. What this means in terms of traditional macro-economic econometric models is that the historical parameters associated with interest rate sensitivity for consumption and investment may be much too high, causing the models to erroneously suggest the possibility of much higher growth rates and job creation rates than are actually likely to occur. This type of corporate behavior appears to have been especially prevalent in the 2010–2012 period after corporate profits had recovered, but job creation was modest. During what we might consider phases two and three of the post-crisis recovery, US corporations built huge cash hoards, much of which were kept overseas due to the peculiar nature of how foreign-earned profits were taxed under US tax law in effect at the time. In short, in evaluating the efficacy of quantitative easing we would definitely not be willing, as Bernanke suggests, "to take as a working assumption that the effects of easier financial conditions on the economy are similar to those observed historically," and we would expect econometric models using historically estimated constant parameters to materially overestimate the effects of LSAPs (Large Scale Asset Purchases) on the economy. Practically speaking, we would strongly suggest that the estimation models aimed at evaluating quantitative easing need to use dynamic techniques with time-varying parameters or at least regime-shifting approaches to have even a fighting chance of producing relevant estimates of the potential effects of quantitative easing on economic activity and job creation in the various phases of recovery after a severe financial shock and deleveraging episode.

Impact of Global Economic Context

Global context matters when evaluating the impact of any policy action. The question of evaluating quantitative easing in terms of its impact on real GDP growth and job creation is whether there have been significant changes in the structure of the world economy compared to the period during which the baseline econometric model was developed relative to the current global environment. This takes us into issues related to the nature of an interconnected global economy and whether simplified domestic-oriented economic models from the 1950–2000 period are still robust enough to use in this new age.

The simplest macro-economic models focus on trade linkages, but these approaches do not do justice to international capital flows that swamp trade flows. There are feedback effects from currency markets, bond markets, equity markets, and commodity markets. Large multinational corporations may have a domicile in one country but get half or more of their cash flow from outside their domestic base. Pension funds, asset managers, and hedge funds manage global portfolios, not domestic ones.

What we can say with confidence is that if large parts of the world are struggling economically in terms of their economic performance, then no country is likely to be an island and not feel some of the effects. While there are many possible approaches to modeling international influences and feedback loops from global markets, what is clear is that there is a need for these effects to be tackled directly and not relegated to simplifying assumptions. This is especially true given the changes in the relative size of various economies over the past decade, especially the relative growth of emerging market nations compared to the mature industrial economies (see Figure 14-5).

Figure 14-5: Global Real GDP Growth

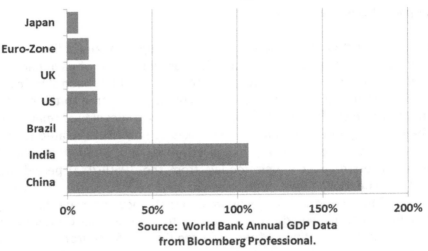

Cumulative Real GDP Growth
from 2001 through 2010

Source: World Bank Annual GDP Data
from Bloomberg Professional.

For example, in 2000, the BRIC nations of Brazil, Russia, India, and China made up only 8% of global GDP, and by 2010 this had expanded to 25%. While one can argue about the nature of international linkages, it would seem an obvious starting point to take the perspective that the relative influence of emerging market nations, such as China, has dramatically increased. From a modeling point of view, this again points to the need for dynamic estimation approaches that allow for time varying parameters, and to carefully avoid assuming constant parameters associated with international feedback effects in this ever-changing world.

There are also concerns regarding the impact of the European sovereign debt crisis during 2010–2012 on evaluating how effective QE2 and Operation Twist were in the US. The European crisis displayed aspects of both a sovereign debt crisis and a banking capital adequacy crisis. As such, the probable impact of the financial uncertainties in Europe may have magnified the direct trade effects emanating from this region in recession or stagnation. Further study is certainly required in this regard, as the "headwinds" from Europe during 2010–2012 for the rest of the world economy, from the US to China as well as other emerging market countries, may have been much more severe due to the impact on capital markets and risk-taking appetites than the real GDP and trade numbers from the Eurozone would initially suggest if these were more normal and cyclical events. That is, in light of the stagnation in Europe and the rapid deceleration of economic growth in emerging markets in 2011–2012, one could build a case that the US economic performance from Q3/2009 through Q3/2012 was quite impressive given the international headwinds, even if real GDP growth averaged only 2.2%.

Demographics, technological progress, fiscal policy shifts

Observing demographic changes is like watching paint dry, but the effects can be truly huge when taken in decades and not years. This presents a serious problem for quantitative economic modeling, since slow moving, yet potentially tectonic effects do not show up in the month-to-month or quarter-to-quarter variations that are the focus of macro-economic statistical models relying on historical data. Yet we know that the policy choices between young and older countries are likely to be strikingly different.

Countries with aging populations or where the number of new retirees equals or exceeds the number of young people entering the work force might focus more on wealth maintenance and health care, such as might be the case for Japan and other older, mature industrial countries. Younger countries with rapidly expanding work forces might focus on job creation and exports with less emphasis on pensions and health care systems, such as Brazil and other relatively young emerging market countries (see Figures 14-6 and 14-7).

Figure 14-6: Japan Population Pyramid

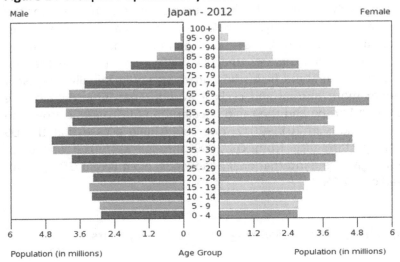

Source: US Census Bureau, International Database.
https://www.census.gov/data-tools/demo/idb/informationGateway.php

Figure 14-7: Brazil Population Pyramid

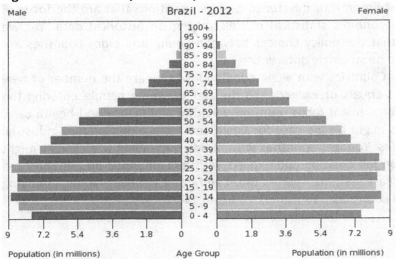

Source: US Census Bureau, International Database.
https://www.census.gov/data-tools/demo/idb/informationGateway.php

An aging nation's policy focus on pensions and health care may well lead to higher labor costs, which possibly develops over time and with the building of a more comprehensive social safety net, partly through mandated charges on workers. [See Chapter 5 for an in-depth discussion of demographics and economic growth.]

Demographics are not the only issues that are powerful in the long-term and hidden in short-term data. Technology can move in jumps, but progress over the decades has been impressive. In particular, the advent of the information age has dramatically improved labor productivity for those firms willing to make the investments in new capital and equipment to take advantages of the leaps forward. A period of rapid technological change, especially of the variety that can increase labor productivity as the world has experienced since the 1980s and is still continuing, can alter the job creation cycle associated with recessions. In particular, recessions tend to weed out the weaker firms that have not taken advantage of technological changes. During decades of rapid technological change, the stronger firms coming out of recessions may not need as many workers for a given level of output, due to their enhanced use of improved labor-productivity capital and equipment (see Figure 14-8).

The quantitative macro-economic question is whether characterizations of how labor markets perform during economic cycles changes with demographic shifts and technological progress or whether it can be safely assumed that structural change does not exist in labor markets. This is highly relevant to the QE debate in the United States because the Fed's objective with QE2, Operation Twist, and QE3 was ultimately to stimulate job creation. If structural changes in labor markets have been important, as argued by Putnam and Azzarello (2012)[9], then these developments need to be taken explicitly into account, which was not done in any of the studies evaluating QE and cited by Bernanke (2012) that were conducted within the Federal Reserve System.

---

[9] Putnam, Bluford H., & Azzarello, Samantha, 2012, "A Bayesian Interpretation of the Federal Reserve's dual mandate and the Taylor Rule", *Review of Financial Economics*, 21(3): 111–119.

Figure 14-8: US Non-Farm Payrolls

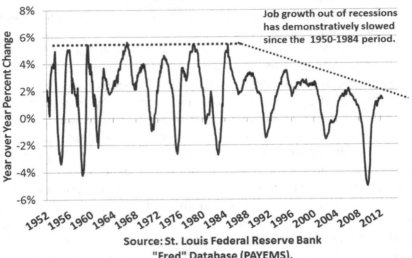

US Non-Farm Payrolls

Source: St. Louis Federal Reserve Bank
"Fred" Database (PAYEMS).

The quantitative macro-economic question is whether characterizations of how labor markets perform during economic cycles changes with demographic shifts and technological progress or whether it can be safely assumed that structural change does not exist in labor markets. This is highly relevant to the QE debate in the United States because the Fed's objective with QE2, Operation Twist, and QE3 was ultimately to stimulate job creation. If structural changes in labor markets have been important, as argued by Putnam and Azzarello (2012)[10], then these developments need to be taken explicitly into account, which was not done in any of the studies evaluating QE and cited by Bernanke (2012) that were conducted within the Federal Reserve System.

When we examine the response of job growth after recessions in the US since WWII, we note a consistency in the patterns during the 1950s, 1960s, 1970s, and through the recession of 1980–82. From the mid-1980s onward, however, there is a new pattern. After each recession, the growth of employment is slower than in the previous

---

[10] Ibid.

recession. Also, it takes longer and longer to return to the previous, pre-recession peak level of employment. Our interpretation of the historical data is that in the US there has been material and substantial structural change in the amount of job growth that is likely for a given recovery in real GDP after a recession, when financially-induced as 2008 or of the more cyclical variety.

The Role of Central Bank Signaling

Central banks can influence rates through signaling their policy intentions as well as through actual asset purchases. Christensen and Rudebusch (2012) compare interest rate responses to quantitative easing in the UK and US, and they explicitly consider central bank signaling. Interestingly, they note that "We find that declines in US Treasury yields mainly reflected lower policy expectations, while declines in UK yields appeared to reflect reduced term premiums. Thus, the relative importance of the signaling and portfolio balance channels of quantitative easing may depend on market institutional structures and central bank communications policies." Certainly, the Fed under Bernanke's chairmanship has made considerable strides to improved communications and signaling.

We note that the signals from the Fed about its intentions for future quantitative easing policies in the period 2009 through mid-2012 were predicated on the potential for weakness in the US economy and a general view that progress in reducing the unemployment rate was insufficient. That is, QE signals and a relatively pessimistic view of the US economic progress went hand in glove. This view is also reflected in White (2012)[11] in his excellent discussion of the myriad potential unintended consequences of ultra-easy monetary policies. The argument is that while the signaling of future QE policies might have caused a more rapid transmission to rates, it came with the potential negative side-effect of depressing consumer and business confidence. Our contention is that the when QE signals embody a pessimistic view of the economy, the signals contribute to breaking the link between

---

[11] White, William R., 2012, "Ultra Easy Monetary policy and the Law of Unintended Consequences". Federal Reserve Bank of Dallas Globalization and Monetary Policy Institute, Working Paper No. 126.

rates and economic activity because they reduce consumer and investor confidence in the future.

Moreover, in the post banking crisis phases of a financially-induced recession, rebuilding confidence in the future is critical to reestablishing a link between lower rates and consumption and business decisions. This view has not gone unappreciated. There were discussions among FOMC members of extending the guidance for the time period for a near-zero federal funds rate regardless of the economic context, so the market would know that accommodative policies would remain in place to support the recovery. Alternatively, and as adopted by the FOMC in December 2012, the near-zero federal funds rate guidance was made conditional, with caveats, on the unemployment rate declining to 6.5%.

Exiting QE

We now turn to our final set of observations, which is to consider exit strategies, also a key topic in White (2012). No investment strategy should be entered into without a plan of exit, and the same applies to policy approaches. The Fed and the ECB both consider their forays into QE as temporary and that the exit from QE is manageable. While we do not doubt that the exit from QE is manageable, we do think it will be highly challenging and contains the distinct possibility, if not certainty, of delaying a return to normal monetary policies.

To the extent that QE has reduced rates, the exit from QE is equally likely to raise rates. But the economic context will be totally different. That is, the entry into QE occurred during the deleveraging phase and lack of confidence phase following a severe financially-induce recession.

These are the periods during which the interest rate sensitivity of consumers and corporations is likely to be very low and even perhaps non-existent. By contrast, the exit from QE is most likely to occur only when the economy has returned to a stable and positive growth path. This means that the exit from QE is likely to occur when the economy has regained a degree of interest rate sensitivity. But in the exit from QE, rates will be rising as assets are sold into the market, and that in turn could spell trouble for a now more interest rate sensitive economy.

There is a strong possibility, although not a necessity, that central banks will delay the exit from QE or extend its time frame to minimize the impact on the economy from high rates. The potential implication of delays from exiting QE once the economy has regained its strength is a weaker currency and the possibility of feedback effects into inflation. In addition, large scale asset sales have the potential to cause price volatility in bond markets. Central bank signaling may be able to reduce the volatility, but at the cost of having the downward price (upward yield) effects occur even faster. Our conclusion is simply that it is much easier to enter QE than to exit QE, and we fear that the long-term costs of QE for the economy and market volatility are easy to under-estimate.

Conclusions

Evaluating QE involves considerable quantitative challenges and our hope is that this research can provide a road map to the problems that are essential to tackle explicitly and avoid the route of assuming that they do not exist. In particular, quantitative macro-economic models designed to evaluate quantitative easing need to explicitly deal with the following issues:

➢ QE1 was applied to an economy with a failing banking system and is a totally different use of QE than the subsequent QE2, Operation Twist, or Q3 applied to an economy already growing again and in recovery. Evaluations of QE must separate Q1 from subsequent applications of QE or their results will be effectively meaningless.

➢ There is evidence of structural change in US labor markets. Can it be safely assumed not to exist? Probably not.

➢ There has been a historic increase in the role of emerging markets in the world economy since 2000. Can domestic economy models without explicit international linkages be used to evaluate QE in the US or elsewhere in this day and age? Probably not.

➤ Internationally, central bank buying of US Treasuries has been measured in the trillions of dollars. The European sovereign debt crisis in 2010–2012 created a number of bouts of market fear and flight-to-quality behavior that may have also lowered US Treasury yields. Research evaluating the impact of QE on US bond yields needs to at least address the possibility that there were material international influences that also worked to lower yields. Domestic-only models of bond yields are totally inappropriate in this context.

➤ There was a material amount of deleveraging by consumers and corporations from 2008 into 2011. Can one safely assume that the 2008–2009 recession was typical of other post-WWII recessions? Certainly not, if one accepts the premises of Reinhart and Rogoff. Even if one rejects the implications of the Reinhart and Rogoff suggestion that "this time is different", one seems obligated to explain why the deleveraging did not materially reduce the interest rate sensitivity of the economy.

Our conclusions from our theoretical considerations and our interpretations of Fed and ECB actions from 2008 through mid-2012 yield the following points:

➤ **QE1 was effective.** Quantitative easing is a very effective tool for central banks to use when combating a failing banking system facing systematic solvency and liquidity challenges.

➤ **Asset purchases are more effective than loans.** Moreover, central bank purchases of securities held by a weakened or failing banking system may be more effective in encouraging a more rapid return to economic growth than other forms of QE such as outright loans to the banking system.

➤ **QE impacts rates.** Quantitative easing in the form of purchases of securities with long-term maturities can have a meaningful effect in terms of lowering long-term interest rates. The opposite effect on rates will occur, however, if and when central banks unwind their expanded portfolios and return to normal monetary policies.

➢ **QE does not necessarily impact economic activity.** Under conditions of deleveraging and a general lack of confidence by market participants, and even in the context of a relatively sound, profitable, and well capitalized banking system, quantitative easing may have little to no positive impact on economic activity or labor markets despite its impact on interest rates. Indeed, using QE when the likely effects are centered on rates and not on economic activity has the distinct potential to be counterproductive in terms of achieving the objectives of the central bank due to the fact that the use of QE sends a powerful signal of economic pessimism to market participants.

➢ **QE exit strategies are likely to be exceedingly challenging.** Exit strategies from QE by central banks may be extremely challenging to implement and have the potential, if not the certainty, to delay a return to the normal conduct of monetary policy to the detriment of longer-term economic growth, currency values, and potential future inflation. That is, the long-term costs to economic activity and financial market stability of QE have the potential to be quite large.

Chapter 15

Financial Crisis:
Lessons from Different
Management Approaches

Blu Putnam[1]

Editor's Note: This chapter was originally published in **The Journal of Financial Perspectives,** *Volume 2, Issue 2, July 2015. The Federal Reserve and the European Central Bank (ECB) chose strikingly different, non-traditional methods to manage the financial panic which began in September 2008. This research contrasts the purchases of assets by the Federal Reserve (Fed) with the emergency term loans extended by the ECB to ensure the liquidity of the banking system. This research argues that the Fed's approach in Q4/2008 was much more effective at putting the US banking system on a solid footing than the approach used by the ECB. – KT*

After the financial panic of September 2008 and the recession that followed, several of the key central banks of the mature, industrial world expanded their balance sheets aggressively, in what has become known as the era of quantitative easing (QE). Yet, there were major differences in the motivations and objectives of central banks for their QE programs, which led to very different approaches to their asset expansion practices. In turn, the different implementation methods resulted in very different outcomes, posing strikingly different

---

[1] **Disclaimer:** All examples are hypothetical interpretations of situations and are used for explanation purposes only. The views expressed here reflect solely those of the authors and not necessarily those of their employer, CME Group or its affiliated institutions. The information herein should not be considered investment advice or the results of actual market experience.

challenges for their respective economies, with critical implications for future central bank policies. Our research compares and contrasts the activities of the Federal Reserve (Fed) and the European Central Bank (ECB). We come to relatively obvious as well as some potentially controversial conclusions, including the following:

> Quick and aggressive Fed and ECB actions after the bankruptcy of Lehman Brothers and badly managed bailout of AIG more than likely prevented another Great Depression.

> Later Fed QE programs adopted from 2011, even as the US economy was already recovering, may not have helped job creation at all.

> The ECB's focus on liquidity loans calmed financial markets, but did not assist banks in shedding distressed assets and may have hindered economic growth compared to the Fed's approach to purchase assets, reducing bank balance and capital requirements and leading to a faster economic recovery.

> The Fed's exit from QE is likely to be highly complex, involving delays in returning to a more traditional short-term interest rate policy, diminished contributions to the US Treasury from central bank net earnings, and the potential for loss of some of the Fed's independence over time as the US Congress increases its oversight concerning the size of the Fed's balance sheet and potentially large unrealized portfolio losses.

> The ECB's initial approach to QE, mostly through loans to the banking system, allowed for the easiest and most natural exit path among the major central banks – just let the loans mature.

Central bank motivations are critical to appreciate. As the financial panic unfolded in September 2008, both the Fed and the ECB focused on the immediate challenge of stabilizing markets. Later, as the economic recovery was taking hold in the US, the Fed shifted its focus to perceptions of fragility in labor markets and set its objective as lowering the unemployment rate at a more rapid pace than would have been otherwise. The ECB, confronted by the sovereign debt crisis, viewed rebuilding the credibility of the single currency as its prime objective.

With different motivations came different methods and approaches. In the initial financial panic of the fourth quarter of 2008, the Fed bought distressed exposures from failing financial institutions. After the economic recovery began in late 2009, and the Fed shifted to worrying about labor markets, it began to accumulate US Treasury securities, extended their maturities and purchased mortgage-backed securities. By contrast, the ECB's focus on rebuilding the credibility of the euro in the face of the sovereign debt crisis meant assuring the liquidity of the financial system. Thus, the ECB prior to 2015 chose mainly to expand its balance sheet with emergency liquidity, low interest term loans to banks, with some, but much less, of an emphasis on purchasing the debt of weaker nations.

Progress toward achieving the objectives has been different as well. The quick and aggressive actions by the Fed, ECB and other major central banks in September 2008 and the following few months probably saved the world from the financial panic spiraling downward into another Great Depression. We will argue, however, that the Fed's QE programs from 2011 onward did little to nothing to assist the US labor market and help in the creation of jobs, and it may well have been a hindrance due to the negative signals it sent about economic confidence. The ECB has enjoyed considerable success in stabilizing the euro and the EU banking system — its primary objectives — yet there has been a lack of meaningful economic growth, although the picture finally appeared to brighten in 2014.

Slowly but surely, the unintended consequences of QE are becoming more apparent. The Fed by end-2016 had a balance sheet equal to about a quarter of one year's nominal GDP and faced severe challenges in how it would manage the exit from QE. By contrast, the ECB saw its balance sheet shrink in 2013-2014 naturally as banks were paying back their emergency term loans relatively aggressively. In 2015, though the ECB embarked on asset purchases which diminished the liquidity of Eurozone government bond markets, making them vulnerable to sharp swings in a crisis, such as Italy in June 2018.

We will adopt the case study approach and examine the Fed and the ECB in turn. We will describe their motivations and methods in detail, and then focus our attention on the results, unintended consequences and implications for the future of their economies. Our concluding section will summarize the lessons learned so far from the QE era and what it means for the future of central banking.

US Federal Reserve

Motivation and implementation. During the financial crisis period, the Fed was led by Professor Benjamin Bernanke, a scholar of the Great Depression of the 1930s.[2] Professor Bernanke was also a critic in the late 1990s of the Bank of Japan's unwillingness to take extraordinary measures, including asset purchases, to counteract the malaise faced by the country's economy after the equity and real estate boom of the 1980s had collapsed.[3]

When the financial panic hit after the bankruptcy of Lehman Brothers and the highly disruptive manner in which AIG was rescued, Fed Chair Bernanke turned to the playbook he had suggested for the Bank of Japan a decade earlier, and aggressively purchased assets.

Phase one of QE-1 (17 September 2008 through 31 December 2008) was all about crisis management. The Fed lowered its target federal funds rate to near zero, and it purchased approximately US$1 trillion of distressed securities and derivative exposures between mid-September and December 2008. We would argue that this part of the QE legacy was critical to the US avoiding a depression, and it was in line with the spirit of the Fed's original charter to be a lender of last resort to the banking system. The Fed used an interpretation of its emergency powers to justify buying the various securities and exposures in QE-1, but it clearly did not want to be a long-term holder of distressed debt and derivative exposures. During the next phase (31 December 2008

---

[2] See: Bernanke, B. S., "Non-monetary effects of the financial crisis in the propagation of the Great Depression," *The American Economic Review*, Volume 73 Number 3, (1983): 257–276. Also, see: Bernanke, B. S., 1994, "The macroeconomics of the Great Depression: a comparative approach," *NBER Working Paper Series*, Working Paper No. 4814, National Bureau of Economic Research, Cambridge, MA.

[3] Bernanke, B. S., 2000, "Japanese monetary policy: a case of self-induced paralysis?" in Mikitani, R., and A. Posen (eds.), *Japan's Financial Crisis and its Parallels to U.S. Experience*, Washington, DC: Institute for International Economics, 149–166.

through 29 December 2010) of the QE era, the distressed assets and exposures were sold at a profit as markets calmed and the economic recovery commenced. The money received from the sale of the distressed assets and exposures was largely used to purchase mortgage-backed securities (MBS).

Figure 15-1: US Federal Reserve Assets

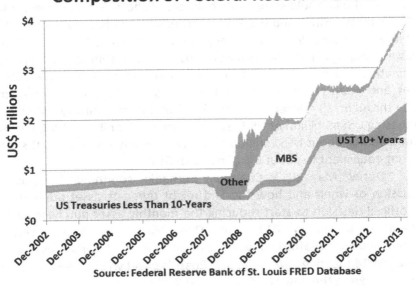

Composition of Federal Reserve Assets

Source: Federal Reserve Bank of St. Louis FRED Database

From 2011 onward, various programs of QE were introduced to expand holdings of US Treasuries and MBS, as well as to lengthen maturities. These next rounds of QE were not motivated by the immediate concerns of financial panic, as was the case in the last quarter of 2008. Equity markets had started a powerful recovery rally in March 2009. Economic growth had commenced in late 2009. Private sector employment growth had begun in early 2010. A second round of asset purchases, QE-2 (29 December 2010 through 6 July 2011), was initiated because the Fed felt the economic recovery was exceedingly fragile and net job growth was painfully slow. QE-2 focused on the purchase of US Treasuries, adding about US$600 billion to its portfolio, of which only US$40 billion were long-term securities of 10-year maturities or more. That is, QE-2 mostly comprised the purchase of short- and medium-term Treasury securities.

Still unhappy with the perceived fragility of the economy, pace of recovery, and labor market conditions, the Fed shifted gears and adopted a Maturity Extension Program (MEP)[4] (6 July 2011 through 26 December 2012) to actively try to lower longer-term US Treasury yields. The MEP was essentially a modern version of the Fed's 1961 attempts to lower long-term bond yields known then as "Operation Twist".[5] In this phase, the Fed sold some of its holdings of short- and medium-term US Treasury securities and used the proceeds to purchase long-term US Treasury securities, dramatically lengthening the maturity profile of its Treasury holdings. In the latter part of 2012, the Fed shifted gears again, terminating the maturity extension program and announcing a new, larger and open-ended asset purchase program, QE-3 (26 December 2012 through 25 December 2013).[6] This phase initially involved purchasing US$45 billion of US Treasuries and US$40 billion of MBS each month, adding about US$1 trillion to the Fed's balance sheet in 2013, an amount equivalent to about 6% of nominal GDP.

During May 2013, Chairman Bernanke commenced a public discussion of when and how the Fed might taper its asset purchases. The official decision to start reducing the monthly asset purchases was made at the December 2013 Federal Open Market Committee (FOMC) meeting and was re-affirmed with further cuts in asset purchases at the January 2014 meeting, when the Fed Board's gavel was handed over by Ben Bernanke to the new Fed Chair, Janet Yellen.

Market impact. The most notable impact on long-term bond yields and probably directly attributable to the Fed's actions occurred with the announcement and implementation of the MEP in 2012 and ended abruptly when Chairman Bernanke initiated his discussion of tapering

---

[4] (Maturity extension program) Federal Reserve Press Release (FOMC statement), Federal Reserve Board, 21 September 2011.
[5] Ross M. H., 1966, "'Operation Twist': A Mistaken Policy?" *The Journal of Political Economy*, 74(2), 195–199.
[6] QE-3 plans, Federal Reserve Press Release (FOMC statement), Federal Reserve Board, 13 September 2012.

the QE program.[7] The Fed's MEP and QE-3 programs temporarily succeeded in lowering 10-year Treasury yields in 2012 below the core inflation rate. Once the "taper talk" began, 10-year Treasury yields immediately rose back above the core inflation rate.

Figure 15-2: Treasury Yields and Core Inflation

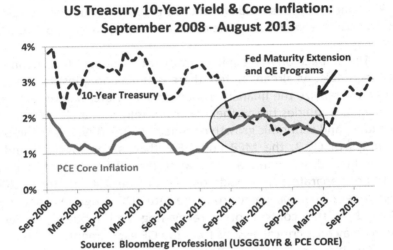

Source: Bloomberg Professional (USGG10YR & PCE CORE)

That is, the Fed's asset purchases in QE-2 of US$600 billion did not appear to make a noticeable difference in bond yields. This was probably because the purchases of long-term bond yields were a relatively small part of the mix. During this period, the Fed purchased mostly short- and medium-term US Treasuries. Since the short-end of the yield curve was already anchored near zero by the target federal funds rate, the impact of these asset purchases on rates further down the yield curve was small to non-existent. Also of note, during the debate, announcement, and implementation of QE-2, bond market

---

[7] QE tapering announced, Federal Reserve Press Release (FOMC statement), Federal Reserve Board, 18 December 2013.

volatility was most probably dominated by the worsening sovereign debt crisis in Europe.

By contrast, when the Fed shifted to the MEP, it was emphasizing purchases at the long end of the Treasury yield curve, and this made a material difference in bond yields. Our estimates, as well as others,[8] put the impact of the Fed's MEP at approximately 100 basis points. This was re-affirmed by the market impact when "taper talk" commenced. At the end of April 2013, the 10-year Treasury was yielding 1.67%. By early July, this yield was more than 2.75%. And for the rest of 2013, the US 10-year Treasury yield traded roughly in the 2.6% to 3.0% range.

The impact on US equities from the various QE programs is highly debatable. As already noted, there is almost no question that QE-1 helped to stabilize the financial system and alleviate market fears of a meltdown. US equities began their recovery rally in March 2009 as the panic faded, and economic growth resumed in late 2009. It is the impact on equities of QE-2, the MEP and QE-3 that is controversial and in question. Indeed, we would argue that studies of US QE that combine and do not separate the impacts of QE-1 in the last quarter of 2008 amidst severe financial panic from the later QE programs that were conducted in the context of a recovering and modestly growing economy may miss critical lessons from the QE experiment.[9]

For his part, Chairman Bernanke in his speech at the annual Jackson Hole conference of August 2012 cited the theory of portfolio balance and asset substitution as the channel by which asset purchases

---

[8] See 1) Christensen, J. H. E., and G. D. Rudebusch, 2012, "The response of interest rates to US and U.K. quantitative easing," *Federal Reserve Bank of San Francisco Working Paper Series*. 2) Kiley, M. T., 2012, "The aggregate demand effects of short- and long-term interest rates," *Federal Reserve Board, Finance and Economics Discussion Series*. 3) Li, C., and M. Wei, 2012, "Term Structure Modeling with Supply Factors and the Federal Reserve's Large Scale Asset Purchase Programs," Preliminary and incomplete version: 7 May 2012, also presented at the 2012 Federal Reserve Bank of New York SOMA Portfolio Workshop.

[9] Putnam, B. H., 2013, "Essential concepts necessary to consider when evaluating the efficacy of quantitative easing," *Review of Financial Economics* 22(1), 1–7.

by the Fed could raise stock prices.[10] On the surface, this seems reasonable and is well supported with economic theory, but there were other things happening, however, that were also likely to have contributed to equity rally. Corporate profits were recovering at a very sharp pace between 2010 and 2012. Based just on the 2010–12 experience, it seems likely that the lower bond yields and reduced bond market volatility attributable to the MEP did aid equity prices, but the credit should be shared with the powerful surge in earnings growth.

That is, to simplify:

Equation 1:

Equity index growth =

(Earnings growth expectations) / (1 + Treasury bond yield + market volatility (risk) premium)

That is, QE was operating mostly in a positive manner on stock prices with its influence on the denominator, lowering the hurdle rate with reduced bond yields and lower volatility. Earnings growth from a recovering economy was a positive factor working through the numerator.

What makes the hindsight analysis of the equity market reaction to QE-2, MEP and QE-3 even more interesting, though, is what happened once Chairman Bernanke commenced his "taper talk" in May 2013. The Treasury bond yield rose as did market volatility, suggesting lower equity prices, subject to earnings growth expectations. Earnings growth was certainly positive in 2013, but the growth rate was decelerating a little from the blistering pace in the first few recovery years. Equity prices, however, appeared to totally ignore the coming end of QE and the rise in Treasury yields. The S&P500 Index went from record high to new record high over the entire second half of 2013.

---

[10] Bernanke, B. S., 2012, "Monetary policy since the onset of the crisis". Speech at the Federal Reserve Bank of Kansas City Economic Symposium, Jackson Hole, Wyoming, 31 August 2012.

Figure 15-3: US Corporate Profits

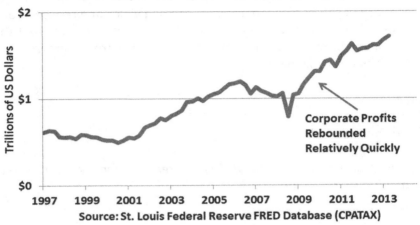

US Corporate Profits After Tax with Inventory Valuation Adjustment and Capital Consumption Adjustment (GDP Basis)

Source: St. Louis Federal Reserve FRED Database (CPATAX)

The performance of US equities in the second half of 2013, in the face of higher bond yields, modestly increased volatility, and slightly slowing observed trailing earnings growth, strongly suggested that there was a very powerful signaling effect in play. Namely, a decision by the Fed to exit its QE program would imply that the Fed had finally come to conclusion that the US economy was strong enough to grow on its own without emergency and extraordinary assistance from the Fed. If this interpretation represents the main influence of QE, then the announcement of the various versions of QE-2, MEP and QE-3 may also be interpreted as having had a depressing influence on economic confidence, and the economy might well have been better off if there had never been the extended and expanded QE programs once the economic recovery had commenced.

For sure, even though a private sector jobs recovery was well under way, major US corporations went on a cash hoarding spree during the first few years of the economic recovery. We would argue that one of the primary incentives to hoard cash came from the negative signaling by the Fed that it thought the economy was so fragile it could easily collapse back into recession and needed an extraordinary, never-before-tried emergency life support. The parallel perspective that QE-2, MEP and QE-3 did not create jobs is given more credence by a look into the details of the labor market data. Under Chairman Bernanke, the Fed appeared to be mostly focused on lowering the unemployment rate and seeing improvements in monthly net new job creation – the payroll employment data.

While the overall picture is one of a more sluggish jobs recovery than in previous cycles, going well back in time, that perspective changes when one divides the employment data into private sector jobs and government jobs. Indeed, private sector jobs in 2010–13 recovered at more or less the same pace as in 2002–06. What was strikingly different in the post-financial crisis period was the behavior of government jobs, driven mostly by state and local governments and to a lesser extent by the US postal service. From the end of 2001 through mid-2007, government jobs grew by 852,000. From April 2009 through March 2013, about 817,000 government jobs were lost. That is, the activity in the government job market was a huge setback for job creation in the post-crisis recovery.

Figure 15-4: US Private Sector Jobs

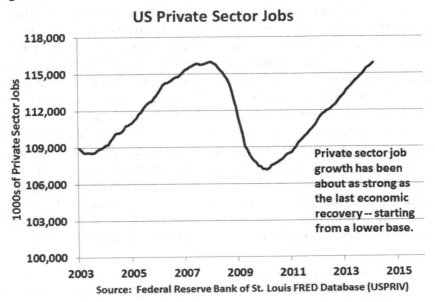

Source: Federal Reserve Bank of St. Louis FRED Database (USPRIV)

Figure 15-5: US Government Jobs

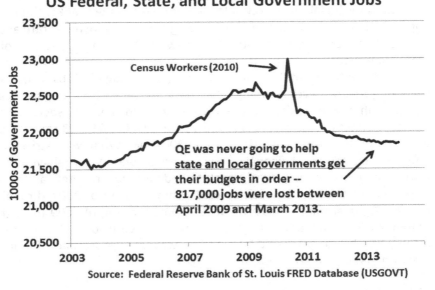

During the housing boom period, property taxes were rising and supporting increased expenditures by local governments in the US Financial recessions are, however, quite different from more typical cyclical recessions due to the role of debt and significant deleveraging that occurs after the crisis.[11] In this case, the high levels of debt were concentrated in the home mortgage market, and the recession saw housing prices plummet. This meant that state and local government revenue expectations had to be reset at much lower levels. Hence, there was substantial retrenchment in government jobs, taking several years to run its course. We would argue that the Fed asset purchases did absolutely nothing to help state and local governments, and that private sector job growth was relatively robust, supported by strong corporate profit growth. There was no need for QE-2, MEP or QE-3, and other than temporarily reducing long-term bond yields in 2012 and

---

[11] Reinhart, C. M., and Rogoff, K., 2009, *This Time is Different: Eight Centuries of Financial Folly*, New Jersey: Princeton University Press.

early 2013, there was little achieved – although the price to be paid in the future may involve some rather serious unintended consequences.[12]

Unintended consequences. Regardless of one's opinions of the success or failure of the Fed's QE programs in meeting their objectives, the Fed's balance sheet and financial situation is profoundly different in the aftermath of the QE experiment. As of the end of 2013, the Fed's total assets stood near US$4 trillion, compared with US$850 billion at the end of August 2008 before the financial panic began. This expansion took the size of the balance sheet from 6% to almost 25% as a share of US nominal GDP.

Figure 15-6: Federal Reserve Assets as Percent of Nominal GDP

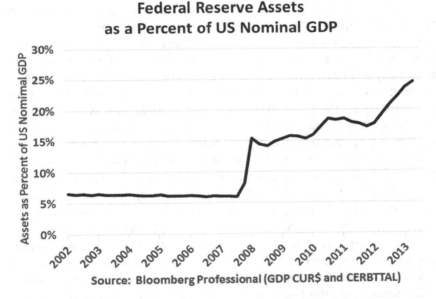

Source: Bloomberg Professional (GDP CUR$ and CERBTTAL)

Within that almost US$4 trillion are US$580 billion US Treasury securities of 10 years or longer remaining maturity as well as US$1.5 trillion in long-term MBS. The interest rate risk embedded in this

---

[12] White, W. R., 2012, "Ultra Easy Monetary Policy and the Law of Unintended Consequences," Federal Reserve Bank of Dallas Globalization and Monetary Policy Institute, Working Paper No. 126.

portfolio is exceptionally large. By illustration, a 10-year Treasury zero-coupon bond equivalent would lose 17.5% of its value if market yields went from 3% to 5%. At some time in the future, should inflation pressures rise and bond yields track upward, then the Fed might sustain some unrealized losses in its bond portfolio – however, the Fed will just keep those securities until they mature; the Fed is unlikely to ever be a seller.

We note that once the Fed began the massive expansion of its balance sheet, its earnings also went up sharply. The Fed contributes most of its earnings to the US Treasury, and this helps in deficit reduction. Prior to the financial panic of 2008, the Fed often contributed around US$20 billion or a little more to the US Treasury each year. In the last few years, those numbers have been much higher – US$76.9 billion in 2011, US$88.9 billion in 2012, and US$79.6 billion in 2013, for example.

The Fed may choose not to consider the impact on the US budget deficit of any decision to start increasing the target federal funds rate from its near-zero level held from late 2008 into 2014. Nevertheless, a decision to raise the target federal funds rate potentially will have an impact on Fed earnings. On the expense side of the ledger, the key item for the Fed is interest expense. The Fed pays zero interest on the US$1 trillion-plus cash outstanding as of mid-2014, but it does pay 25 basis points on the required and excess reserves of the banking system (i.e., the federal funds deposits held by the banking system on account at the Fed to satisfy reserve requirements or in excess of those requirements). Under a longer-term scenario where the core inflation rate rises to 2.0% (the Fed's target), if economic growth was positive, the Fed might choose to raise its federal funds target to roughly equal the core inflation rate. Under this circumstance, the Fed would raise the rate paid on reserves to enforce the new federal funds target rate. Thus, the Fed might see a US$60 billion or more increase in its interest expense on its US$3 trillion of required and excess reserves. At the same time, the Fed would be getting the old, low coupons from its holdings of longer dated Treasury securities and MBS, with some small increases in rates received on the short-term bills it might be rolling over. So, even before considering the potential unrealized losses on the portfolio, the carrying costs would be zooming upward. Fed accounting does, however, consider unrealized losses, which are taken as a charge against earnings for the purpose of calculating the contribution to be made to the US Treasury. Put another way, if inflation pressures emerge, if the Fed responds by raising the target federal funds rate and if bond yields rise with inflation pressures, then the Fed's contribution to the US Treasury will start to trend lower.

The guidance from the Bernanke Fed was that it planned to hold its long-term securities to maturity, so any losses would remain unrealized. Future Fed leadership will probably take the same view. And, the Fed has considerable discretion as to how fast it might want to shrink its balance sheet even without selling its longer-term Treasury securities and MBS. As already noted, when the Fed starts to raise its target federal funds rate, it may need to pay higher rates on excess reserves to achieve its new target rate in the marketplace. All of these complicated questions surrounding the QE exit strategy will come into sharp focus once the Fed starts raising its target federal funds rate.[13]

European Central Bank

The ECB faced immediate liquidity issues in its financial system during the 2008 crisis, but then also had to deal with the additional pressures on an undercapitalized banking system during the sovereign debt crisis in 2011 and 2012. The ECB chose to focus most of its balance sheet expansion on liquidity loans to the financial system to preserve the banks' ability to survive the sovereign debt crisis with less of an emphasis on outright sovereign debt purchases, although some debt was bought. The largest motivating factor for the ECB was probably the "do anything it takes" attitude to preserve the euro as the single currency for the subset of nations in the currency zone of the European Union (EU). After all, the ECB was explicitly created to be the central bank for the euro.

Providing banking sector liquidity. The ECB's choice to lend to banks rather than to buy distressed assets from banks as the Fed did was classic central banking. Serving as a lender of last resort to secure the safety and integrity of the whole banking system is one of the primary purposes of central banks. Notably, the Fed had been created in 1913,

---

[13] Editor's Note: This chapter was reprinted from a 2014 article, and we note that as the Fed started raise short-term interest rates in 2016, 2017, and into 2018, these complex issues became exceptionally relevant. --KT

following the Panic of 1907, because at the time the US had no central bank and no method for providing the liquidity to banks to stop a run on a few banks from cascading into a run on the whole system. The first big crisis after the Fed was created came with the stock market crash of 1929, and the Fed totally failed in its mission, did not serve as a lender of last resort and allowed a stock market crash to bring down the banking system and the economy, with the Great Depression as its result. Unlike the ECB, though, as the Financial Panic of 2008 emerged, Fed Chairman Bernanke went down the path of buying distressed assets instead of making emergency liquidity loans.

Figure 15-7: European Central Bank Assets

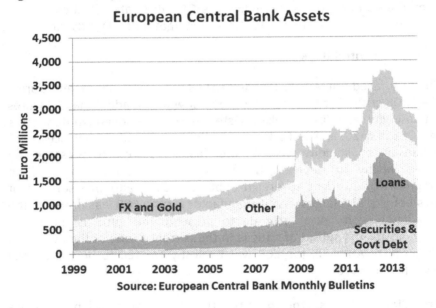

Source: European Central Bank Monthly Bulletins

There are similarities and differences in the two approaches. Buying assets immediately shrinks the size of the balance sheet of financial institutions, providing them cash as well as reducing their capital needs. Lending to banks solves the immediate liquidity challenges, but does not relieve banks of their distressed assets or reduce their balance sheets and capital needs. That is, both methods address the immediate liquidity crisis, but have different impacts on balance sheet sizes and capital needs.

We would argue that taking a US$1 trillion of distressed assets and exposures out of the system, as the Fed did in its QE-1 program, turned out to help the US banking system rebound faster since it also reduced the size of bank balance sheets. The ECB's method of providing low-interest term liquidity loans did not get the distressed assets off the balance sheets and left European banks in a very difficult capitalization posture. This had economic consequences, because the longer banks remain undercapitalized, the less new lending they can do. And, economies simply do not grow in a healthy manner without a well-functioning financial system.

The implications for exit strategies differ, too. As banks regain financial health, even if it takes longer, they can repay their loans, thus shrinking the balance sheet of the central bank in a quite natural manner and with no issues about potential portfolio losses at the central bank. This is what started happening with the ECB in 2013. As banks repaid their emergency liquidity loans, the ECB's balance sheet started contracting rather dramatically. Of course, part of the motivation for repaying the loans was the bank stress tests the ECB conducted in the second half of 2014. Banks perceived that they would perform better on the stress tests if they could show they did not need the emergency liquidity loans. Thus, these stress tests worked to depress bank lending in the second half of 2014, at least until the ECB announced the results.

Sovereign debt crisis. The emergence of the sovereign debt crisis in Europe as a follow-on impact of the Financial Panic of 2008 has its roots in two historical developments. First, banks in Europe tend to hold large portfolios of sovereign debt and are also lenders to municipalities for their public development projects. This is not so much the case in the US, where banks are not a primary source of funds for the US Federal Government and issuance in the municipal debt market is used to finance local public projects. The role of European banks as long-term holders of sovereign debt complicated the crisis, by tightly linking the need for government fiscal reform with EU-wide banking reform.

And second, when the single currency system was created, to entice more members into the Eurozone system, it was agreed that for regulatory and credit risk purposes the debt of any sovereign nation in the EU would be treated the same as any other country in the EU. That is, there would be no capital risk haircut when amassing a portfolio of higher yielding sovereign debt from EU nations with weaker economies. We would argue that if the euro was born with a birth defect, it was not the lack of common fiscal policy as typically cited; instead, it was the lack of an EU-wide bank capital policy that evaluated risk appropriately and selectively by country.

Figure 15-8: Spanish and German Government Bond Yields

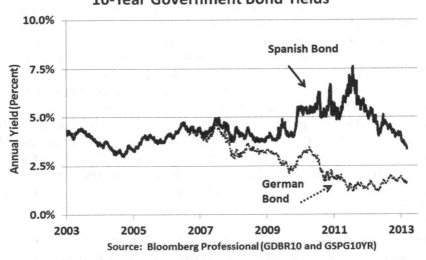

As the sovereign debt crisis worsened and its scope spread well beyond Greece, the ECB lent money to the central banks of nations in distress as well as bought some of the weaker sovereign debt securities to calm the markets. Since this was essentially a government fiscal crisis, there were limits to what the central bank could do. The task fell to the EU finance ministers to hammer out programs in order to bail out countries. And, the individual countries had to take very tough fiscal austerity measures to get their financial houses in order. In the midst of this severe fiscal deleveraging by the weaker countries in the Eurozone, the ECB was mainly focused on avoiding any implosion of the banking system and stabilizing the euro.

We would also note that what sovereign debt securities the ECB did buy were largely of the distressed variety with low prices and high yields. Consequently, as the crisis faded into the background with yields falling and prices rising, and the ECB made a nice profit.

We will return to this topic in the concluding section, but it makes a big difference whether a central bank is buying the distressed assets that are part of the immediate problem or whether the central bank is buying the most liquid, low-rate, flight-to-quality assets in the financial system, as the Fed was doing in its QE-2, MEP and QE-3 programs.

Figure 15-9: Euro (USD per EUR) Exchange Rate

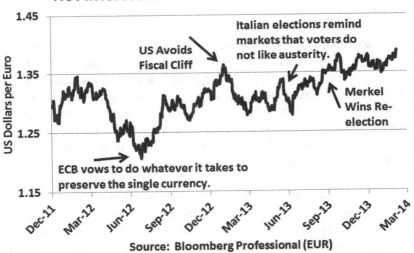

Euro Trades Politics and Policy Commitments, Not Interest Rate Differentials: 2011-2013

Source: Bloomberg Professional (EUR)

"Do whatever it takes (to preserve the euro)". Shortly after becoming the president of the ECB, Mario Draghi famously told the markets that the ECB would do whatever it takes to preserve the euro. At this point, the worst was already over for the sovereign debt crisis, but markets were still unsettled. The media and financial analysts were regularly speculating on whether Greece and possibly other countries would drop out of the Eurozone. The Eurozone, however, has no protocol for kicking a country out of the club. And, arguably, Germany's economy had been one of the largest beneficiaries of the Eurozone, with its implicitly fixed exchange rate removing currency risks from German exports to other

EU countries. In any case, the commitment to do whatever it takes was credible, and so the ECB did not actually have to do much, and the euro bounced upward and stabilized relatively quickly after President Draghi's remarks.

Lessons Learnt (or Perhaps Not)?

Stick to using QE only for crisis management. Given the general consensus that the first round of QE as the Financial Panic unfolded in September 2008 may well have saved the world from another Great Depression compared with the distinct controversies and unintended consequences of later QE efforts by the Fed after economic growth has already resumed, one lesson might be for central banks to only use QE for crisis management.

Have an exit plan. One key lesson for central bankers from the QE era is that large experiments with new methods of conducting monetary policy are likely to have equally large unintended consequences. This does not mean central banks should not be willing to act quickly and aggressively in a financial crisis, but absent a crisis, and certain during a period of modest, if not robust economic growth, one would hope the lesson had been learned to have an exit plan at the time the new strategy is implemented.

The Fed went into uncharted waters when it adopted asset purchase programs even as the economy was already in recovery mode (i.e., QE-2, MEP and QE-3). The Fed faces extremely complex exit issues that may well cause it to delay going back to a more tradition short-term interest rate policy as it faces more intense oversight from the US Congress and sharply diminished net earnings and lower contributions to the US Treasury. By contrast, the ECB's use of term liquidity loans has a natural exit strategy as banks pay back the loans.

Central bank profits and losses. Another interesting observation has to do with nature of the assets being bought in any QE program and the potential for central bank portfolio losses. In QE-2, MEP and QE-3, the Fed bought US Treasuries and MBS when core inflation was close to 1%. If the US economy were to achieve to Fed's long-term objective of a 2%

core inflation rate, and its shorter-term objective of 2.5% core inflation, this would imply rising bond yields and unrealized losses on the Fed's portfolio. That is, according to the Fed's business plan, economic success would mean huge portfolio losses on its bond purchases. By contrast, since the ECB primarily used term liquidity loans, and as these are paid back, the ECB faces no portfolio losses. And, when the ECB did buy assets, it tended to buy the weaker sovereign debt securities in the midst of the crisis, so as the crisis faded, the ECB holdings produced a tidy profit. The question facing central bankers is whether any QE program that will generate losses if economic success is achieved is worth the risk to its credibility and political independence.

QE and its role in helping banks recover. The Fed's choice in QE-1, during the height of the crisis in late 2008, was to buy distressed assets from the financial system and take them out of play. Arguably, the Fed's initial QE program allowed banks to reduce their balance sheets, lower their capital requirements and recover much faster — leading to faster economic improvement. The ECB's choice to focus on term liquidity loans meant that it did not provide any assistance to help banks reduce their balance sheets and meet their capital requirements. As a result, the European banking system was much slower to recover and considerably less able to assist in any economic recovery.

The future of central banking: our best assessment is that as more and more research is done to evaluate QE and as the unintended consequences continue to play out, that there may be a diminishing appetite for the Fed's experiment with QE during times of economic growth, even if the growth is modest. By contrast, the successes of both the ECB and the Fed in containing the Financial Panic in 2008, and later the ECB's success in helping stabilize the euro during the European sovereign debt crisis, more than justifies future crisis management. If anything, both the Fed and the ECB can look back and take great credit for not allowing the Financial Panic to turn into a prolonged and deep depression.

Chapter 16

Taylor Rule.
A Bayesian Interpretation of the
Federal Reserve's Dual Mandate

Blu Putnam[1] and Samantha Azzarello[2]

Editor's Note. An earlier version of this chapter was originally published in the **Review of Financial Economics,** *Volume 21, June 2012. One of the more famous rules to guide the conduct of monetary policy is the "Taylor Rule." This research takes a Bayesian dynamic estimation approach to evaluate Federal Reserve monetary policy in light of their dual mandate to encourage full employment and price stability. This dynamic analysis yields some surprising conclusions, compared to fixed period regression analysis, and shows how interest rate policy has shifted over the decades. And, while this research lost relevance in near-zero rate years, 2009–2016, the research returned to relevance as the Fed normalized its policy in 2017–2018. – KT*

After the Panic of 1907, the US Congress moved to establish a central bank with the powers to serve as a lender of last resort and prevent runs on banks turning into full-fledged financial crises. The Federal Reserve came into being in 1913, and its charter mandated that the new central bank "promote an elastic currency." The term "elastic" in the opening words of the charter was intended to underscore the need for a

---

[1] **Disclaimer:** All examples are hypothetical interpretations of situations and are used for explanation purposes only. The views expressed here reflect solely those of the authors and not necessarily those of their employer, CME Group or its affiliated institutions. The information herein should not be considered investment advice or the results of actual market experience.

[2] At the time this research was published in June 2012, Samantha Azzarello was a colleague of Blu Putnam at CME Group.

robust banking system that could withstand shocks and not collapse upon itself. There was no mention whatsoever of a dual mandate of promoting price stability and encouraging full employment. The dual mandate concept emerged after World War II, as the US Congress reflected on the Federal Reserve's near total abrogation of its assigned duties in the 1930s with its failure to serve as a lender of last resort as had been intended.

Congress passed the Employment Act of 1946, and later the Full Employment and Balanced Growth Act of 1978 (Humphrey-Hawkins), along with other amendments to the Federal Reserve Act, which collectively and over time enshrined the dual mandate of encouraging price stability and full employment into law. Since the 1950s and well before the Humphrey-Hawkins Act of 1978, the Federal Reserve had become highly involved in the management of the economy of the United States to serve both inflation and full employment objectives.

In 1993 Professor John Taylor set forth an elegant and simple framework (aka, the Taylor Rule) for analyzing the interest rate policy of the Federal Reserve in terms of its dual mandate. Our Bayesian Inference methodology allows for a sophisticated and nuanced quantitative perspective of how the Federal Reserve shifted its management of its twin objectives over time and in response to the different economic challenges it faced.

To highlight the research implications, our interpretation of our empirical results suggests the following:

➢ Our Bayesian approach broadly confirms that the Federal Reserve pays active attention to balancing the inflation and full employment of its dual mandate more or less along the lines suggested by the original Taylor Rule.

➢ The Federal Reserve typically puts more emphasis on output and employment data than inflation data. However, we believe this is because the Federal Reserve in its collective wisdom appears to use its output and employment projections as a critical input into whether it is willing to project rising or falling inflation for the future. This dependence of inflation projection on the output/employment projection is a severe complication for estimation techniques that assume that the output and inflation factors are truly independent, when they may not be.

➤ We also note that from time to time in the past, there appears to have been short periods when inflation pressures pre-occupied the Federal Reserve. Periods such as in the late 1960s or the 1979–1982 period were interesting, because during these periods the Federal Reserve may well have been willing to risk (or even cause) a recession to get better control of inflation. In the same vein, the Federal Reserve appears to have acted in the periods following the 2008 financial crisis in a manner that suggests the Federal Reserve was either worried about deflation or actively would like to have encouraged a little more inflation.

➤ These nuanced observations and interpretations are made possible by the use of the Bayesian dynamic linear modeling approach which treats the beta coefficients as time-varying parameters to be estimated as they evolve through time. This Bayesian approach allows for a much more sophisticated and rich interpretation of the Federal Reserve's interest rate decision process than could have been obtained by standard regression analysis techniques that assume away the possibility of time-varying beta coefficients in the first place.

This chapter is organized into five sections. Section One presents a brief synopsis of the Taylor Rule literature and presents the original equation describing how the Federal Reserve might target its interest rate policy decisions to meet its dual mandate of price stability and full employment.

Section Two focuses on how we structure the equations for our empirical analysis and describes the data used in the study.

Section Three answers the question of why we decided to apply Bayesian inference methods and chose a one-step-ahead dynamic linear modeling process.

Section Four presents our findings and provides possible interpretations.

Section Five concludes the paper with some observations about how Federal Reserve decision making may change in the coming decade and point toward potential paths for future research.

Original Taylor Rule Formulation from the Economic Literature

What has become known as the Taylor Rule was first set forth in Taylor (1993, 1993)[3], with later modifications by Taylor (1994, 1996)[4]. While the modifications to the Taylor Rule are interesting, the original formulation provides an extremely clear framework for analyzing how a short-run interest rate policy might be conducted to balance the trade-offs of the dual mandate to promote price stability and encourage full employment. The original Taylor Rule formulation was as follows:

(EQ-1) Target Federal Funds Rate = Actual Inflation Rate - Short-Term Real Rate Assumption + 0.5 x (Actual Inflation – Desired Inflation) + 0.5 x (Output Gap in Percentage Terms)

With the Taylor Rule framework in hand, one could compare the target federal funds rate as implied by the Taylor Rule to the effective federal funds rate that prevailed in the short-term money markets over time (see Figure 16-1).

The usefulness of the Taylor Rule as a framework for analyzing the trade-offs involved in the dual mandate of the Federal Reserve is probably nowhere better underscored than the mere fact that such a straightforward equation became widely known as the Taylor Rule. Indeed, there have been numerous Taylor Rule studies, including Woodford (2001)[5], Smets (2002)[6], and Orphanides (2003)[7], which contain many more references to previous studies.

---

[3] Taylor, J., 1993, "Discretion Versus Policy Rules in Practice," *Carnegie-Rochester Series on Public Policy*, North-Holland, Vol 39, pp. 195–214. And also: Taylor, J., 1993, "The Use of the New Macroeconometrics for Policy Formulation", *American Economic Review, Papers and Proceedings*, 83(2), May 1993, pp. 300–305.
[4] Taylor, J., 1994, "The Inflation-Output Variability Tradeoff Revisited," in Jeffrey Fuhrer (ed.) *Goals Guidelines, and Constraints Facing Monetary Policymakers*, Federal Reserve Bank of Boston. And also: Taylor, J., "Policy Rules as a Means to a More Effective Monetary Policy", *Monetary and Economic Studies*, Bank of Japan, 14(1), July 1996, pp. 28–39.
[5] Woodford, M. (2001). "The Taylor Rule and Optimal Monetary Policy." *The American Economic Review*, 91(2), 232–237.
[6] Smets, F. (2002). "Output Gap Uncertainty: Does it matter for the Taylor Rule?", *Empirical Economics*, 27(1), 113–129.

Figure 16-1: Actual Federal Funds Rate versus Taylor Rule

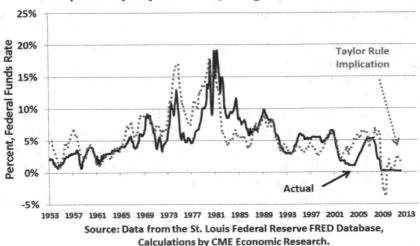

Actual versus Target Federal Funds
Implied by Taylor Rule (using PCE Deflator)

Source: Data from the St. Louis Federal Reserve FRED Database,
Calculations by CME Economic Research.

The overriding message from the economic literature is that the Taylor Rule is a great starting point for analyzing Federal Reserve interest rate policy decisions, and then expanding the analysis into the subtleties of how the Federal Reserve measures and monitors the data informing its policy decisions. That is, for example, on the full employment side, is the Federal Reserve more focused employment data, unemployment data, or output gap data? On the inflation side, the data monitoring questions revolve around the use of the personal consumption expenditure deflator, core consumer prices excluding energy and food, or the generally inclusive consumer price index. There are also different formulations of the Taylor Rule, to look at changes in the trends for employment or inflation to add more information and nuance to the original equation.

What has been missing from the literature is a dynamic estimation approach that allows one to analyze how the Federal Reserve's adherence to the Taylor Rule has changed over time or in

---

[7] Orphanides, A. (2003). "Historical Monetary Policy Analysis and the Taylor Rule". *Journal of Monetary Economics*, 50(5), 983–1022.

response to different economic conditions. The dynamic linear modeling approach utilized here is the one-step ahead Bayesian methodology with its theoretical originals outlined succinctly in Harrison and West (1997)[8], which is based on their earlier work from the 1980s. An applied example of the one-step Bayesian dynamic linear modeling methodology is contained in Harrison, Pole, and West (1994)[9]. Early applications of the Harrison and West one-step-ahead Bayesian approach to financial modeling problems were pioneered by Putnam and Quintana (1994)[10] and Putnam, Quintana, and Wilford (1998)[11], among others.

Our approach is to combine these different strands of literature. We pair the study of the Federal Reserve's interest rate decision process using the Taylor Rule as the basic framework for analysis with dynamic Bayesian statistical methods. Using this dynamic estimation approach we can observe how the Federal Reserve shifted its emphasis from full employment to inflation or to some other external factor given the economic context.

Estimation Equations and Data Sources and Transformations

Our first estimation equation using the Taylor Rule framework to analyze Federal Reserve behavior is simply to compare the target federal funds rate as specified by the original Taylor Rule (equation #1) with the observed effective federal funds rate. Our initial estimation equation is as follows:

---

[8] Harrison, J.& West, M., 1997, *Bayesian Forecasting and Dynamic Models*, New York: Springer-Verlag.

[9] Harrison, J., Pole, A. & West, M., 1994, *Applied Bayesian Forecasting and Time Series Analysis*, New York: Chapman and Hall.

[10] Putnam, B., & Quintana, J., 1994, "New Bayesian Statistical Approaches to Estimating and Evaluating Models of Exchange Rates Determination", *Proceedings from Annual Meeting of the American Statistical Association '94, Section on Bayesian Statistical Science*, Toronto, ON.

[11] Putnam, B., Quintana, J., & Wilford, S., 1998, "Mutual and Pension Funds Management: Beating the Markets Using a Global Bayesian Investment Strategy", *Proceedings from Annual Meeting of the American Statistical Association '98, Section on Bayesian Statistical Science*. Dallas, TX.

(EQ-2) Level of Federal Funds Rate = $\beta(1)$ x Target Federal Funds Rate Given by the original Taylor Rule + error term

While this basic estimation equation yields some interesting insights as described later, we also wanted to decompose the Taylor Rule framework into its two parts representing the dual mandate for price stability and full employment. Specifically, our decomposition estimation equation is as follows:

(EQ-3) Adjusted Level of Federal Funds Rate = $\beta(0)$ x Constant + $\beta(1)$ x (Inflation − Desired Inflation) + $\beta(2)$ x (Output Gap) + error term

Where, the Adjusted Level of Federal Funds Rate = Actual Level of Federal Funds Rate - Actual Inflation Rate + Short-Term Real Rate Assumption. This adjustment takes us back to the original Taylor Rule equation so that we can assess whether the estimated $\beta(1)$ and $\beta(2)$ are stable and close to their expected values of 0.5 given the Taylor Rule or not as well as to learn from their evolution through time.

Our last formulation is to focus on whether shorter-term data that provides the Federal Reserve with information about how inflation and employment trends are evolving, such as toward the Federal Reserve's objectives or away from them, could further influence the interest rate decision process. The estimation formulation we chose to investigate is specified as follows:

(EQ-4) 6-Month Change in the Adjusted Federal Funds Rate (according to the original Taylor Rule) = $\beta(0)$ x Constant + $\beta(1)$ x (6-Month Change in Inflation, measured by the year-over-year rate, lagged two months) + $\beta(2)$ x (6-Month Change in Employment Growth, lagged two months) + error term

This gives us three estimation equations looking at the following research questions:

➤ How does the actual federal funds rate track the implied target rate from the original Taylor Rule?

➤ What additional insights into the relative emphasis the Federal Reserve applies to its dual objectives can be obtained from decomposing the inflation and employment parts of the Taylor Rule?

> ➤ And finally, does an examination of recent inflation and employment data trends add further to our understanding of the Federal Reserve's interest rate decision process?

Our choice of data is important. Where possible, we prefer to look at the data the Federal Reserve prefers. Also, in a Bayesian next-step-ahead framework we want to try as much as possible to look at the data available to the Federal Reserve at the time the rate decisions were made. Where appropriate we use two month lags for the explanatory factors in the estimation equation to approximately capture this available information criteria. We do not, however, attempt to go back in time and re-create the originally released data prior to later revisions, as that is beyond the scope of this research study. Since we believe that data revisions on average and over time are not necessarily biased and do not change the observed volatility of the data, we do not feel that the use of published economic data as revised at the time of this research study presents a material problem.

For the price stability mandate we have chosen to use inflation data based on the personal consumption expenditure (PCE) deflator. Different measures of inflation make little difference over time. There is a little less volatility, however, in the target rule using the PCE deflator than consumer prices. Using core inflation data excluding energy and food prices can also reduce the volatility of the implied Taylor Rule target federal funds rate. To avoid potential head fakes in the price data, the Federal Reserve has a general preference for the PCE Deflator or core CPI. For this study, however, the choice of inflation data is not material.

For the short-term real rate assumption required by the original Taylor Rule, we interpret the assumed short-term real rate as the desired target spread on the federal funds rate, on average and over time, relative to the lagged rate of inflation. The justification for this spread is that over the business cycle it should be associated with the concept of the economy's average real return on capital. There is probably a time dimension at play in average real return on capital, so that the short-term real return should be lower than the long-term real return. We have used the assumption of 2%. If this assumption is far off the mark, it will be observed as a positive or negative estimated coefficient associated with the constant (or drift term in the Bayesian world).

Our interpretation of the assumption required for desired inflation goes back to the 1950s. Professor Milton Friedman had argued at the time that because prices and wages did not adjust easily to the downside, that the long-term target inflation rate should be around 2%, not zero (or absolute price stability).[12] We note that the 2% target inflation rate or something close to it is typical of the long-run average inflation target of most major industrial countries. We follow this convention here and note again that if this assumption is off the mark we may observe this as a positive or negative estimated coefficient associated with the constant (or drift term in the Bayesian world). As an aside, while the 2% target inflation rate seems reasonable for mature industrial countries, such as the US, we would strongly caution against using the 2% inflation objective for dynamic, emerging market countries. As they build a robust middle class, the target inflation rate should probably be set higher, say 5%, to recognize the frictions in that phase of economic development.

For the real GDP output gap we use the difference in percentage points between the actual real GDP relative to potential real GDP, or the difference in logarithms, where the Output Gap = ln(Real GDP) – ln(Potential Real GDP). Professor Taylor in his initial research suggested that potential real GDP should be estimated with a time trend based on an averaging or distributed lag process. More recent work uses the estimates of potential real GDP provided by the US Congressional Budget Office (CBO). We follow this convention and use the CBO estimates for potential real GDP. For the historical period under study the way the output gap is calculated does not seem to matter very much, but as we will highlight later, this may not be true in the future. The reason we expect more controversy in the future is that some market analysts perceive that the long-term average growth rate of potential real GDP was lower in the 2000–2010 period than suggested by the CBO and that potential GDP also is slowing more than suggested by the CBO as labor force growth diminishes and the workforce ages.

We also looked at the question of whether we should use employment or output gap data. To adhere to the original formulation of the Taylor Rule we use output gap data in our estimation equations

---

[12] Friedman, Milton, 1969, *The Optimum Quantity of Money*, Macmillan.

looking at the level of the target federal funds rate and also for the decomposition into the two parts of the dual mandate. For our last estimation equation which focuses on recent data trends, we shift to the use of employment data. Payroll employment data in the US is generally released on the first Friday of the new month for the jobs situation in the previous month. It is well recognized that the monthly release of the payroll data has the attention of the markets and the Federal Reserve since it is always the first economic activity indicator released that sheds light on the previous month.

We have chosen a monthly time frequency. Where data is released quarterly we produced a monthly interpolation that preserved the quarterly averages from the original data series. Using monthly data gives us a better match with the Federal Reserve's schedule of having about eight meetings of the Federal Open Market Committee (FOMC) each year. Also, when conditions require, the Federal Reserve may hold meetings in between its scheduled meetings, so there are somewhere between 8 and 10 meetings a year, more in line with a monthly perspective than a quarterly frequency.

Our monthly data set starts in 1953. It takes several periods for a next-step-ahead Bayesian dynamic linear model to calibrate itself, as we initiate the next-step-ahead process with the naïve priors of zero for the estimated beta coefficients and priors for the variances of 10,000. That is, we are clueless at the start and let the model learn, which it does quite quickly.

All data used in this study was obtained from the "FRED" Database of the Federal Reserve Bank of St. Louis.

Why Bayes?

Before going into our estimation results, we want to discuss why a Bayesian inference process appears an appropriate statistical tool for our research into the Federal Reserve's interest rate decision process. Essentially, the thought process embedded in Bayesian inference appears to follow the same steps as used by many financial practitioners. First, one develops a hypothesis based on available information/theories and assesses one's confidence in the projections. Second, one receives new information which is used to evaluate errors in terms of the previous hypothesis. New information can include new data on factors thought to be important to the projections or they can be actual observations of the projected data so that errors can be determined. Finally, with the new information, one invokes Bayes' Theorem as part of the process of updating one's priors. That is, one revises the old hypothesis and develops a new hypothesis, a new projection and a new confidence assessment. These three steps are continually repeated. The nature of the Bayesian updating process and its intuitive appeal in economics and finance has a long history pioneered in part by the work of Zellner (1980, 1997).[13]

The Bayesian dynamic linear modeling (DLM) process makes the assumption that the estimated beta coefficients for the explanatory factors are time varying parameters. We think this is the appropriate assumption to make, and indeed, this is part of the research question we want to answer. If one assumes, as a standard least squares regression approach does, that there is one fixed and true value for the beta coefficients for the whole time period under study, one has assumed away the possibility of time-varying parameters. Our historical analysis of the Federal Reserve certainly leads us to believe that the relative weights applied to price stability and full employment over time have undergone some important changes. Hence, standard regressions are an inappropriate statistical tool for analyzing this question unless one can provide evidence of stable beta coefficients, and as we will discuss, that is not our finding.

The constant term in the Bayesian DLM is sometimes known as the drift term and measures the residual momentum after taking account of the explanatory factors. A standard regression equation can either include a constant term or omit it. In the Bayesian DLM framework, we have the same choice, although it is specified slightly differently. A term, $\beta(0)$ x Constant, is included or not in the estimation equation. The constant is represented by a vector of 1's (or some other fixed, non-zero number for each observation period) and then one dynamically estimated the time-varying drift term as the evolution of $\beta(0)$ through time as new information is received and parameter estimates are revised. In some sense the Bayesian drift term is a measure of our ignorance. Estimated values substantially above or below zero would indicate that the explanatory factors are missing something important, and that possibly there are missing factors or the

---

[13] Zellner, A., 1980, revised 1997, *Bayesian Analysis in Econometrics and Statistics.* The original version was published by North Holland in 1980 and a revised version by Edward Elgar in 1997 with some additional material.

relationship among the existing factors and the dependent variable is not linear.

A Bayesian DLM system also gives us the ability to time decay the information value in our data. That is, in a standard regression equation each observation has the same weight in estimating the fixed parameter values. In a next-step-ahead Bayesian DLM process, we can exponentially time decay information so that more recent information effects our time-varying parameter estimates more than older data. For our estimation in this research we assume a time decay parameter of 0.985 for monthly data, which is more or less the equivalent of a 5-to-6-year window of memory weighting more recent information more heavily than the older information. While we studied incrementally higher and lower time decay parameters, we judged that the 5-to-6-year window of memory weighting seemed appropriate for this study. Future studies may wish to explore this aspect of the Bayesian process in more detail.[14]

The dynamic estimation process adds one data period at a time, and revises its estimate of the each time-varying parameter with each step using Bayes' Theorem. For each observation period we get an estimate for each beta coefficient in our estimation equation as well as a standard error or confidence interval around that estimated beta coefficient. Just as the estimated beta coefficient changes through time, so does its standard error. This makes the presentation of the estimation results very different than for standard regression. We are not looking at R-squares or even T-Statistics for each estimated beta coefficient. Instead, we draw graphs that show the evolution of the time-varying beta coefficient estimates, and where appropriate we can draw upper and lower confidence bands around the estimated values. In this study, where we draw confidence bands, we have chosen to show the one standard deviation confidence band. Visually, one can easily see where the time-varying beta estimates are getting less or more confident (i.e., statistically significant).

---

[14] Editor's Note: There is an R package for Bayesian dynamic linear modeling: "dlm: an R package for Bayesian analysis of Dynamic Linear Models" by Professor Giovanni Petris, University of Arkansas, Fayetteville AR, 2009-01-14. The authors of this research developed their own R code for their Bayesian dynamic linear modeling to incorporate the time decay parameters.

Empirical Results and Interpretation

As noted earlier we will estimate three equations. We start with the question of the general adherence of the actual federal funds rate to the target rate as determined by the original Taylor Rule. We then decompose the Taylor Rule into its parts to examine what is happening under the surface. Finally, we examine the influence of changes in the short-term data trends to see what impact they may have on the rate setting decision process at the Federal Reserve.

The Actual Federal Funds Rate and the Taylor Rule. We start with the basic analysis from equation #2 of the evolving pattern of adherence to the target federal funds as implied by the original Taylor Rule when compared with the effective federal funds rate. This estimation equation does not contain a constant or Bayesian drift term, as we are looking only at the estimates of the beta coefficient associated with the implied federal funds rate. An estimated beta coefficient of positive one indicates that the effective federal funds rate and the Taylor Rule are in perfect alignment. Estimated beta coefficients that are positive but less than one indicate that the Taylor Rule is being followed in a dampened form while estimates above one indicate a magnified application of the Taylor Rule.

As one can observe in Figure 16-2, the estimated beta coefficient for Taylor Rule adherence ranged from +0.4 to +1.4 during the 1954 to March 2012 period. This is highly consistent with the casual observation of that the eye perceives from Figure 16-1, which showed the actual and desired federal funds rate.

What is more interesting and can be tracked with our Bayesian updating process is the evolution of the estimated beta coefficient. There is a rise in adherence to the Taylor Rule from the 1950s into the 1960s, with the estimated beta coefficient moving into the 0.8 range, and with a relatively tight confidence interval (one standard error bands are shown in Figure 16-2). There was then a dip in the estimated coefficient in the 1970s as the first OPEC-driven spike in crude oil prices disturbed, inflation, output, and Federal Reserve policy decision making. In August 1979, then President James Earl (Jimmy) Carter appointed Paul Volcker as Chairman of the Federal Reserve and one can observe a clear rise in the estimated coefficient from that point forward into the

1980s when the estimated coefficient stabilized for a time around the value of one — near perfect adherence to the Taylor Rule.

Alan Greenspan was appointed Chairman of the Federal Reserve in August 1987 by then President Ronald Reagan, and the estimated beta coefficient remained close to one until the latter half of the 1990s when the Federal Reserve became concerned about the "irrational exuberance" of the stock market, which is reflected by a magnification of the Taylor Rule with the estimated coefficient rising almost to 1.4. The "Tech Wreck" collapse of stocks, especially high-tech companies, in 2000, and then the terrorist attack on the US of September 11, 2001, gave way to a much more accommodative policy that the Taylor Rule would have suggested, and the estimated beta coefficient collapsed toward +0.6 and did not move back upward toward unity until the Federal Reserve abandoned its emergency 1% federal funds rate and starting hiking rates in a step by step progression in 2005–2006.

Figure 16-2: Adherence to the Taylor Rule

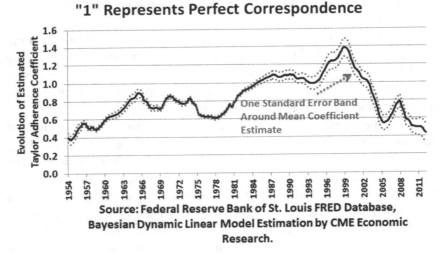

Estimated Adherence to Taylor Rule with Confidence Bands:
"1" Represents Perfect Correspondence

Source: Federal Reserve Bank of St. Louis FRED Database, Bayesian Dynamic Linear Model Estimation by CME Economic Research.

President George W. Bush appointed Benjamin Bernanke as Federal Reserve Chairman in 2006 and the estimated beta coefficient moved toward a +0.8 until the financial panic created in part by the

Federal Reserve's and US Treasury's handling of the Lehman Brothers bankruptcy and AIG bailout in September 2008. As the federal funds rate was lowered to near zero and held there, the estimated beta coefficient collapsed as well toward its low value of 0.4 and falling. Also, one can observe that the standard errors associated with the estimated beta coefficient widened markedly after the financial crisis that started in 2008. In general, standard errors were narrower in the early periods and wider during the Greenspan and Bernanke periods.

One possible interpretation of wider standard errors is that the Federal Reserve was looking at more factors than just inflation and output to determine its rate policy. Certainly, the Greenspan-Bernanke era includes such volatile events as the stock market crash of October 1987, the savings and loan debacle of 1990–1992, the failure of hedge fund LTCM (Long-Term Capital Management) in the summer of 1998, the collapse of technology stocks in 1999–2000, the 9-11 terrorist attack in 2001, the sub-prime mortgage crisis of 2007, and the financial panic of September 2008. We could produce a long list for the previous periods too, but it appears that the Greenspan-Bernanke period was more likely to have been influenced by special events than previously.

Bayesian Decomposition of the Taylor Rule. We now turn with Figure 16-3 to the Bayesian decomposition of the relative influence of inflation and economic growth in our estimation of equation #3, where we obtain estimates of beta coefficients associated with a constant term, the spread between the actual inflation rate and the desired inflation rate, and the output gap, following the prescription in the original Taylor Rule formulation.

Compared to the relative simplicity of Figure 16-2 with the target federal funds rate based on the Taylor Rule compared to the actual federal funds rate, there is clearly a lot happening beneath the surface that warrants investigation given the relative instability of the estimated coefficients in the decomposed estimation equation. In this estimation equation, adherence to the Taylor Rule would imply a zero estimated beta coefficient for the constant term, that is the Bayesian drift term. And, we would see estimated beta coefficients of 0.5 on both the inflation and output gap factors if the Taylor Rule was being followed tightly.

Figure 16-3: Taylor Rule Decomposition

Decomposition of Taylor Rule Attirbution into Inflation, Output Gap, and Drift Components

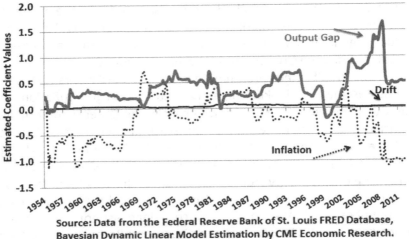

Source: Data from the Federal Reserve Bank of St. Louis FRED Database,
Bayesian Dynamic Linear Model Estimation by CME Economic Research.

We do see that the Bayesian drift term hovers near zero, which allows for the possible interpretations that our assumptions for the real rate of interest and long-term inflation objectives are more or less appropriate, as well as the interpretation that we are not missing any major additional factors.

The estimated beta coefficients on the output gap are generally positive evolving in a rather wide band around the 0.5 coefficient set by the Taylor Rule. There are several periods where the estimated coefficient moved toward zero. During the initial tightening of monetary policy under the Volcker Federal Reserve and the subsequent 1980–1982 recession the Bayesian decomposition suggests that for a short period that taming inflation was the only objective and that the Federal Reserve viewed the recession as part of the medicine needed to get inflation on a declining path. The output gap was also less important in 1998–1999 in the run-up phase of the technology stock boom, as the Greenspan Federal Reserve appeared to worry about the potential for an over-heating economy based on stock market performance and not actual output gap data. The 2003–2007 period is also interesting in that the estimated beta coefficient on the output gap moved well above 0.5, indicating a pre-occupation with economic growth. On the whole, though, the output gap estimated coefficient evolves broadly in line with a Federal Reserve that is paying considerable attention to output related data, including employment data and other indicators of economic activity.

The estimated coefficients for inflation, however, present a much more complex picture for interpretation. For the most part the estimated inflation coefficients are negative, not the positive 0.5 imposed in the original Taylor Rule. There are some key periods, though, when the inflation estimated beta coefficient moves into positive territory. Two of those periods, the late 1960s and the early 1980s, are associated with rising inflation and a primary desire on the part of the Federal Reserve to tackle those inflation pressures even if it meant risking a recession. The other positive estimated beta coefficient occurs in the 2002–2004 period when the Federal Reserve was deciding when it could abandon its 1% federal funds rate emergency policy and move back to a more balance policy. The pattern of inflation in that period appears to have been a key driver in the decision to start raising rates again.

The interpretation of the generally negative values for the estimated inflation beta coefficient while the output gap estimated beta coefficient is positive is more nuanced. In an estimation equation, we are assuming that the explanatory factors are exogenous variables and not interdependent. Our interpretation of the Federal Reserve's approach to economic analysis is that the Federal Reserve often takes the view that negative output gaps are associated with falling inflation and positive output gaps indicate possible economic over-heating and are associated with rising inflation. What this means is the output gap is the more important factor in Federal Reserve decision making because it is the output forecast that also determines the projection as to whether inflation is likely to rise or fall. Thus, only when the Federal Reserve is solely focused on dampening perceived inflation pressures and willing to risk (or even cause) a recession will the estimated beta coefficient for inflation move into positive territory.

Indeed, the 2009–2011 period reinforces this interpretation, since the Federal Reserve's preoccupation in the aftermath of the 2008 financial panic was to err on the side of a more accommodative monetary policy so as not to take any unnecessary risk of the economy slipping back into recession. In this period, we see the inflation estimated beta coefficient moving to minus one, indicative of a Federal Reserve either afraid of deflation or actively hoping for some inflation.

What this Bayesian decomposition shows is that the decision process at the Federal Reserve can appear to roughly adhere to the Taylor Rule on the surface (Figures 16-1 and 16-2) while hiding a much more complex decision process underneath the final rate outcome. This observation points the way toward research that more thoroughly explores the inflation-output trade-off when output is thought (whether or not true) to determine the future acceleration or deceleration of inflation.

Shifting Short-Term Data Trends.   Within the minutes of the Federal Open Market Committee (FOMC) and the press releases from the Federal Reserve after each meeting of the FOMC, there is an abundant supply of evidence that the Federal Reserve is actively watching and is influenced by short-term trends in the US economy. Given the focus on the dual mandate framework of the Taylor Rule, we decided to use the Bayesian approach to look at how six-month trends in inflation and employment might be impacting the interest rate decision process.

Our estimation equation derived earlier, EQ-4, is obtained as first differences from the estimation equation used in the previous section. The dependent variable is no longer related to the level of the federal funds rate, but now to its 6-month change. For data on the output side, for the 6-month perspective, we move from using the output gap data of the original Taylor Rule and switch to using the 6-month first difference in the year-over-year payroll employment data, which is one of the most intensely observed data releases by the Fed-watching community on Wall Street. Employment data is typically released on the first Friday of the new month for the previous month, making it the first economic indicator for the previous month. For inflation, we are using the 6-month first difference in the year-over-year personal expenditure deflator. The explanatory factors are both lagged by two months to more or less approximate the information available to the Federal Reserve at the time the FOMC meets, although these meetings occur at different times of the months so our 2-month lag is mainly to avoid the use of "future" information.

If the Federal Reserve is following an interest rate decision path more or less in adherence to the Taylor Rule, then we would expect to see positive estimated beta coefficients on both the 6-month changes (first differences) in the inflation rate and the 6-month changes (first differences) in the year-over-year percentage change in employment.

This dynamic estimation with 6-month change of trend data verifies that employment gains and losses are a very good short-term indicator associated with Fed policy decisions. For the whole period, 1954 – March 2012, the estimated employment data beta coefficient was positive, and since the 1970s, the estimated beta coefficient was above 1, until the financial panic of 2008 and the advent of quantitative easing (balance sheet expansion) by the Federal Reserve.

Figure 16-4: Fed Rate Decisions, Inflation, and Employment

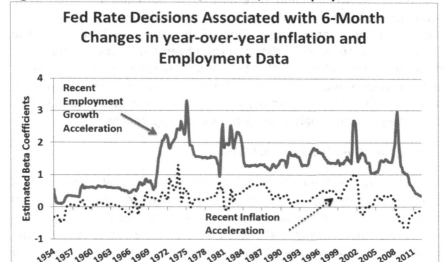

The shift to a 6-month first difference estimation equation brings the estimated beta coefficient for inflation into positive territory for much of the analysis period. Nevertheless, we view the higher estimated beta coefficients on the employment factor compared to the inflation factor as supportive of our earlier interpretation that the Federal Reserve typically uses its view of the employment or output picture to color its projections of whether inflation is likely to decline or rise. This interdependence of the explanatory factors with the employment or output factor being the more important is a critical complication to analyzing the dual mandate of the Federal Reserve and deserves further research. That is, we believe this business cycle perspective on inflation forecasting is the reason that the employment factor seems more important to the Fed than the inflation factor, not that the Federal Reserve considers its inflation objective less important than its full employment objective.

In the 2009 – March 2012 period following the financial panic of 2008, both the estimated beta coefficients start to head for zero. Once adopting an emergency near-zero rate policy for the federal funds rate in late 2008 and embarking on a massive program of balance sheet expansion known as quantitative easing, the correlation of the federal funds rate effectively went to zero, since the dependent variable flat-lined after the financial crisis. One of the very nice features of the Bayesian DLM approach is that one can observe this type of episode as it evolves, depending on the time decay parameter that has been chosen. With standard regression techniques to see the same effect, one is stuck with splitting up the periods, since each observation has an equal weight in the analysis using regression approaches.

Looking Past the 2008 Financial Crisis

As we look to the future[15], we believe the post-financial crisis period is going to embody two major research challenges for those seeking to understand the interest rate decision process of the Federal Reserve. Moreover, both of these challenges may weaken the application of the Taylor Rule framework or at least complicate it immensely. The two challenges are, first, whether or not the expanded balance sheet of the Federal Reserve impacts the interest rate decision process, and second, whether the CBO estimates of the future potential real GDP growth path become more controversial, making the output gap a less informative economic indicator.

---

[15] Editor's Note: The authors are looking to the future from the perspective of the Spring of 2012 when the original research was written.

Fed Balance Sheet Challenges. During the 2008–2009 financial crisis, the Taylor Rule suggested the need for negative short-term interest rates. As part of its response to the financial disarray, the Federal Reserve had taken the federal funds rate to near zero, and then went further to dramatically expand its balance sheet (Quantitative Easing) as shown in Figure 16-5. As the economy stabilized and output started to expand again the Taylor Rule's guidance for rates moved back into positive territory. Using the original Taylor Rule (equation #1), by March 2012, when this data set ends, the Taylor Rule was suggesting a Federal funds rate of 1.5% while the Fed was still holding rates at near zero and suggesting it might do so through the end of 2014.

Figure 16-5: Federal Reserve Assets

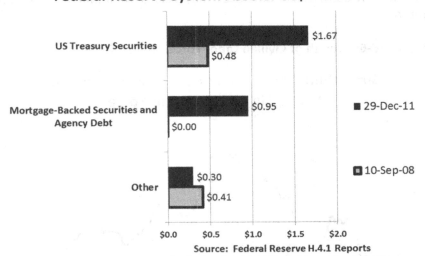

Federal Reserve System Assets: US$ Trillions

Source: Federal Reserve H.4.1 Reports
for September 10, 2008, and December 29, 2011.

We believe that one of the hidden agenda reasons that the Fed may have been reluctant to raise rates was that it did not want to begin the process of selling assets and shrinking its balance sheet while it viewed the gains in employment as fragile and the economic growth as not necessarily sustainable. Understandably, the Federal Reserve was worried about the fiscal policy in the US and 2010–2011 sovereign debt crisis in Europe that was still impacting markets in 2012.

In the future beyond 2012, even during periods of positive real GDP growth and employment gains, we see the strong possibility of federal funds rate decisions being heavily and jointly impacted by the decisions on how to unwind quantitative easing. This will become especially critical to the Federal Reserve once the federal funds rate exceeds 2% and a large part of the Fed's US$1.5 trillion portfolio of Treasury securities moves underwater or in a negative carry position — assuming the Federal Reserve raises the rates it pays on excess reserve in parallel with decisions to raise the target Federal funds rate.

Lack of Labor Force Growth Poses Additional Challenges. The US population is aging and the labor force is growing more slowly than in the past, as illustrated in Figure 16-6. Moreover, US immigration policy is in flux, and the rise of emerging markets and development of robust middle classes in these countries may also slow immigration in the future.

Figure 16-6: Growth of Civilian Labor Force

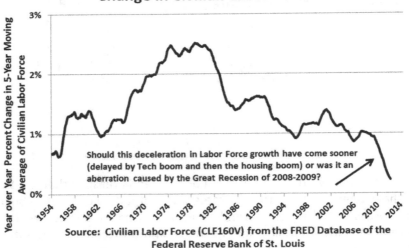

Source: Civilian Labor Force (CLF160V) from the FRED Database of the Federal Reserve Bank of St. Louis

Countries that have very slow or stagnant labor force growth are not likely to be able to post long-term average economic growth rates at the same pace they did when there was a younger and faster growing labor force. That is, looking ahead, US long-term average economic growth rates may slow. The CBO estimates of potential output appreciate this observation and take it into account, at least in part.

But there is more potential controversy ahead. There is a reasonable case that can be made that the technology boom of the 1990s and the low rate policy of the Greenspan Federal Reserve in the 2001–2004 period, which helped to expand the economy and propel the housing boom, both drew many workers into the labor force that would not normally have been working, masking the slower growth of the population. This means that there is a possibility the full employment equilibrium labor force was over-estimated by the CBO in the 1995–2007 period and by a material amount. Given the declining population and labor force growth rate, reduced immigration, and aging of the US population, future labor force may be slowing faster than anticipated. The implication for the potential real GDP estimates is that the CBO may need to reduce them, including backward revisions downward for 1995–2012 and forward revisions downward for 2012–2020.

Conclusions

In conclusion, our research focused on the Federal Reserve's interest rate decision process using the framework of the Taylor Rule with a next-step ahead Bayesian dynamic linear model provides some supporting evidence that the Federal Reserve broadly adheres to the inflation and economic growth trade-offs of its dual mandate suggested by the original Taylor Rule. There are, however, some important nuances to consider when looking more deeply into how the decision making has evolved during different economic contexts.

Specifically, we have interpreted our results to indicate that the Federal Reserve typically puts more emphasis on output and employment data than inflation data, in no small part because we believe that the Federal Reserve in its collective wisdom appears to use its output projections as a critical input into whether it is willing to project rising or falling inflation for the future. This dependence of inflation projection on the output projection is a severe complication for estimation techniques that assume that the output and inflation factors are truly independent, when they may not be.

We also note that from time to time in the past, there appears to have been short periods when inflation pressures pre-occupied the Federal Reserve. Periods such as in the late 1960s or the 1979–1982 period were interesting, because during these periods the Federal Reserve may well have been willing to risk (or even cause) a recession to get better control of inflation. In the same vein, the Federal Reserve appears to have acted in the periods following the 2008 financial crisis in a manner that suggests the Federal Reserve was either worried about deflation or actively would like to have encouraged a little more inflation.

These nuanced observations and interpretations are made possible by the use of the Bayesian dynamic linear modeling approach which treats the beta coefficients as time-varying parameters to be estimated as they evolve through time. This Bayesian approach allows for a much more sophisticated and rich interpretation of the Federal Reserve's interest rate decision process than could have been obtained by standard regression analysis techniques that assume away the possibility of time-varying beta coefficients in the first place.

About the Authors

Blu Putnam is the Chief Economist and Managing Director at CME Group, the operator of futures and options exchanges, including the Chicago Mercantile Exchange, the Chicago Board of Trade, the New York Mercantile Exchange, and COMEX. He is responsible for leading economic analysis on global financial, commodity, and agricultural markets. Blu's career has ranged from central banking (Federal Reserve Bank of New York) to investment research (Morgan Stanley and Kleinwort Benson) to portfolio management (Bankers Trust and Caisse des Dépôts et Consignations). Blu earned his Ph.D. in economics from Tulane University in New Orleans. He has five books on international finance and portfolio management to his credit as well as many academic articles, in such journals as The American Economic Review, the Journal of Finance, American Statistical Association, and the Journal of Applied Corporate Finance, among others.

Erik Norland is Executive Director and Senior Economist of CME Group. Prior to joining CME Group, Erik gained experience in the financial services industry working for investment banks and hedge funds both in the United States and in France. He most recently served in sales and research at BEAM Bayesian Efficient Asset Management LLC, and previously as Director of Research at EQA Partners, both global macro hedge funds. He also worked for IXIS Corporate & Investment Bank in Paris (now called Natixis), covering central banks and supra-nationals for the fixed income sales business, and also worked as a market economist and strategist. He began his career at Bankers Trust, Global Investment Management in New York working with the tactical asset allocation group. Erik holds a bachelor's degree in economics and political science from St. Mary's College of Maryland and an M.A. in statistics from Columbia University. He is also a CFA Charter holder.

K.T. Arasu is a Director on the economics team at CME Group. Prior to joining CME Group, KT was a world-class news and business reporter and editor with global news and information service Thomson Reuters, having covered flashpoints such as the independence movement in East Timor, the Asian financial crisis of the 1990s, the fall of the Suharto regime in Indonesia and the Great Recession in the United States as part of his journalist assignments in over a dozen countries that began in his home country of Malaysia.

List of Figures

Figure 1-1. US Inflation 2
Figure 2-1. Most Debt has Been Issued by the Private Sector,
   not the Public Sector 15
Figure 2-2. Debt Levels have Soared in Most Nations 16
Figure 2-3. Japan had Fun Levering Up During the 1980s —
   Paying for it Ever Since 19
Figure 2-4. Productivity in the US 22
Figure 2-5. Supply-Side Economics Lowered Inflation, Increased
   Inequality and Sent Debt Soaring 23
Figure 2-6. Tax Rates and Inequality 24
Figure 2-7. Productivity Soared, Wages Stagnated. Debt Helped
   Consumers to Buy the Excess Production 24
Figure 2-8. UK Debt Ratio Stabilized but Didn't Fall Much in the
   10 Years After Crisis 26
Figure 2-9. Eurozone Debt Ratios Remained Above Pre-Crisis Levels
   for at Least a Decade 27
Figure 2-10. With Near Zero Rates and Aggressive QE, UK and US
   Expansions Led the Way 29
Figure 2-11. China Joins the Club 30
Figure 3-1. Laffer Curve 35
Figure 3-2. US Top Marginal Tax Rates 37
Figure 3-3. US Economic Expansions 38
Figure 3-4. US Government Receipts and Expenditures 39
Figure 3-5. US National Debt 40
Figure 3-6. US Federal Corporate Taxes and Profits 42
Figure 4-1. The 1980s Cycle 48
Figure 4-2. The 1990s Boom Extended With a Productivity Revolution. 48
Figure 4-3. Yield Curve — 2004–2018 49
Figure 4-4. The Mid-1990s Expansion to Mid-2000s 50
Figure 4-5. The 2006–2018 Cycle 52
Figure 4-6. Equity Volatility and Yield Curve Cycle — 1990–1999 55
Figure 4-7. Equity Volatility and Yield Curve Cycle — 2000–2008 55
Figure 4-8. Equity Volatility and Yield Curve Cycle — 2009–2018 56

Figure 5-1. US real GDP — 1952 through 2017........................61
Figure 5-2. US Expansion periods..61
Figure 5-3. US in 1980 62
Figure 5-4. US in 2025 62
Figure 5-5. Japan in 1980 63
Figure 5-6. Japan in 2025 63
Figure 5-7. Japan Real GDP since the 1950s 63
Figure 5-8. China in 1990 65
Figure 5-9. China in 2025 65
Figure 5-10. China Employment Growth 66
Figure 5-11. China Real GDP 66
Figure 5-12. India in 2025 Figure 5-13. Brazil in 2025............67
Figure 6-1. US Inflation Expectations....................................71
Figure 6-2. US Population over 65 72
Figure 6-3. US Working Age Population..................................73
Figure 6-4. US Workers — Younger vs Older 74
Figure 6-5. US Working Age Population..................................74
Figure 6-6. US Jobs by Sector 75
Figure 6-7. US Service Sector 76
Figure 6-8. US Jobs by Pay Scales..77
Figure 7-1. Elastic Supply (Left) is Less Price Volatile Than Inelastic
        Supply Markets (Right)..82
Figure 7-2. Inelastic Expansion and Slowing Growth of Bitcoin Supply..83
Figure 7-3. The Cost of Mining Gold 85
Figure 7-4. Bitcoin Mining Difficulty and Price........................86
Figure 7-5. Does Bitcoin Volume Drive Price? 88
Figure 7-6. Relation Between Prices and Transactions................89
Figure 7-7. What Level of Bitcoin Transaction Costs Can the Market
        Sustain? 90
Figure 7-8. Relation of Prices to Transactions Costs.................91
Figure 9-1. Stock and Bond Volatility....................................110
Figure 9-2. Government Bond Yield Comparisons.....................112
Figure 9-3. Job Growth by Category 113
Figure 9-4. Major Country Oil Production...............................114
Figure 9-5. US Oil Consumption 114
Figure 10-1. The Reverend Thomas Bayes (a common rendering,
        although no one knows if it is accurate) 125

Figure 10-2. Bayes' Billiard Table Example 128
Figure 11-1. The Impact of Brexit on the USD-GBP Exchange Rate 137
Figure 11-2. Market Worry Indicator. Before/After
        Brexit Referendum 140
Figure 11-3. Hypothetical Risk-Return Probabilities Pre-Brexit............143
Figure 12-1. Pavnuty Chebyshev (from Wikipedia) 151
Figure 12-2. UK Brexit Referendum 152
Figure 12-3. S&P500® Futures 156
Figure 12-4. Drought Monitor for August 2012 157
Figure 12-5. Corn Futures Prices...158
Figure 13-1. Monetarism Worked in the 1970s.......................................166
Figure 13-2. Monetarism Failed in the 1980s and onward.....................167
Figure 14-1. TED Spread..174
Figure 14-2. Factors Supplying Reserves to the US Banking System 176
Figure 14-3. US Financial Profits 178
Figure 14-4. US Consumer and Commercial Credit 182
Figure 14-5. Global Real GDP Growth...186
Figure 14-6. Japan Population Pyramid 188
Figure 14-7. Brazil Population Pyramid...188
Figure 14-8. US Non-Farm Payrolls 190
Figure 15-1. US Federal Reserve Assets..201
Figure 15-2. Treasury Yields and Core Inflation 203
Figure 15-3. US Corporate Profits 206
Figure 15-4. US Private Sector Jobs 207
Figure 15-5. US Government Jobs..208
Figure 15-6. Federal Reserve Assets as Percent of Nominal GDP.........209
Figure 15-7. European Central Bank Assets 212
Figure 15-8. Spanish and German Government Bond Yields...............214
Figure 15-9. Euro (USD per EUR) Exchange Rate 215
Figure 16-1. Actual Federal Funds Rate versus Taylor Rule..................223
Figure 16-2. Adherence to the Taylor Rule 232
Figure 16-3. Taylor Rule Decomposition..234
Figure 16-4. Fed Rate Decisions, Inflation, and Employment..............237
Figure 16-5. Federal Reserve Assets. 239
Figure 16-6. Growth of Civilian Labor Force 240

Index

artificial intelligence, 119

baby boomer generation, 58, 70
Bank of Japan, 7, 19
Bayes, The Reverend Thomas, 123
bi-modal, 151
binary age, 109
bitcoin, 79
bitcoin cash, 89
black swan, 116
blockchain, 90, 91

central bank, 206
chess, 120
Commodity Futures Trading Commission, 94
corporate destruction, 113
correlation, 116
correlation, 167
Cotton Futures Act, 94
credit, 14
crypto-currencies, 90

debt-to-GDP ratio, 16
delveraging, 173
demographics, 57, 187
derivative markets, 93
distributed ledger, 91
diversification, 116

Dodd-Frank Act, 95, 97, 99, 121

ethereum, 90
European Central Bank, 6, 206
event risk, 116
event risk, 150
expected correlations, 133
expected returns, 133
expected volatilities, 133

facial recognition, 120
Federal Reserve, 1, 77, 94, 206
feedback loops, xv
fiat currency, 14, 82
financial panic, 171
flight-to-quality, 178, 192
forks, 81

garbage in, garbage out, 134
Generation X, 70
Great Recession, 67

household debt, 23

implied volatility, 147
inelastic supply, 80
inflation, 1, 173
in-sample, 161
instability, 113
interest-rate risk, 5

investor protection, 105

Laffer Curve, 33
Laffer, Arthur, 32
Lehman Brothers, 171
lender of last resort, 173
linear models, xv
Long-Term Capital
Management, 49

machine learning, 119, 130, 144
marginal tax rates, 32, 35
market integrity, 105
Markowitz, Harry, 131
Marshall, Alfred, xvi
maturity extension program,
169
mean-variance, 131
millenials, 60, 70
Minsky moment,15
modern portfolio theory,130
monetarist models,164
money supply,3
Mynsky, Hyman, 13

non-linear behavior, 122

one-child policy, 63
operation twist, 184
optimization, 129
options, 116, 127
out-of-sample, 161

pattern recognition, 146
productivity growth, 22
prudential regulation, 4, 103

quantitative easing (QE), 2, 169,
205
quantitative investment
strategies, 159
quantum computers, 91, 130,
143

regression techniques, 127
risk assessment, 129
risk management, 117
rural-to-urban migration, 62

savings & loan crisis, 5
Securities and Exchange
Commission, 94
simulations, 160
simultaneously determined,
167
sovereign debt, 184, 192
standard deviation, 107
standard deviation, 147
supply-side economics, 20, 22
systematic risk, 105

time-varying, 127

uncertainty, 107
unintended consequences, 197
unsupervised learning, 145

VIX, 52
volatility, 107

West, Geofrey, 114

yield curve, 6, 43